D0793164

The Deconstitutionalization of America

WITHDRAWN
UTSA LIBRARIES

The Deconstitutionalization of America

The Forgotten Frailties of Democratic Rule

Roger M. Barrus, John H. Eastby,
Joseph H. Lane Jr., David E. Marion,
and James F. Pontuso

LEXINGTON BOOKS
Lanham • Boulder • New York • Toronto • Oxford

Library
University of Texas
of San Antonio

LEXINGTON BOOKS

Published in the United States of America
by Lexington Books
An imprint of The Rowman & Littlefield Publishing Group, Inc.
4501 Forbes Boulevard, Suite 200, Lanham, Maryland 20706

PO Box 317
Oxford
OX2 9RU, UK

Copyright © 2004 by Lexington Books

All rights reserved. No part of this publication may be reproduced,
stored in a retrieval system, or transmitted in any form or by any
means, electronic, mechanical, photocopying, recording, or otherwise,
without the prior permission of the publisher.

British Library Cataloguing in Publication Information Available

Library of Congress Cataloging-in-Publication Data

The deconstitutionalization of America : the forgotten frailties of democratic rule / Roger
M. Barrus ... [et al.].
   p. cm.
  Includes bibliographical references and index.
  ISBN 0-7391-0834-4 (cloth : alk. paper) — ISBN 0-7391-0835-2 (pbk : alk. paper)
  1. Democracy—United States. 2. Constitutional law—United States. 3. United
States—Politics and government. I. Barrus, Roger Milton.
JK1726.D44 2004
320.973—dc22   2004004699

Printed in the United States of America
♁™ The paper used in this publication meets the minimum requirements of American
National Standard for Information Sciences—Permanence of Paper for Printed Library
Materials, ANSI/NISO Z39.48–1992.

Library
University of Texas
at San Antonio

CONTENTS

PREFACE AND ACKNOWLEDGMENTS

This book was born during the impeachment crisis of 1999. President Bill Clinton was impeached by the House of Representatives for having an affair with a White House intern, Monica Lewinski, and then lying about it under oath and getting others to lie about it as well. The President was tried by the Senate, which after an acrimonious debate, refused to convict him. The crisis touched off a great debate on the nature and responsibilities of leadership in the American system of constitutional democracy. In many ways the debate was confusing and contradictory. Republicans who had been willing to overlook lying or at least convenient lapses of memory from President Ronald Reagan during the Iran-Contra scandal now were insisting that any lying by the President was an impeachable offense. Democrats who had demanded the removal of President Richard Nixon from office for covering up a third-rate burglary now were emphatic that nothing President Clinton had done in covering up a tawdry sexual affair rose to the level of criminality required by the Constitution for deposing the nation's chief executive officer. The most persuasive argument of the President's supporters was that, in spite of his admitted misdeeds, his popular support as measured by public opinion polls remained strong, so he should be allowed to continue in office. This argument apparently persuaded not only Democrats but also many Republicans in the Senate, who seemed to want nothing more than to get Clinton's trial over with as quickly as possible.

There was something profoundly, albeit unconsciously, thought provoking about this last argument. No one, not even Clinton's harshest critics, noticed that the line of reasoning implied a whole new extra or even non-constitutional theory of presidential power—that such power is based on the immediate will or mandate of the American people, expressed informally through opinion polls. This new political theory, completely alien to the spirit of the original Constitution, influenced the impeachment debate in many ways. For example, the President's lawyers frequently cautioned members of Congress against reversing the results of two national elections, overlooking the fact that the President is not now and never has been directly elected by the people as a whole, but rather is indirectly elected by the Electoral College. More to the point, they were apparently unaware that the Constitution's framers established the Electoral College precisely to preclude the President's direct dependence on the people—the very situation they were pointing to as justifying Clinton's continuation in office. Such dependence, the framers believed, would make the President both too weak and too strong for stable democratic government: it would inhibit him from acting decisively, when necessary, for the people's interests but against their passions; at the same time, it would give him a dangerous degree of influence over the people. The solution to this problem was the Electoral College and other constitutional forms, which created a distance between the President and the people.

The President's supporters spoke quite unselfconsciously about his "mandate" from the American people, adopting the terminology of European-style parliamentarism. Rhetorically, they were superimposing the British theory of parliamentary democracy—the party that wins a majority in the legislature selects its leader as the chief executive, with the expectation that he will carry out the policies articulated in the party's platform—on the institutions of American constitutional democracy—in particular, the separation of powers and the system of checks and balances. The imported theory does not square well with our institutional forms. The President is not elected by Congress, as the Prime Minister is by the House of Commons. The President cannot control the Congress by threatening to dissolve it and call new elections, as the Prime Minister does the Commons. Apropos the impeachment crisis, Congress cannot remove the President by a simple vote of no confidence, as the Commons can the Prime Minister. The impeachment procedures in the Constitution—which make removal of the President a very difficult task by requiring a two-thirds vote in the Senate—are an important part of the system of checks and balances.

The new theory raises a number of questions for the practice of American government: what legal restraint is a popular president subject to in the exercise of his power? What is the role of Congress and the courts, neither of which can pretend to the kind of popular mandate claimed by the President, in the making of policy? How can the President's mandate be gauged between the quadrennial elections set by the Constitution? One extraordinary effect of the new theory is to give the non-governmental institution of opinion polls a crucial role in government.

The President's supporters did not, of course, develop this new theory of American government for the occasion of the impeachment crisis. They were appealing to an understanding of democratic government that was already widely accepted. It has been developing for some time, certainly through much of the twentieth century, as political power for many causes has shifted to the presidency. The apparent acceptance of the new theory represents something truly momentous in American politics, however. The "real constitution" is not the document enshrined in the National Archives in Washington, D.C. Rather, it is the understanding of the American people about the purpose, structure, and mode of operation of their government. The "real constitution" has traditionally been based on the documentary Constitution. The impeachment debate demonstrated how very far the "real constitution" has come to diverge from the documentary one. The change, which has taken place piecemeal over time, has occurred almost completely unnoticed by the American people, and perhaps also by their political leaders. The people have even less understanding of the consequences—the costs as well as the benefits—of this change for the actual functioning of their government.

The Clinton impeachment crisis was an embarrassingly low point in American political history, but it had one redeeming feature: it led people to take seriously again the question of the meaning of the Constitution. One of the most interesting reactions to the crisis was that of legal theorists who previously had argued that the Constitution is a living, ever-changing thing whose original meaning, defined by the intentions of the framers, can never be ascertained. Each generation, they claimed, defines the Constitution for itself, in light of its own needs and values. This argument justifies the federal courts in making policy, bypassing Congress and the state legislatures, through their interpretation of the evolving Constitution. Those arguing for the "living Constitution" are most often those enchanted by the idea of progress and therefore tend to be liberals. The threat of impeachment of a Democratic President by a Republican Congress led to a change of thinking, however. Some of the same legal theorists now argued that Clinton could not be removed from office because whatever moral or even legal offenses he had committed, they did not rise to the level of the "high crimes and misdemeanors" specified by the framers as grounds for impeachment—almost as if the Constitution had a determinate meaning that could and indeed should be applied in political practice. The "living Constitution" suddenly went into eclipse, if only temporarily. The present opportunity, to think seriously about the meaning of the Constitution and the nature and purposes of constitutional government, must not be allowed to slip away. This book is intended as a contribution to what should be a great national discussion.

We would like to thank the Committee on Professional Development at Hampden-Sydney College for its financial support of this book. Rosalind Warfield-Brown and Sheila-Katherine Zwiebel did their usual excellent job editing the manuscript. We also appreciate the patience and encouragement that Serena Leigh Krombach at Lexington Books gave to this project.

INTRODUCTION

For democracy, the beginning of the twenty-first century is both the best of times and the worst of times. It is the best of times because democracy, in one form or another, has now triumphed throughout the world. In place of the many different government forms that previously existed—monarchies, tyrannies, aristocracies, oligarchies, and mixed regimes, along with democracies—only various kinds of democracy are presently found—American-style presidential democracies, European-style parliamentary democracies, Third World developing democracies, Islamic republics, and even a few remaining Marxist people's democracies. Political leaders no longer claim the right to rule because of personal qualities such as wisdom, virtue, descent, and wealth, or by divine grace; rather, they govern as representatives of the people, their title to wield depending on victory in some kind of election, even if only one party or one candidate is on the ballot.

The present is the worst of times for democracy for exactly the same reason: it is universally triumphant. With all governments claiming to be democratic, modern democrats—and that includes just about everyone—find it difficult if not impossible to understand the nature and problems of democracy. Since most everyone lives within a democratic horizon, they have nothing to compare democracy to and no one to point out its faults. In this way, they are hampered in dealing with their social and political problems, some of which might be the result of contradictions inherent in the democratic principle itself. The solution to democracy's ills might not be, after all, more democracy.

Democracy was not always so favorably embraced. Until relatively recently, it was held by most political thinkers to be an inherently defective form of government. In his taxonomy of regime forms, Plato ranked democracy fourth, after aristocracy, timocracy, and even oligarchy. He considered only tyranny a worse form of government, and it typically arose out of the decay of democracy. The best Plato could say about democracy was that, because it left its citizens largely free to follow their own interests, it allowed the few individuals who were endowed by nature with the ability and the disposition to pursue philosophy. He was also painfully aware, of course, that democratic Athens had put his teacher Socrates to death for subverting the city by philosophizing.[1] Aristotle classified democracy as one of the bad regime forms, along with tyranny and oligarchy. It was the best of the bad forms, to be sure, but still it was inferior to the good regimes: monarchy, aristocracy, and polity—the mixed regime.[2]

Democracy, according to the ancient philosophers, was defective because it was rule by the poor, the *demos*, who were relatively uneducated, uncultured, and politically inexperienced. The *demos* claimed the right to rule because, as freeborn citizens, they were equal to those with superior wealth or virtue. The *demos* demonstrated their incapacity for rule, however, by their capriciousness. By constantly changing the laws that they themselves had made, they clearly proved that they lacked the wisdom necessary for good government.[3] According to the ancients, the best form of government—the good form most likely to be established, given the defects of human nature and the human condition—was a mixed regime that combined democracy, oligarchy, and aristocracy, sharing power among the many poor, the few rich, and the even fewer well-bred.

The early modern political philosophers, while in many ways disagreeing with the ancient philosophers, agreed with them completely in their estimation of democracy. Niccolo Machiavelli argued that, while all forms of government were in some way defective, democracy was especially so. It "was never of long duration, and lasted generally only about as long as the generation that had established it; for it soon ran into that kind of license which inflicts injury upon public as well as private interests."[4] Thomas Hobbes argued that democracy was inferior to monarchy, and perhaps also to aristocracy. The three forms of government did not differ in their rights or power but only in their "Convenience," that is, their "Apptitude to produce the Peace, and Security of the people; for which end they were instituted." Monarchy was the best form of government because it most closely tied the private interest of the ruler to the public interest of the state. No king could be "rich, nor glorious, nor secure" whose people were "either poore, or contemptible, or too weak through want, or dissention, to maintain a war against their enemies." The rulers in a democracy could become rich and powerful, however, by ignoring or even betraying their state. In addition, Hobbes believed that monarchy was immune to the most dangerous disease of democracy, factional conflict among the rulers.[5] Even John Locke, who insisted that all legitimate government rested on the consent of the governed, was not a partisan of democracy. The people could consent to the creation of any form of government that prudence might dictate—monarchy, aristocracy, or democracy—entrusting the supreme, legislative power to one, few, or many. Locke, who praised the "wise and godlike" Prince who "by established laws of liberty" could provide "protection and incouragement to the honest industry of Mankind against the oppression of power and narrownesse of Party," clearly saw some advantages to monarchy.[6] The best form of government for Locke was a kind of mixed regime, in which the legislative power, which did not have to always be in session, would be exercised by a representative assembly, while the executive power, which did have to always be present and functioning, would be exercised by a monarch.[7]

These philosophers' understanding of democracy was grounded on the historical record. The fall of Athens, chronicled by Thucydides in his history of the Peloponnesian War, epitomized the problems of democratic government. At the height of its power at the beginning of the conflict, Athens was dependent for its success on the leadership of one man, Pericles, who—because of the respect the people had for him—could speak the truth to them, even when it contradicted their fondest hopes or their deepest fears. Not having to pander to the people, he could lead them rather than being led by them. As war with Sparta approached, he counseled the Athenians to follow a strategy of caution, and in particular to refrain from attempting to expand their empire until they had defeated the Spartans.

Unfortunately, Pericles died very early in the conflict, leaving a political vacuum in Athens. There followed an intense struggle for power among would-be leaders who, instead of restraining the people, courted their favor by flattering them and catering to their political whims. Spurred on by the demagogues, who were more interested in their own power than the city's, the Athenians ignored Pericles' wise counsel and undertook a series of risky military ventures, culminating in the invasion of Sicily. The catastrophic failure of this enterprise, which was in large part the result of factional political conflict back home, doomed Athens to defeat in the war, loss of its empire, and waning of its power.[8] The defects of Athens' democracy were starkly illuminated in one tragic episode in the Sicilian invasion. When the military campaign had obviously failed, but before the invasion force had been annihilated, the Athenian commander Nicias considered withdrawal but decided against it, knowing how his political enemies would use such an action against him. Rather than be "put to death on a shameful charge and unjustly at the hands of the Athenians," he determined to "fight and die, if so he must, his own death at the hands of the foe." Of course, in choosing to remain in Sicily, he condemned not only himself but his whole command to destruction.[9] Thus Nicias, whom Thucydides judged to be the most virtuous of all the Athenians, was in effect compelled by the dynamic of democratic politics to betray the true interests of Athens and become a virtual traitor to his cause.

The problems of democracy were well known to the framers of the American Constitution, who were close students of history and political philosophy. James Madison summarized the historical record in the observation that the ancient democracies were "as short in their lives" as they were "violent in their deaths."[10] Alexander Hamilton declared that it was "impossible to read the history of the petty republics of Greece and Italy without feeling sensations of horror and disgust at the distractions with which they were continually agitated, and at the rapid succession of revolutions by which they were kept in a state of perpetual vibration between the extremes of tyranny and anarchy." The "momentary rays" of democracy's "glory," such as Athens' golden age, while dazzling with "a transient and fleeting brilliancy," only induced a profound sorrow "that the vices of government should pervert the direction and tarnish the luster" of such "bright talents and exalted endowments" as Pericles and Nicias. Indeed, the ancient democracy's failures had given the "advocates of despotism" persuasive reasons for rejecting not only the "forms of republican government" but also the "very principles of civil liberty."[11] The framers criticized the practice of democracy not because, as they sometimes have been accused, they were aristocrats or oligarchs at heart, but because they were dedicated democrats who wanted to make democratic government really work. Like Abraham Lincoln decades later, they saw the establishment of American democracy as a great experiment in the possibility of rational self-government. The American people, according to Hamilton, were apparently called upon "to decide the important question, whether societies of men are really capable or not of establishing good government from reflection and choice, or whether they are forever destined to depend for their political constitutions on accident and force." [12]

Only against the backdrop of democracy's historical failures is it possible to understand the intention, and the achievement, of the American framers. They set out to accomplish something that not only had never been done before, but also that the most eminent thinkers had claimed could never be done: establish a stable and effective democracy. [13] The framers believed that they could succeed where others had failed because of the invention of a new political science found in the books of liberal philosophers such as Hobbes, Locke, and Baron de la Brède et de Montesquieu. The new science included a number of devices that could be employed—contrary to the explicit purpose of the liberal philosophers, who were not democrats—to make democracy work. Among these devices were representation, separation of powers, checks and balances, and an independent judiciary. They were "powerful means," according to Hamilton, "by which the excellencies of republican government may be retained and its imperfections lessened or avoided." [14] The framers in effect used the political institutions of liberalism to restrain the excesses of democracy, while using democracy to give liberalism, which is dedicated to private freedom, a public purpose. Charged with saving the United States from the anarchy which resulted from the democratic government of the Articles of Confederation, the framers ultimately accomplished much more: they redeemed democracy itself, making it possible for reasonable people to consider it a good form of government. Showing how "the public good and private rights" could be secured in a political system that preserved both the "spirit and form of popular government," the framers achieved what Madison called the "great desideratum by which alone" democracy could be "rescued from the opprobrium under which it has so long labored and be recommended to the esteem and adoption of mankind." [15]

The present favorable opinion of democracy is the result of the political success of the United States. The Americans' victory in the Revolutionary War against Great Britain demonstrated that a democratic people could defeat a powerful monarchy. The establishment of the Constitution proved that such a people could organize a government for themselves by a democratic process of debate and decision. In the same year that George Washington was inaugurated first president under the Constitution, a democratic revolution broke out in France, inspired in part by the Americans' accomplishments. As the French Revolution descended into factionalism, military adventurism, terror, and finally dictatorship, however, it seemed to confirm the traditional understanding of democracy. The French Revolution recapitulated, in virtually every particular, the tragic experience of ancient Athens. The modern revival of democracy might well have ended with the defeat of Napoleon in 1815 were it not for the continued success of the United States, which in the early nineteenth century was busy expanding across the North American continent. In the same year that it completed that process, 1848, the monarchies of Europe were shaken by a wave of democratic revolutions. Over the next few decades, even the most autocratic European governments were compelled to adjust to demands for democratic political change, for example by establishing popularly elected legislatures. By the end of the nineteenth century, the United States had emerged as one of the world's great powers, proving that a democracy could compete effectively in the international struggle for power and prestige. Its status was in large part due to the productivity of its free market economic system. All the great powers began to become democratized to some degree, with more or less effective institutions for mass political participation. By the end of the twentieth century, after winning three world wars—two "hot" and one "cold"—the United States emerged as the world's sole superpower, the only nation with global interests and the global reach to defend them. Its victories over its most powerful ideological enemies—victories won as much by its economic productivity and social dynamism as its military might—corresponded to the general acceptance of democracy not just as *a* good form of government, but as the *only* good form of government.

Dazzled by the successes of the United States and other democratic societies, modern democrats tend to look at the rise and eventual triumph of democracy as inevitable.[16] This view is highly distorting, of both past and present politics. On more than one occasion in the past, the fate of democracy has hung in the balance; there was nothing inevitable about its success. For example, without the resolve of Lincoln, the North might have given up the war against Southern secession, the Union would have been divided, and a powerful nation with the justification of human slavery as its raison d'etre might have become a military and ideological adversary of democracy. Britain and France could easily have lost World War I before the intervention of the United States tipped the balance in their favor, leaving the German Empire, with its autocratic nationalist regime, to dominate Europe. Between the World Wars, the economic failures of the United States and the other Western democracies led many people to look to the Soviet Union as the hope of the future, and to demand the establishment of a similar regime in their own societies, even as Stalin was murdering millions in his labor camps. Perhaps only the determination of Winston Churchill kept Great Britain from negotiating a peace with Nazi Germany after the fall of France and before the United States entered the war. Without Churchill's resolve, a new dark age of barbarism would have descended over Europe. During the Cold War, the NATO alliance established to contain the Soviet Union could have split over what might have appeared to Europeans as American arrogance or to Americans as European anti-Americanism, the same causes that today in the post-Cold War world have the potential to split the broader alliance of democratic societies in the war on terror.

The misunderstanding of democracy's past might not be so important if it did not contribute to a potentially dangerous misunderstanding of its present. Failures occur in the putatively inevitable progress of democracy. A new democracy disintegrates in ethnic or tribal violence and is overthrown by a military leader promising to restore order who then, to secure public support, embarks on an aggressive foreign policy. In crisis circumstances, a fanatic religious movement develops that can take power by democratic means and can be prevented from doing so only by military intervention and the suspension of civilian government. An established democracy is so paralyzed by party factionalism that it is unable to respond to pressing economic, social, or even security problems; the people become disaffected and look for someone able to get the country moving again, and reward him with dictatorial power. When these situations arise, they are typically dismissed as temporary setbacks along the path to democracy. No thought is given to the possibility that such situations, which are eerily reminiscent of the political conditions in post-Periclean Athens, represent dangerous tendencies inherent in democracy itself. They are at least as likely to be caused by too much democracy as by too little. Democracies can fail, catastrophically, if they are not properly organized. The tragic errors of Western policy in Bosnia, Rwanda, and other so-called developing nations, where the Western powers failed to foresee, much less to prevent, the slaughter of hundreds of thousands of those nations' ethnic minorities, arguably have been the result of the inability to recognize democracy's inherent dangers.

The universal triumph of democracy has led many to take it for granted, and nowhere is that thoughtlessness more apparent than in the United States, the principal source of democracy's present ascendance. The thoughtlessness takes the form of utopian expectations about what democratic government can accomplish to abolish poverty, ignorance, war, disease—any and every human problem. Nothing seems to be Impossible. Franklin D. Roosevelt articulated the sense of boundless possibility when he told the American people, in his first inaugural address, that "the only thing we have to fear is fear itself."[17] That attitude was a source of strength during the Great Depression, but in other circumstances it can be dangerous. When problems do not get resolved, frustrated citizens turn against the nation's political leaders, who appear to be failing in their responsibilities, and even against its governing institutions, which appear to be unresponsive and ineffective in addressing the people's needs.

For example, in the 1990s, the general feeling was, "If we could win the Cold War, then why can't we do something about _____?"—with just about any economic, social, or political problem filling the blank. This assumption was manifest in the 1992 presidential campaign, when a brief and mild recession (that actually ended months before the election) energized a "radical center" to demand an immediate solution to the nation's economic problems. The radical center found its champion in Ross Perot, a businessman with no significant political experience who promised to use the presidency to force Congress to devise a new economic program. All discussion of constitutional forms—of the powers and responsibilities of the President and the Congress—were dismissed as campaign rhetoric designed to obfuscate the real issues. During the campaign, Perot spoke of the possibility of governing through a national "electronic town meeting," using the technology of the computer and the Internet to let the people instantaneously decide questions of public policy. Such an arrangement would in effect have replaced the American system of representative democracy with a form of the direct democracy of ancient Athens, but in a vastly larger and substantially more impersonal version of the Athenian Assembly. Neither of Perot's opponents, President George Bush or Bill Clinton, was able or willing to defend the forms of limited, constitutional government. In the end, Perot received almost 20 percent of the national vote.[18] Bill Clinton, the "New Democrat" who won the 1992 election, never forgot its lesson, and governed as if every problem in American society was his concern as president, and he had a plan to solve it. His successor, the "Compassionate Conservative" George W. Bush, came into office governing the same way, which lasted until the attack on the World Trade Center on September 11, 2001, a crisis that reemphasized his constitutional responsibilities as president.

The American people now have largely forgotten the most profound insight of the Constitution's framers, garnered from their study of both philosophy and history, concerning the nature and problems of democracy: In Madison's words, "Had every Athenian citizen been a Socrates, every Athenian assembly would still have been a mob."[19] The history of democratic government demonstrates that in order to work it requires representative institutions that refine and enlarge public opinion and insulate political decision-makers from the momentary whims of popular passion. The success of representative democracy endangers such forms, however, by blinding the people to their necessity. The American system of government requires a great deal of political understanding on the part of the people. Without it, the system must degenerate. Alexis de Tocqueville, who came to the United States in the early 1830s to study democracy, held that the American Constitution is "the best of all known federal constitutions," but confessed that "it is frightening to see how much diverse knowledge and discernment it assumes on the part of the governed." American government rests on "legal fictions." Constructed of "artificially contrived conventions," de Tocqueville concluded, it is "only suited to a people long accustomed to manage its affairs, and one in which even the lowest ranks of society have an appreciation of political science."[20] Like every other form of government, democracy has its intrinsic and characteristic deficiencies, which must be counteracted if it is to function properly. It cannot be left to follow its natural inclinations, but must be restrained by reason and prudence. In part, this means that the people must defend representative institutions against efforts to alter or abolish them in order to make government more democratic. The belief in democracy's inevitable triumph has led the people to abdicate their responsibility, however. The result of this abdication can be seen in what might be called the "deconstitutionalization" of American government, a process that has been going on for more than a century, but whose practical consequences are only now becoming apparent in the pathologies of contemporary American politics, of which the Perot phenomenon is only one example. To reverse the process of deconstitutionalization, the American people must learn once again to think seriously about democracy, and in particular about the problems that necessitated the founding of constitutional government in the first place.

NOTES

1. For Plato's characterization of democracy, see *Republic* VIII, 555b-562a.

2. For Aristotle's discussion of the nature of democracy, see *Politics* Bk. III.

3. See Plato, *Minos* 317b.

4. Niccolo Machiavelli, *Discourses on the First Ten Books of Titus Livius*, in *The Prince and the Discourses*, ed. Max Lerner (New York: Modern Library, 1940), I: 2, 114.

5. Thomas Hobbes, *Leviathan, or The Matter, Forme, and Power of a Commonwealth, Ecclesiastical and Civill*, ed. C. B. Macpherson (New York: Penguin Books, 1981), II: 19, 241-243.

6. John Locke, *Two Treatises of Government*, ed. Peter Laslett (Cambridge, U.K.: Cambridge University Press, 1988), II: 42, 132; 298, 354.

7. See ibid., II: 150-154, 367-370.

8. See Thucydides, *History of the Peloponnesian War*, trans. by Charles Foster Smith, 4 vols. (Cambridge, MA: Harvard University Press, 1969), II: 65; vol. 1, 375-379.

9. Ibid., VII: 48, 86; vol. 4, 95, 177.

10. Alexander Hamilton, James Madison, and John Jay, the *Federalist Papers*, http://libertyonline.hypermall.com/, #10, hereafter cited as *Federalist*.

11. *Federalist* #9.

12. *Federalist* #1.

13. The one exception was Benedict Spinoza, who argued for democracy as the best regime based on the principle that "might makes right"—that everything has a natural right to do whatever it is naturally conditioned to do—which means in human affairs that "as the wise man has sovereign right to do all that reason dictates, or to live according to reason, so also the ignorant and foolish man has sovereign right to do all that desire dictates, or to live according to the laws of desire" (See *Theological-Political Treatise*, ch. 16.). The American framers, if they knew of Spinoza's argument, did not appeal to it to support their establishment of democratic government.

14. *Federalist* #9.

15. *Federalist* #10.

16. See Francis Fukuyama, "The End of History?" *The National Interest* 16 (Summer, 1989): 3-18.

17. "Franklin D. Roosevelt's First Inaugural Address," in *Documents of American History*, ed. Henry Steele Commanger, 2 vols. (New York: Appleton, Century, Crofts; 1963), II: 240.

18. On the constitutional consequences of the 1992 election, see *America through the Looking Glass: A Constitutionalist Critique of the 1992 Election*, eds. Roger Barrus and John Eastby (Lanham, MD: Rowman & Littlefield, 1994).

19. Madison in *Federalist* #55.

20. Alexis de Tocqueville, *Democracy in America*, ed. J. P. Mayer, trans. George Lawrence (Garden City, NY: Doubleday, 1969), 164-165.

CHAPTER 1

JAMES MADISON'S CONSTITUTION OF FREEDOM

Introducing the section of the *Federalist Papers* that discusses the democratic character of the United States Constitution—"The conformity of the proposed Constitution to the true principles of republican government," according to the outline of the work in *Federalist #1*—James Madison declared that if the constitution should "depart from the republican character," then it must be abandoned as "indefensible" because no other form of government is "reconcilable with the genius of the people of America; with the fundamental principles of the Revolution; or with the honorable determination which animates every votary of freedom to rest all our political experiments on the capacity of mankind for self-government."[1] The genius, or general character, of the American people he defined in another place as a "vigilant and manly spirit" that "nourishes freedom, and in return is nourished by it."[2] Madison is, of course, the Constitution's principal architect, as well as one of the authors of the *Federalist Papers*, the authoritative commentary on the Constitution. It is significant, then, that he holds that there is a moral purpose guiding the construction of the Constitution, and that it must ultimately be judged by how well it fulfills that purpose. It is not merely an apparatus for governmental decision-making. The moral purpose of the Constitution is, stated succinctly, freedom—or self-government—which the experience of the Revolution led the American people to demand as their right, and the most patriotic Americans to dedicate themselves to as the greatest of all political causes.

The Constitution establishes a complex system of government because self-government is a complicated affair, involving the reciprocal actions of the passions, virtue, and reason. Just how complicated is indicated in the Declaration of Independence, the definitive statement of the principles of the American Revolution. These principles are the "self-evident truths" with which the Declaration opens its defense of the American colonists' rebellion against British rule:

> that all men are created equal; that they are endowed by their Creator with certain unalienable rights; that among these are life, liberty, and the pursuit of happiness. That, to secure these rights, governments are instituted among men, deriving their just powers from the consent of the governed; that whenever any

form of government becomes destructive of these ends, it is the right of the people to alter or abolish it, and to institute new government, laying its foundation on such principles, and organizing its powers in such form, as to them shall seem most likely to effect their safety and happiness.

Each of the Declaration's self-evident truths represents a kind of self-government, or an element of self-government, properly—that is, comprehensively—understood. Human beings are equal because nature does not distinguish among them as it does between them and other animals. According to Thomas Jefferson, author of the Declaration, "the mass of mankind has not been born with saddles on their backs, nor a favored few booted and spurred, ready to ride them legitimately, by the grace of God."[3] They are thus left free by nature to govern themselves—to decide what ends to pursue, and how to attain them—without having to answer to anyone else for their decisions. The greatest goods are incorporated in the natural rights of life, liberty, and the pursuit of happiness. Self-government, in one sense, is the exercise of these rights. As such, it accords with the most powerful passions in human nature. There is more to self-government than following the passions, however. The founding of political society, which, according to the Declaration, is necessary to secure the rights granted by nature, involves the exercise of a more austere kind of freedom. Founding political communities requires at least certain individuals to transcend their natural inclination, to care for their own good, and to concern themselves with the good of others as well as their own. They must, like the signers of the Declaration, dedicate their "lives, fortunes, and sacred honor" to the achievement of the common good. The people must possess some of the same virtue—the same ability to control the passions for the sake of something higher—in order to properly exercise the ultimate power of self-government, to rationally decide if, when, and how their system of government should be changed. Prudence dictates that "governments long established" should not be changed for "light and transient causes." To rationally deliberate on the need for a change—assessing the advantages and disadvantages of the existing government, and of a possible replacement for it—the people must be able to look beyond their immediate, private concerns to the common good.

In his insistence that the Constitution of the United States must be republican, Madison went beyond the idea of self-government articulated in the Declaration of Independence. The Declaration does not specifically require that American government be democratic. It left this issue to be resolved by the American people once they had attained their political independence from Great Britain. They would be able to make a choice after prudently considering their situation in domestic and foreign affairs. In principle, they could choose to establish a monarchy, aristocracy, or other non-democratic form of government, suspending the exercise of their political freedom in the very act of employing it, allowing it to remain dormant until they were again compelled to deliberate on the need for revolution and a change of regime. Madison understood that the democratic spirit of the Americans, nurtured in the experience of the Revolutionary War, has essentially answered the question of what kind of government should be created for them. Proud of the ability to govern themselves that they demonstrated in the war, and suspicious of all monarchic and aristocratic political institutions, the Americans are not going to consent to any form of government but a democratic one. Not even a mixed regime such as the British, combining monarchic and aristocratic with democratic elements, will be acceptable to them. Madison was not a democratic dogmatist: he did not claim that all peoples will or even should try to govern themselves democratically. He did not even claim that the American people will necessarily succeed in their attempt. All historical experience indicates that the issue is very much in doubt. Democratic government, he held, "presupposes the existence" of "those qualities in human nature which justify a certain portion of esteem and confidence" to a "higher degree than any other form."[4] These qualities, of moral self-restraint and rational self-control, were frequently absent from the politics of the ancient democracies. Democracy, for Madison, is by no means synonymous with self-government. It can descend into the unrestrained pursuit of private advantage, along with the political demagoguery that such behavior encourages. The passions of pride and fear, according to Madison, led the Americans to embrace democracy after the Revolution. What they needed to do next was demonstrate that their action was reasonable, by adopting and implementing a democratic Constitution that would foster "public and personal liberty," that is, self-government in both its essential forms.[5]

FOUNDING THE DEMOCRATIC REPUBLIC

Founding a new government, after the old one has been overthrown by revolution or some other event, is the supreme act of self-determination, requiring the exercise in the highest degree of the noble qualities of human nature. Founders must possess political wisdom—an understanding of the nature, purposes, and problems of politics—along with the prudence necessary to apply that understanding to the conditions of a given place and time. They must also possess moral virtue. Laying down the fundamental laws that will give form to society and govern its most important activities, they are presented with virtually limitless opportunities to profit themselves and gratify their passions. To do their job well, they must be able to subordinate their private interests to those of society as a whole. Perhaps even more than other political leaders, founders are animated by the desire for fame, what Alexander Hamilton called "the ruling passion of the noblest minds."[6] The best way for them to get what they want is to create a government that will secure the people's peace, freedom, and prosperity. They must recognize the common good as identical to their own, and act accordingly. Not all founders rise to this level of understanding—a kind of self-interest properly understood—and that is one reason why many foundings fail. In other cases, the founders lack the necessary knowledge of politics to organize an effective government. Certainly there is nothing inevitable about founding: a government may be destroyed and no replacement successfully established. Because of the failures of their would-be founders, some societies are trapped in a condition of perpetual revolution or anarchy.

The United States was more fortunate in its political origins. Its republican form of government did not just fall together, its elements combining by political gravity, or grow from simpler forms, its elements developing incrementally by a process of political evolution. Rather, it was founded by a small number of able, knowledgeable, and public-spirited individuals who took advantage of a growing crisis in the country to bring about a fundamental political transformation. The founders did not attempt to impose their new Constitution by force or fraud, but, true to the principles of self-government articulated in the Declaration of Independence, they proposed it to the people to be established by their consent. In his discussion of the workings of the constitutional convention, in particular in *Federalist* #37 and 38, Madison showed the intellectual and moral qualities of the American Founders that enabled them to succeed where so many others have failed.

The framers were elected as representatives to a convention to make recommendations for revising the Articles of Confederation, in order to establish an effective national government and preserve the union of the states.[7] Under the influence of Madison and others, the convention concluded that no revision to the Articles could correct its deficiencies because it was based on a fundamentally flawed theory of federalism. A federation, from this point of view, was a union of states that retained their sovereignty in all matters except those expressly granted to the general government, typically in the area of foreign affairs. Furthermore, to protect the sovereignty of the states, the general government was prohibited from legislating directly for the people; it could legislate only for the states. The people were subject only to the laws of the states. A federation was understood to differ from a national or consolidated government in both these respects. The result of the application of traditional federalist theory in the Articles, as the framers understood the situation, was political chaos: the federal government was too weak to compel the states to fulfill their financial and other obligations to the union or to keep them from fighting and engaging in trade wars with each other. The union was in serious danger of breaking up.[8] The framers then took a bold step: recognizing that whatever plan they put forward would have to be approved by the same people who had delegated them to revise the Articles, they decided to scrap the existing government and develop an entirely new plan, carrying over almost nothing except the names of the principal political institutions. Because it was founded on "principles which are fallacious," the old government had to be changed in its "first foundation," and so did the whole "superstructure" resting on that foundation.[9] The framers' plan involved elaboration of a new theory of federalism, according to which a federation was a mixture of national and federal—afterwards called "confederal"—elements. The new Constitution was nationalist in apportioning membership in the House in accordance with population and allowing the Congress to legislate directly for the people; it was federalist in granting an equal representation to the states in the Senate and restricting the general government to certain enumerated

powers, leaving much authority to the states. It was both nationalist and federalist in the amending procedure, which allowed Congress to propose amendments,
but placed the final ratification responsibility in the states.[10] Exercising "a manly
confidence in their country," the framers then submitted their plan to the nation
for approval, with many of them entering into the ratification debates in the
states. The most active were Madison and Hamilton, who wrote the *Federalist
Papers* to persuade the voters of New York.

The intellectual and moral qualities of the framers can be deduced, according to Madison, from a consideration of the great number and intractable nature
of the difficulties they had to overcome in putting together the new Constitution.
Perhaps the most important of the difficulties was the absolute "novelty" of their
undertaking. History and the political experience of the United States offered no
example of a strong and stable union of democratic states, but only examples of
shaky confederations that, like beacons along a rocky shore, warned of dangers
to be avoided. At the level of democratic political theory, the framers confronted
the problem of reconciling "stability and energy in government with the inviola-
ble attention due to liberty and to the republican form." Liberty seems to require
that "all power should be derived from the people"; that it should be held in "not
a few, but a number of hands"; and that it should be granted for only a "short
duration."[11] Stability, in contrast, seems to require the very opposite in the number and tenure of government offices, if not in the very source of government
power. Earlier republics had attempted to solve the problem of stability by "creating a will in the community independent of the majority—that is, of the society itself."[12] These republics were mixed regimes composed of a monarchical or
aristocratic element combined with the democratic. The American government,
however, was to be wholly democratic, or popular. On the level of political practice, the framers confronted the problem of defining the relationship between the
federal and state governments. Traditional political science, which had not even
been able to clearly distinguish among the legislative, executive, and judicial
powers of government, or among the different branches of the law, offered little
help in solving this problem. With nothing to guide them in devising their federal system, the framers also had to contend with what Madison called the "interfering pretensions of the larger and smaller States," the demands of the states
for either equality or superiority of representation, depending on their particular
circumstances. With all these issues before them, it was not remarkable that in
the new federal system the framers created there were "some deviations from
that artificial structure and regular symmetry which an abstract view . . . might
lead an ingenious theorist to bestow on a Constitution planned in his closet or in
his imagination."[13]

Even more remarkable from the point of view of political history, Madison
argued, was the singular unanimity of the framers in drafting, revising, and approving the proposed Constitution. This circumstance should lead to the "aston-
ishment" of anyone who considers it candidly. He went even further: the unanimity of the constitutional convention must lead any "man of pious reflection"
to "perceive in it the finger of that Almighty hand which has been so frequently

and signally extended to our relief in the critical stages of the revolution."[14] As miraculous in its own way as the military victories of the upstart, ragtag American army over the better trained and equipped British at Trenton, Saratoga, and Yorktown was the unprecedented level of political agreement achieved by the delegates at the convention. Madison compared the experience of the convention with all previous "councils and consultations held among mankind for reconciling their discordant opinions, assuaging their mutual jealousies, and adjusting their respective interests." Almost without exception, these efforts broke down in "factions, contentions, and disappointments." They represent some of the "most dark and degrading pictures which display the infirmities and depravities of the human character." The unanimity of the convention, in contrast, showed that the delegates to it "enjoyed, in a very singular degree, an exemption from the pestilential influence of party animosities—the disease most incident to deliberative bodies and most apt to contaminate their proceedings."[15] The extraordinary character of the American framers, Madison argued, is indirectly confirmed by the history of the great founders of classical antiquity. Whenever the ancient Greeks or Romans, who prized liberty above all other goods, were compelled to reorganize their societies politically, they entrusted the task to one man: Minos, Theseus, Lycurgus, Solon, Romulus, Brutus, and others. Why would the Athenians, who would not send out an army commanded by fewer than ten generals, allow one man, even one as wise as Solon, to lay down new laws for their society? The only possible answer, Madison claimed, is that they feared "treachery or incapacity in a single individual" less than they feared "discord and disunion among a number of counsellors."[16] The American framers, in devising their Constitution by the process of free, rational deliberation, accomplished something that the ancients, celebrated through the ages for their civic virtue, never dared attempt. Critics of the Constitution might consider the ancients' problems with lawgiving a caution against rashly embarking on another attempt at constitution making. The circumstances the next time, including the quality of the political leadership, might not be so propitious for founding a new government.

RATIONALIZING DEMOCRACY

Madison summarized the problem of establishing a decent and effective democracy in a famous passage from *Federalist* #51, on the separation of powers:

> Ambition must be made to counteract ambition. The interest of the man must be connected with the constitutional rights of the place. It may be a reflection on human nature that such devices are necessary. But what is government itself but the greatest of all reflections on human nature? If men were angels, no government would be necessary. If angels were to govern men, neither external nor internal controls on government would be necessary. In framing a government which is to be administered by men over men, the great difficulty lies in this: you must first enable the government to control the governed; and in the next place oblige it to control itself. A dependence on the people is, no doubt, the

primary control on the government; but experience has taught mankind the necessity of auxiliary precautions."[17]

Angels are immortal beings, without physical needs or passions. Government is necessary because human beings are not like the angels in this respect. Good government is possible because human beings share something very important with the angels, the power of reason. The establishment of good government involves both the angelic and the non-angelic—both the rational and the passionate—elements of human nature. Reason must rule over the passions, but with due regard for their power. It cannot suppress them, nor should it even try, since they give individuals and societies their vitality. Rather, it must rule them indirectly, by guile or cunning. The strategy Madison adopted for bringing about the rule of reason is to turn the passions against themselves. The means for this purpose are the forms of constitutional democracy: representation, federalism, legislative bicameralism, the system of checks and balances, and other institutions of modern republicanism. He analyzed the political problem of the passions, and shows how reason can be made to rule over them, in his discussion of factionalism, in particular in *Federalist* #10 and 51.

Factionalism, for Madison, is the most important political manifestation of the problem of the passions in democratic societies. It is the cause of the "instability, injustice, and confusion introduced in the public councils" that have been the "mortal diseases under which popular governments have everywhere perished." Madison defined a faction as "a number of citizens, whether amounting to a majority or minority of the whole, who are united and actuated by some common impulse of passion, or of interest, adverse to the rights of other citizens, or to the permanent and aggregate interests of the community."[18] The causes of faction are "sown in the nature of man," specifically in the "reciprocal influence" of "his reason and his self-love," or "his opinions and his passions." Passions become politically active through people's zeal for their political or religious beliefs; through people's attachment to political leaders or others "whose fortunes have been interesting to the human passions"; and last but certainly not least, by "the various and unequal distribution of property" among debtors and creditors, and manufacturing, mercantile, landed, and moneyed interests, who inevitably divide themselves into "different classes, actuated by different sentiments and views."[19] Since the problem of faction is rooted in human nature, it cannot be rationally resolved by eliminating its causes. Removing the causes of faction, Madison reasoned, could be accomplished either by destroying the liberty necessary for its existence, or by giving all citizens the same passions, interests, and opinions. The first method—political despotism—is a cure worse than the disease, since liberty is essential to the good life for individuals, as well as for societies. The second method—essentially traditional republicanism—is "as impracticable as the first is unwise."[20]

For both philosophers such as Plato and statesmen such as Lycurgus, the necessary means for establishing the good society was a process of political education that would in effect transform human nature itself, reconstituting self-

interested individuals as selfless social beings. Plato's *Republic* and Plutarch's
"Life of Lycurgus," both of which were well known to Madison, make clear just
how comprehensive and intrusive this process must be. In the *Republic* the rulers prescribe the tales and even the music the young will hear. The purpose is to
shape the opinions and tastes of the people so that they will think and act as true
citizens, more dedicated to the common good than to their individual interests.
Each individual is to be trained for one particular job, one which is most consistent with his natural abilities, either a trade such as farming, or the military, or
government. The society will be a genuine community, with each doing his job
as well as possible and contributing the fruits of his labors to the whole. Madison might well reject the traditional approach—which, if effective, would cul-
minate in the creation of a "philosophical race of kings," if not exactly a "nation
of philosophers"[21]—not only because it is impracticable, but also because it is
inimical to freedom. It ignores the real "diversity in the faculties of men," even
though "the protection of these faculties is the first object of government."[22]
Human beings are not endowed by nature with the ability to do just one job, and
one purpose of freedom is to allow them the opportunity to develop their various
talents.[23]

The only sensible solution to the problem of faction, Madison maintained, is
to control its effects. How this is to be accomplished depends on the factions
that arise. Minority factions can be handled relatively easily, by the operation of
the democratic principle of majority rule. A majority faction is more difficult to
deal with, and more dangerous, because it acts in accordance with the democratic principle. Democratic peoples, for whom the will of the majority is just by
definition, frequently do not recognize that a majority can constitute a faction.[24]
A majority functions as a faction, however, when it sacrifices "to its ruling passion or interest both the public good and the rights of other citizens."[25] The problem of majority faction can be solved, consistent with the requirement of majority rule, in two ways: by inhibiting a majority from coalescing around a
dangerous passion, or by preventing a majority stirred by such a passion from
acting on its intention. Both are facilitated by enlarging the political community
in territory and population, and increasing the number and variety of interests
while dispersing these factions geographically. Madison claimed that the problem of majority faction is simply irresolvable in the kind of democratic society
that existed in antiquity, "a pure democracy . . . consisting of a small number of
citizens, who assemble and administer the government in person." Such a society must be limited in both population and territory, in order for the citizen body
to be able to meet together regularly to conduct the business of government. In
this situation, "a common passion or interest will, in almost every case, be felt
by a majority of the whole," and nothing will "check the inducements to sacrifice the weaker party or an obnoxious individual." As a result, the ancient democracies were "spectacles of turbulence and contention," and "as short in their
lives" as they were "violent in their deaths."[26] Given the actual experience of
direct democracy, Madison took "theoretic politicians who have patronized this
species of government" to task for mistakenly believing that "by reducing man-

kind to a perfect equality in their political rights, they would at the same time be perfectly equalized and assimilated in their possessions, opinions, and their passions."[27] Even in a "republic," a democratic society employing the modern principle of representation, a majority faction can develop if the society is too small. The election of representatives offers the advantage of refining and enlarging public opinion, by passing it through "the medium of a chosen body of citizens," distinguished by their wisdom, justice, and patriotism.[28] This advantage is negated in a small republic, however, in which the representatives will be too closely associated with and dependent on local interests. Rather than being checks on a tyrannical majority, representative institutions in a small republic will tend to be its instruments.

While representation does not solve the problem of the tyranny of the majority, according to Madison, it is an essential element of the solution. The real advantage of representation is that it allows for enlargement of a democratic society beyond its natural limit, which is the number of citizens that can actively participate in government, located in an area small enough that those farthest from the center can attend the general assembly as often as required. A representative republic, in contrast, can expand to the point where the people's representatives, a small part of the whole, journey to the center to conduct government business.[29] The advantage of such an extension of the boundaries of the union is that it brings in a much greater diversity of interests, scattered over much greater distances, making it "less probable that a majority of the whole will have a common motive to invade the rights of other citizens; or if such a common motive exists, it will be more difficult for all who feel it to discover their own strength and to act in unison with each other."[30] Tyrannical factions may arise in one state or section of the country, but their influence will be diluted in the nation as a whole. A "flame" may kindle in one state, but a "general conflagration" is not likely to engulf the Union.[31] Of course, national majorities will form: that is required for democratic government to function. However, the majorities will be moderated, tempered, or rationalized. "In the extended republic of the United States, and among the great variety of interests, parties, and sects which it embraces," Madison purposed, "a coalition of a majority of the whole society could seldom take place on any other principles than those of justice and the general good."[32] The purpose of multiplying and diversifying factions is not to thwart the will of the majority—as if the "majority" were a fixed thing, with a fixed character—but rather to encourage the development of the right kind of majority, one capable of ruling justly and wisely. "Justice is the end of government," Madison claimed, and "[i]t ever has been and ever will be pursued until it be obtained, or until liberty be lost in the pursuit." This applies to democracy as much as to other forms of government. "In a society under the forms of which the stronger faction can readily unite and oppress the weaker," he argues, "anarchy may as truly be said to reign as in a state of nature."[33]

Madison conceived of the extended republic as a mélange of interests of diverse types and purposes, locked together in a ceaseless struggle for wealth, power, and other goods. Ironically, in this situation, reason can exercise its greatest possible political influence. In the dynamic equilibrium created by the never-ending competition of interests, reason is able to exercise decisive influence. It is the center point around which the whole can be organized and made to revolve. Society will be "broken into so many parts, interests and classes of citizens," Madison stated, "that the rights of individuals, or of the minority, will be in little danger from interested combinations of the majority."[34] Between the many different interests in society, justice will "hold the balance."[35]

The system of checks and balances has the same general purpose. It sets ambition against ambition, not to suppress it, but to induce it to submit to rational control. On many different levels, the forms established in the Constitution set the passions against themselves and against each other, and thus give reason the leverage it needs to rule over them. The Constitution's strategy of creating equilibrium among rationally controllable social forces reflects a more general human reality. "This policy of supplying, by opposite and rival interests, the defect of better motives," Madison argued, can "be traced through the whole system of human affairs, private as well as public." It is "particularly displayed in all the subordinate distributions of power, where the constant aim is to divide and arrange the several offices in such a way as that each may be a check on the other—that the private interest of each individual may be a sentinel over the public rights."[36] Madison saw operating in a well-constructed republic the same kind of "invisible hand" that Adam Smith insisted is at work in a properly functioning free market economy, something that induces individuals—even against their immediate intentions—to act rationally for the good of all.[37] The balance of political forces in Madison's republic makes it necessary for individuals and groups to listen to and heed the voice of reason in order to secure their own interests. Government officials will learn that if they are to accomplish anything, they must exercise the arts of persuasion, negotiation, and compromise. Interest groups will learn that, in order to form the majority necessary to win elections and influence government, they must ally with other groups by finding a good they all share in. Everyone will learn something about the need to subordinate passion to reason. Madison thus found, in the "extent and proper structure of the Union," a "republican remedy for the diseases most incident to republican government."[38] The cause of these diseases is the power of the passions in human nature. The remedy for them is the subjection of the passions to reason, through the operation of the forms of constitutional government, in the political environment of the large republic. Madison's rational state perhaps lacks the noble simplicity of Plato's *Republic*, with its ordered classes of citizens, all dedicated to the common good. But it has the more than offsetting advantage of being practically achievable, because it is structured by and around the most powerful forces in human nature.

DEMOCRATIC SELF-GOVERNMENT

It hardly needs saying that the American framers did not establish their new democratic republic just to experience of freedom of self-government them-

selves, during the brief period of the founding. The political system they established was intended to make self-government possible for all, for generations to
come. In spite of appearances, the framers did not set out to create a "machine
that would run itself." Their system, which makes use of the spirit of faction
that, according to Madison, was singularly absent from their own deliberations,
has a certain mechanical character to it. Faction is set against faction in society,
as ambition is set against ambition in government, in order to create a dynamic
equilibrium in which reason can and indeed must rule. Self-government is a
problem because reason is too weak to rule directly over the passions. The very
existence of government—which Madison called the "greatest of all reflections
on human nature"—attests to the magnitude of the problem. The solution to the
problem is not to invent a political system that obviates the need for reason, but
rather one that creates an environment in which reason can be effective. The
system the framers established depends for its operation on the passions, which
give it energy. However, they did not expect that it would function only by the
passions. Speaking for himself, Madison claims that he trusts the "great republican principle, that the people will have virtue and intelligence to select men of
virtue and wisdom." He did not place "unlimited confidence" in elected officials. If there is no virtue among the people, he declared, then

> we are in a wretched situation. No theoretical checks, no form of government,
> can render us secure. To suppose any form of government will secure liberty or
> happiness without any virtue in the people, is a chimerical idea. If there be suf-
> ficient virtue and intelligence in the community, it will be exercised in the se-
> lection of these men; so that we do not depend on their virtue, or put confidence
> in our rulers, but in the people who are to choose them.[39]

His constitution is intended to make the exercise of virtue and intelligence possible and even necessary.

Madison indicated how this will occur in his discussion of the Senate, in
Federalist #62 and 63. "Good government," he argues, "implied two things:
first, fidelity to the object of government, which is the happiness of the people;
secondly, a knowledge of the means by which that subject may be attained."[40]
That is, it must combine a good will—virtue in its simplest and most essential
form—with wisdom. With a view to the necessary conjunction of virtue and
wisdom, Madison treated the Senate as the central institution in the structure of
government, the part that holds the whole together and directs its movements.
Senators are fewer and elected for a longer term of office than members of the
House of Representatives, and their terms are staggered in order to insure continuity in the Senate's membership. The Senate fulfills a number of absolutely
essential governmental roles. Without the upper chamber to check it, the House
would be prone "to yield to the impulse of sudden and violent passions, and to
be seduced by factious leaders into intemperate and pernicious resolutions."
Without a body of experienced members, the legislative branch would lack "due
acquaintance with the objects and principles of legislation." Without a "stable

institution in the government," the "public councils" of the nation would be excessively changeable in their opinions and their policies. Without a "select and stable member of the government," a "due sense of national character" would be absent from the "national councils." Finally, without a continuing body in the national government, the people could not hold anyone politically responsible for the success, or failures, of governmental policies.[41] With its smaller numbers, longer term of office, and special powers in the areas of foreign affairs and executive and judicial appointments, the Senate is designed to be attractive to individuals of ability, accomplishment, and gravity. It gives such individuals an appropriate arena to display and exercise their best qualities. And the American political system cannot function properly without such people in the Senate. Undoubtedly the greatest benefit of the Senate, for Madison, is "as a defense to the people against their own temporary errors and delusions." "As the cool and deliberate sense of the community ought . . . ultimately prevail over the views of the rulers," he argues,

> so there are particular moments in public affairs when the people, stimulated by some irregular passion, or some illicit advantage, or misled by the artful misrepresentations of interested men, may call for measures which they themselves will afterwards be the most ready to lament and condemn. In these critical moments, how salutary will be the interference of some temperate and respectable body of citizens, in order to check the misguided career and to suspend the blow meditated by the people against themselves, until reason, justice, and truth can regain their authority over the public mind? What bitter anguish would not the people of Athens have often escaped if their government had contained so provident a safeguard against the tyranny of their own passions? Popular liberty might then have escaped the indelible reproach of decreeing to the same citizens the hemlock on one day and statues on the next.

A senate in Athens might well have saved the cause of "popular liberty" from the "indelible reproach of decreeing to the same citizens the hemlock on one day and statues on the next."[42]

Madison explained how the constitutional system is supposed to work in *Federalist* #49, one of a series of papers on the delicate problem of maintaining the separation of powers among the legislative, executive, and judicial departments of government. The underlying theme of *Federalist* #49—in which Madison criticized, very gently, a proposal by his friend Jefferson for calling a new constitutional convention whenever the departments differ about the division of powers—is the interplay between reason and the passions in a properly constructed democracy. Madison agreed that "[t]he accumulation of all powers, legislative, executive, and judiciary, in the same hands, whether one, few, or many, and whether hereditary, self-appointed, or elective, may justly be pronounced the very definition of tyranny." He stated the problem in such a way as to make it clear that an improperly structured democracy is a tyranny, something that democrats need to be reminded of, so that they will accept and support the complicated political arrangements necessary to make democracy work. The problem with Jefferson's proposed solution to the problem, which would lead to the "frequent reference of constitutional questions to the decision of the whole society," is that it would disturb "the public tranquility by interesting too strongly the public passions." The people would inevitably divide in accordance with "the spirit of pre-existing parties, or of parties springing out of the question itself," supporting the legislature because it is the people's branch of government, or the president because he is the people's defender against their enemies. In sum, "[t]he *passions* . . . not the *reason*, of the public would sit in judgment." This is the direct contrary of the way that democratic government should function. In a decent democracy, "it is the reason, alone, of the public that ought to control and regulate the government. The passions ought to be controlled and regulated by the government."[43] Madison's system of checks and balances—setting ambition against ambition—is a better way to maintain the division of powers, because it cools rather than inflames the passions. It puts the people in the proper frame of mind for self-government.

Jefferson's plan, under which constitutional confrontations would be resolved by public debate and majority vote, appears as the height of rationality. In reality, it is profoundly irrational, because it does not take into account the power of the passions. Its inevitable consequence would be to undermine the people's support for their government. Madison claimed that frequent appeals to the people, every one of which carries "an implication of some defect in the government," would "deprive the government of that veneration which time bestows on everything, and without which the wisest and freest governments would not possess the requisite stability." In a "nation of philosophers," he admits, this issue would not be a concern. In such a society, enlightened reason would be sufficient to sustain the government and the laws. A nation of philosophers, however, is no more to be expected than the "philosophical race of kings wished for by Plato." Taking human beings as they really are, even "the most rational government will not find it a superfluous advantage to have the prejudices of the community on its side." Government rests on a foundation of opinion, and opinions derive their strength from the number of people who hold them and the length of time that they have been held. Reason is "timid and cautious when left alone, and acquires firmness and confidence in proportion to the number with which it is associated." And when "the examples which fortify opinion are *ancient* as well as *numerous*, they are known to have a double effect."[44]

According to Madison, it is reasonable for reason, recognizing its own weakness in the face of the passions, to enlist unreasoning belief in its cause. Indeed, it would be irrational to do otherwise. If the people hear their government constantly criticized by its most authoritative spokesmen, they will lose their respect for and attachment to it. The eventual result will be a change of government, and probably not for the better. The constitutional system, forged in the struggles of the Revolution and the chaos of the Articles of Confederation, was created "in the midst of danger that repressed the passions most unfriendly to order and concord"; in almost universal respect for the political leadership, which "stifled the ordinary diversity of opinions on great national questions"; and in a general antipathy to the existing government. That is, it was formed at a time when, as a result of chance circumstances, the passions of the people supported the establishment of good government.[45] And reason says that such circumstances are not likely to repeat themselves in the future.

Some time after the Constitution had been ratified and had gone into effect, Madison wrote a short essay in which he placed the new government in historic and comparative perspective. This essay was one in a series he published, anonymously, in Philip Freneau's *National Gazette*, which he and Jefferson founded to counter John Fenno's *Gazette of the United States*, the organ of Hamilton and his Federalist Party. Madison, who was a member of the House of Representatives, had broken with Hamilton, who was Secretary of the Treasury, over the funding of the Revolutionary War debt and the establishment of a national bank. Madison's essays laid out the principles of the developing opposition party, the Republicans—later the Democrats. The purpose of the party was to defend the Constitution against what Madison saw as the "monarchist" tendencies of Hamilton and the Federalists. In the essay on the "Spirit of Governments," Madison indicated what was at stake in this conflict by explaining what the Constitution meant in the long sweep of human history. There are three "species" of government, he argues, defined by "their predominant spirit and principles." The first and most common kind, "under which human nature has groaned through every age," operates by "a permanent military force." Such force is "at once the cause of burdens on the people, and of submission in the people to their burdens." Virtually all the governments of Europe, "the quarter of the globe which calls itself the cradle of civilization and the pride of humanity" are of this type. The second kind operates by "corrupt influence, substituting the motive of private interest in place of public duty, converting its pecuniary dispensations into bounties to favorites or bribes to opponents . . . in a word, enlisting an army of interested partisans . . . whose active combinations, by supplying the terror of the sword, may support a real domination of the few, under an apparent liberty of the many." Although Madison did not say so explicitly, this seems to be the type of government that he fears will result from the policies of Hamilton and the Federalists. The third and best kind derives its "energy from the will of the society" and operates "by reason of its measures, on the understanding and interest of the society." Madison claimed that such a government, which "it is the glory of America to have invented, and her unrivalled happiness to possess," is that "for which philosophy has been searching and humanity fighting from the most remote ages." It represents the fulfillment of the dream of rational freedom. All that remains is for the nation's "happiness to be perpetuated by a system of administration corresponding with the purity of the theory," which is what Madison understood as the function of the political party he was founding.[46]

NOTES

1. *Federalist* #39.

2. *Federalist* #57.

3. Letter to Roger C. Weightman, June 24, 1825, in *The Life and Selected Writings of Thomas Jefferson*, eds. Adrienne Koch and William Peden (New York: Modern Library, 1944), 729-730.

4. *Federalist* #55.

5. *Federalist* #10.

6. *Federalist* #72.

7. On the charge to the Constitutional Convention, see *Federalist* #40.

8. On the deficiencies of the Articles of Confederation, as a result of its adoption of the traditional theory of federalism, see *Federalist* #15, by Hamilton. He refers to the "imbecility" of the existing government.

9. *Federalist* #37.

10. See *Federalist* #39.

11. *Federalist* #37.

12. *Federalist* #51.

13. *Federalist* #37.

14. Ibid.

15. Ibid.

16. *Federalist* #38.

17. *Federalist* #51.

18. *Federalist* #10.

19. Ibid.

20. Ibid.

21. *Federalist* #49.

22. *Federalist* #10.

23. Plato at least is aware of the problem that nature presents to traditional republicanism, that it does not create human beings like bees or ants, fit for only one purpose. The citizen education he outlines in the *Republic* culminates in what he specifically calls a "noble lie," a story which ascribes the class division of society not to the rulers and the laws, but to God and nature. See *Republic* 414b-415d.

24. Jefferson in his first Inaugural Address reminded the American people of the "sacred principle, that though the will of the majority is in all cases to prevail, that will, to be rightful, must be reasonable; that the minority possess their equal rights, which equal laws must protect, and to violate which would be oppression." Thomas Jefferson's first Inaugural Address at http://www.yale.edu/lawweb/avalon/presiden/inaug/jefinau1.htm

25. *Federalist* #80.

26. *Federalist* #81.

27. *Federalist* #81.

28. *Federalist* #82.

29. *Federalist* #14.

30. *Federalist* #10.

31. Ibid.

32. *Federalist* #51.

33. Ibid.

34. *Federalist* #51.

35. *Federalist* #10.

36. *Federalist* #51.

37. See Adam Smith, *The Wealth of Nations* (New York: Modern Library, 1937), Bk. I, ch. 2, "Of the Principle which Gives Occasion to the Division of Labor," 13-16. This chapter includes Smith's famous observation, "It is not from the benevolence of the butcher, the

brewer, or the baker, that we expect our dinner, but from their regard to their own interest" (14).

38. *Federalist* #10.

39. Quoted in Martin Diamond, "The American Idea of Man: The View from the Founding," in *The Americans: 1976*, eds. Irving Kristol and Paul H. Weaver (Lexington, MA: Lexington Books, 1976), 16-17.

40. *Federalist* #62.

41. *Federalist* #62-63.

42. *Federalist* #63.

43. *Federalist* #49. The italics are Madison's.

44. Federalist #49.

45. Ibid.

46. James Madison, "Spirit of Governments," in *The Mind of the Founder: Sources of the Political Thought of James Madison*, ed. Marvin Meyers (Hanover, NH: University Press of New England, 1981), 183-184.

CHAPTER 2

ABRAHAM LINCOLN'S NEW BIRTH OF FREEDOM

As the primary authors of the Declaration of Independence and the Constitution, Thomas Jefferson and James Madison are the most authoritative interpreters of American political principles and the American system of government. After them, the next is probably Abraham Lincoln. He achieved his eminence by leading the United States through its greatest trial, when its very existence was threatened in the Civil War. In his speeches and writings, he portrayed the war as not just a clash of arms and interests but as a conflict of principles. It was inevitable that these issues would arise when the United States—founded on philosophic premises, the Declaration's self-evident truths that "all men are created equal"; that "they are endowed by their Creator with certain unalienable rights," including the rights of "life, liberty, and the pursuit of happiness"; and that "to secure these rights, governments are instituted among men, deriving their just powers from the consent of the governed"—descended into internecine war. Both sides claimed only to be defending their rights under the Constitution and laws. The victory of the Union, which was due in no small part to Lincoln, gave credibility to his distinctive and more equalitarian understanding of American political principles.

Lincoln did not set out, when he entered politics in the 1830s, or when he became a national political figure in the 1850s, to bring about such a fundamental change in American thought and practice. To the extent that he had an overarching purpose, it was conservative—to perpetuate the form of government established by the founders, which he, like they, understood to be an example of freedom and opportunity and the best hope for rest of humanity that had experienced neither. In the conflicts over slavery in the 1850s, which brought him to national attention and eventually to the presidency, Lincoln looked to the founders for guidance, and especially to Jefferson, whom he considered "the most distinguished politician" in American history.[1] Lincoln insisted that his whole purpose was to reestablish Jefferson's policy on slavery: not to abolish it immediately, but to engineer its extinction by leaving it to be regulated by the states where it existed but to prevent its expansion into new territories. This policy was embodied in the Ordinance of 1787, authored by Jefferson, which prohibited slavery in the Northwest Territory. It was continued, according to Lincoln, in the

Missouri Compromise of 1820, which prohibited slavery in the Louisiana Purchase north of latitude 36° 30'. The Missouri Compromise was repealed, however, by the Kansas-Nebraska Act of 1854, and declared unconstitutional in the *Dred Scott* decision of 1857. Lincoln's immediate objective was therefore the restoration of the Missouri Compromise, which was also the main platform plank of the Republican Party, the anti-slavery party he helped establish. He considered the Republicans to be the true heirs to Jefferson and his party, the Democratic-Republicans, rather than the Democrats who claimed lineal descent from them. The Republicans, like Jefferson, were dedicated to "the *personal* rights of men, holding the rights of *property* to be secondary only," while the Democrats, who were responsible for the repeal of the Missouri Compromise and supported the *Dred Scott* decision, held "the *liberty* of one man to be absolutely nothing, when in conflict with another man's right of *property*."[2] Looking beyond the immediate conflicts, Lincoln also took from Jefferson his ultimate solution to the slavery problem—gradual, compensated emancipation followed by the expatriation of the former slaves. As late as December 1862, within a month of issuing the final Emancipation Proclamation, he proposed to Congress a plan for compensated emancipation.[3] Only a few months before, he had met with a delegation of free blacks to urge on them a plan for foreign colonization.[4]

Lincoln did not change his policy when he became president in 1861, even as the nation descended into Civil War. In his first Inaugural Address, which he delivered after a number of southern states had seceded but before any shots had been fired, he assured southerners, "I have no purpose, directly or indirectly, to interfere with the institution of slavery in the States where it exists. I believe I have no lawful right to do so, and I have no inclination to do so."[5] He did not back down, however, from his opposition to the extension of slavery into the territories. Even as the war raged, he declared, "My paramount object in this struggle *is* to save the Union, and is *not* either to save or to destroy slavery. If I could save the Union without freeing *any* slave I would do it, and if I could save it by freeing *all* the slaves I would do it; and if I could save it by freeing some and leaving others alone I would do that." At the same time, he reaffirmed his "oft-expressed *personal* wish that all men everywhere could be free."[6] He resisted all attempts to turn the war into an anti-slavery crusade; he went so far as to reverse the emancipation orders of Union military commanders.[7] He even ignored a law passed by Congress that allowed the taking of rebels' slaves as captives of war and their subsequent emancipation.

The restoration of the status quo ante bellum remained his policy until late in 1862, after months of bloody warfare, when Lincoln decided that as a matter of military necessity, to win the war, he would have to free the slaves. Even then he did not act immediately, but issued a warning in the form of the preliminary Emancipation Proclamation. In it, he declared that as of January 1, 1863,

> all persons held as slaves within any state, or designated part of a state, the people whereof shall then be in rebellion against the United states shall be then, thenceforward, and forever free; and the executive government of the United

States, including the military and naval authority thereof, will recognize and maintain the freedom of such persons, and will do no act or acts to repress such persons, or any of them, in any efforts they may make for their actual freedom.[8]

Lincoln's final Emancipation Proclamation was derided by many in the North as too timid, since it freed slaves only in those areas that the national government did not control, while leaving untouched the slaves in those areas that it did. The critics missed entirely the meaning of the Proclamation. Its practical limitations were dictated by the constitutional authority under which Lincoln acted, that of Commander in Chief of the armed forces: as "a fit and necessary war measure," and "an act of justice, warranted by the Constitution, upon military necessity," intended to bring to an end the rebellion, it could only apply to those states or parts of states that were actually rebelling.[9] To do more would be to act outside the bounds of his constitutional authority as president, that is, as a tyrant or despot.

The real significance of the Emancipation Proclamation was that it elevated the abolition of slavery to a goal of the war—an end to be achieved by military victory, along with—or rather inseparable from—saving the Union. After its issuance, there was no chance of a return to the old order. If the North won the war—and that was a question very much in doubt at the beginning of 1863—slavery would be abolished everywhere in the United States, since it could not continue to exist in the four border states that had not seceded if it were destroyed by military action in the eleven southern states that did. For Lincoln, the Proclamation represented not just a change of tactics in the war, but a fundamental change in its meaning. The war had already cost more in blood and treasure than anyone imagined when it began, and it was showing no signs of ending. It could not be won except by attacking southern society at its foundation. Slavery was not, as Jefferson seemed to believe, simply a relic from the United States' colonial past, incompatible with its modern democratic principles, and hence destined to die out with its progress. Somehow slavery had been able not only to survive, but perhaps even to grow stronger under democratic government. To save the Union—not only to win the war but also to bring about a lasting peace—slavery would have to be extirpated from it. That required, in addition to the military success of the North, a new understanding of the principles of American politics, which Lincoln supplied in his great wartime speeches. What was involved in this "new birth of freedom," as Lincoln referred to it in the Gettysburg Address, was reflected in his characterization in that speech of the United States as a "new nation, conceived in Liberty, and dedicated to the proposition that all men are created equal"—a peculiar reversal of the order in Jefferson's Declaration of Independence.

THE PERILS OF POLITICAL REFORM

Lincoln was criticized for being too conservative and also for being too radical. For Abolitionists, he was too slow and cautious in attacking slavery. They despaired that he would ever actually do anything to end it. For Stephen Douglas, author of the Kansas-Nebraska Act, and his supporters among northern Democrats, to say nothing of southern slaveholders, Lincoln was out to start a sectional war, if not a race war. As his conduct of the Civil War would prove, however, the critics from both sides were wrong. When the time was right, he struck directly and with deadly effect against slavery. And although he urged his military commanders to fight the war as vigorously as possible to bring it to an end as speedily as possible, he also did everything he could to cool the hatreds engendered by it. His critics misunderstood Lincoln because they failed to connect his political thought and political practice. He did not advocate a slow and cautious approach to the problem of slavery, as the Abolitionists believed, because he was conservative by disposition. In that respect he was a radical—literally, one who goes to the root of things. His radicalism was first and foremost a matter of thought: he sought to understand the changing issues of politics in light of unchanging first principles.

It was precisely his way of thinking that led Douglas and southerners to fear Lincoln. They dismissed his statements on policy, which, if implemented, would have taken decades—if not generations—to actually eradicate slavery, as empty rhetoric intended to disguise his real intentions. He pledged to uphold the constitutional provisions relating to slavery, which protected it in the states but allowed the federal government to prohibit it in the territories. The critics refused to believe that he would compromise his principles and obey the law. Once in power, he would show himself to be just like the Abolitionists, with no compunction about violating the law and even ignoring the Constitution. He was a dangerous fanatic like Elijah Lovejoy, the Abolitionist editor who was murdered by a mob in Alton, Illinois, in 1837, or like John Brown, the Abolitionist insurrectionist who was hung by the state of Virginia in 1859. What these critics did not understand, however, was that his very thought about first principles led Lincoln to recognize the need for compromise and above all for obedience to the law. His thought on these needs was reflected in two speeches early in his political career, well before he entered national politics and became involved in the national controversy over slavery.

The first of these speeches Lincoln delivered to a Young Men's Lyceum meeting in Springfield, Illinois, in January 1838. His topic was "The Perpetuation of Our Political Institutions."[10] He gave it in the immediate aftermath of the murder of Lovejoy, which occurred just over two months before in a town only sixty miles from Springfield. Even though his main concern was mob violence, he did not speak directly about the incident, but mentioned it only in passing, referring to the throwing of printing presses into rivers and the shooting of editors.[11] He confined himself to discussing two mob incidents from farther away: the lynching of a number of gamblers in Vicksburg, Mississippi, and the burning of a black man who killed a police officer in St. Louis, Missouri. He left the Lovejoy murder in the background in order to calm his audience rather than inflame their passions. In this, he illustrated the most important point of his speech, which was the need to control the passions for the perpetuation of democratic self-government.

The challenge for the American people, Lincoln declared, was to preserve the advantages handed down from the founding generation, including "a system of political institutions, conducing more essentially to the ends of civil and religious liberty, than any of which the history of former times tells us." As a Whig, concerned more about internal improvements than foreign expansion, he denied that the danger that had to be confronted was from the outside: "All the armies of Europe, Asia and Africa combined, with all the treasure of the earth (our own excepted) in their military chest; with a Bonaparte for a commander, could not by force, take a drink from the Ohio, or make a track on the Blue Ridge, in a trial of a thousand years."[12] The great danger must come from the inside. "As a nation of freemen," Lincoln argued, the Americans would "live through all time or die by suicide." Already there was a harbinger, in the form of the waves of mob violence, in Mississippi, Missouri, and elsewhere. The distressing events showed an "increasing disregard for law" and "growing disposition to substitute the wild and furious passions, in lieu of the sober judgment of Courts; and the worse than savage mobs, for the executive ministers of justice."

The evil of mob actions was not so much in their direct effects, which were of comparatively minor importance, but in their indirect effects, which included encouraging "the lawless in spirit" to become "lawless in practice," alienating good citizens "who love tranquility" and "desire to abide by the laws," and undermining the "attachment" of the people to their government.[13] In this circumstance, supremely ambitious individuals, those "of the family of the lion, or the tribe of the eagle," would see their chance to win immortal fame for themselves. Appearing as defenders of public order, they would overthrow the existing government and establish a new one, with themselves at its head. This cycle of events had been the typical pattern of the destruction of previous democracies, as attested by the examples of Alexander, Caesar, and Napoleon.

Lincoln even indicated how, in the United States, such an ambitious individual might create the conditions of chaos necessary for taking power, either by "emancipating slaves" or "enslaving freemen."[14] Here was the great danger in the Abolitionist movement of the 1830s that had culminated in the murder of Lovejoy in Alton. While its cause might have been noble, it was unleashing passions among both its supporters and its opponents that were dangerous in the extreme. The only defense against an American Caesar was for the people to adhere to a "political religion" of obedience to law, "to swear by the blood of the Revolution, never to violate in the least particular, the laws of the country; and never to tolerate their violation by others." Even bad laws should be obeyed until they could be removed from the statute books. No grievance was so great that it could legitimately be redressed by mob action.[15]

Lincoln's argument about the danger of mob rule was a subtle analysis of the problem of the passions in democratic society. The danger did not emerge until the 1830s because before, during the Revolution and its aftermath, the passions supported democratic government. The great leaders of the revolutionary

generation earned fame by establishing a successful democracy, something that
had never been accomplished before. Their received their own measure of the
same good. In this circumstance, the passion for fame suppressed the destructive
passions of human nature, such as envy and avarice. Now, however, the Revolutionary generation—the pillars of American democracy—was rapidly dying off.
With their passing, the relation between the passions and democratic government was changing. Fame could most readily be gained by overthrowing what
the founders had created. The condition of peace and prosperity that followed
the Revolution had begun stimulating other dangerous passions.

With the passions now arrayed against democratic government, the only
power that could be relied on to preserve it was reason.[16] It was this power to
which Lincoln appealed in his call for a political religion of obedience to law.
The American people would have to learn to curb their passions, even their noble passions, in order to preserve their government and society. "Reason, cold,
calculating, unimpassioned reason," Lincoln concluded, "must furnish all the
materials for our future support and defense. Let those materials be moulded
into *general intelligence, sound morality*, and, in particular, *a reverence for the
constitution and the laws*."[17] Lincoln's position in the sectional crisis of the
1850s—opposing both the southern firebrands who wanted to spread slavery
into the territories as well as the Abolitionists who wanted to destroy it in the
states, both of whom were dangerously inflaming the nation over the issue of
slavery—reflected his thought on the problem of the passions in the 1830s.

The second speech was delivered by Lincoln to the Washington Temperance Society of Springfield in February, 1842.[18] The Washingtonians, a society
of reformed drunkards, was a new element in the temperance movement, which
in the 1840s was at least as powerful a cause as Abolitionism. Invited to address
the group on Washington's birthday, Lincoln took the opportunity to discuss the
general questions of the ends, strategy, and tactics of political reform. He concentrated on the temperance movement, but not far in the background was the
anti-slavery movement, as he indicated in his peroration, where he looked forward to the day "when the victory shall be complete—when there shall be neither a slave nor a drunkard on the earth—how proud the title of that *Land*, which
may truly claim to be the place and cradle of both those revolutions, that shall
have ended in that victory."[19] Indeed, he seems to have crafted the speech to
make it apply to slavery and Abolitionism as much as to liquor and the temperance movement.

Lincoln described the liquor trade in terms that fit trafficking in slavery just
as well if not better: "Wagons drew it from town to town—boats bore it from
clime to clime, and the winds wafted it from nation to nation; and merchants
bought and sold it, by wholesale and retail, with precisely the same feelings, on
the part of the seller, buyer, and bystander, as are felt at the selling and buying
of flour, beef, bacon, or any other of the real necessities of life. Universal public
opinion not only tolerated, but recognized and adopted its use." He dated the
appearance of the temperance movement to twenty years before, putting it in the
same time period as the beginning of Abolitionism, which emerged out of the

first great slavery conflict, the struggle over Missouri's admission as a slave state, when the possibility of the dissolution of the Union between free and slave states first arose.[20] Most important, the strategy and tactics of the temperance movement, or at least one phase of it, were identical to the strategy and tactics of Abolitionism, which, if it was to be successful, needed to change directions as the other movement had.

Lincoln praised the Washingtonians as the most effective promoters of temperance, and then, seeking to discover the "rational causes" for their success, contrasted them with earlier participants in the movement. These were preachers, lawyers, and hired agents who, in addition to having suspect motives, employed methods that were "impolitic and unjust." They were impolitic in approaching those they wished to correct, the sellers and users of the evil commodity, "in the thundering tones of anathema and denunciation," rather than in "the accents of entreaty and persuasion," treating them as if "*they* were the authors of all the vice and misery and crime in the land," and "the manufacturers and material of all the thieves and robbers and murderers that infested the earth." The reformers did not take into account human nature, which is "God's decree, and can never be reversed." Human nature resists being driven to any end, especially when "such driving is to be submitted to, at the expense of pecuniary interest, or burning appetite."[21] It was no wonder that denunciations of the reformers were in turn met with denunciations—that is, that they succeeded only in inciting anger at themselves and their cause.

The earlier reformers were unjust in that they demanded an immediate abandonment of a practice that was legal, had existed from time immemorial, and was accepted by most people as right and good. It was not just to attack people for doing something that was sanctioned by "the universal *sense* of mankind," in particular, when they were impelled by "interest, fixed habits, or burning passions." Again the reformers did not understand human nature. They "damned without remedy" those opposed to them, so that "the grace of temperance might abound to the temperate *then*, and to all mankind some hundreds of years *thereafter*." The benefits of reform were too far off, however, to engage many in the cause. "What an ignorance of human nature does it exhibit," Lincoln inquired, "to ask or expect a whole community to rise up and labor for the *temporal* happiness of *others* after *themselves* shall be consigned to the dust, a majority of which community take no pains whatever to secure their own eternal welfare, at a no greater distant day?" The Washingtonians were successful because they avoided the errors of the earlier reformers, not because they understood the causes of the errors—otherwise, Lincoln would not have had to explain the causes to them—but because their own experiences made them more sympathetic toward those they wanted to reach. They practiced a "more enlarged philanthropy": "*They* go for present as well as future good. *They* labor for all *now* living, as well as all *hereafter* to live. *They* preach *hope* to all, *despair* to none. As applying to *their* cause, *they* deny the doctrine of unpardonable sin."[22]

The earlier temperance reformers, whose conduct was identical to that of leading Abolitionist such as Elijah Lovejoy and William Lloyd Garrison, represented for Lincoln a profound danger in social and political reformism. Their conduct was so manifestly counterproductive from the perspective of their avowed purposes—neither drunks nor slaveholders were ever going to reform by being denounced as demons, and, in fact, would likely react by defending and holding more tightly to their respective vices—that some deeper cause had to account for it. Lincoln recognized a profound vanity operating in these reformers. They were more concerned about maintaining their own moral purity, and displaying it for all to see, than they were about improving society and the conditions of individuals in it. This vanity was, if anything, more dangerous among the Abolitionists than the earlier temperance reformers. Slavery was protected in the Constitution. In particular the fugitive slave clause guaranteed that "No Person held to Service or Labour in one State, under the Laws thereof, escaping into another, shall, in Consequence of any Law or Regulation therein, be discharged from such Service or Labour, but shall be delivered up on Claim of the Party to whom such Service or Labour may be due." This notorious provision led Abolitionists like Garrison to denounce the Constitution as "a covenant with death and an agreement with hell," and made them willing to see it destroyed.

If what Lincoln said about the Washingtonians, who were the temperance movement's most effective spokesmen because of their sympathy for the victims of intemperance, were applied to the Abolitionists then its most effective spokesmen would be freed slaves and former masters rather than northern preachers, politicians, and editors. Such spokesmen would have been more moderate and humane, and thus ultimately more successful than those who had traditionally carried the Abolitionist cause. Abolitionism never changed its organization and methods, however. In fact, it became even more strident, with heroes like John Brown, whom Lincoln despised as an "enthusiast" brooding over the oppression of the slaves until he fancied "himself commissioned by Heaven to liberate them," but managing to accomplish nothing but getting himself killed.[23] Abolitionists in the 1850s were effectively in the same camp as southern slavery advocates, both willing to destroy the Union in order to get what they wanted. "No union with slaveholders" was Garrison's platform. It did not trouble the Abolitionists that if the Union should be divided, by civil war or otherwise, the slaves would remain permanently in bondage. Lincoln's position at that time—to adhere strictly to the Constitution's guarantees on slavery while restoring the Missouri Compromise—was intended to contain the fanaticism on both sides.

SLAVERY IN THE TERRITORIES

Lincoln was a successful state politician in the late1830s and the1840s, winning four terms in the Illinois legislature and one in the U.S. House of Representatives. He did not run for reelection to the House after his term expired in 1849, and because of his opposition to the Mexican War, he did not appear to have much of a political future. He was thus largely out of politics when the great conflicts over slavery broke out in the 1850s. As a member of the House, he voted many times in favor of the Wilmot Proviso, which would have prohibited slavery in any lands gained from Mexico as a result of the war. He was not in Congress, however, to participate in the furious debate that erupted when California, part of the Mexican Cession, applied for admission as a free state. Neither did he give any public addresses on issue. Again there was talk about dissolution of the Union. The crisis passed when Congress approved the Compromise of 1850, in large part through the influence of Henry Clay, who was also the architect of the Missouri Compromise. It admitted California as a free state, while organizing Utah and New Mexico as territories under the principle of "popular sovereignty," leaving "all rightful subjects of legislation"—most important, slavery—to the territorial legislatures. It also abolished the slave trade in the District of Columbia, gave the South a more stringent fugitive slave law, and adjusted the western boundary of Texas.

The most significant speech Lincoln delivered in his period of political retirement was a eulogy to Clay, who died in 1852. He praised Clay for opposing not only those

> who would shiver into fragments the Union of these States; tear to tatters its now venerated constitution; and even burn the last copy of the Bible, rather than slavery should continue even a single hour" but also those "who for the sake of perpetuating slavery, are beginning to assail and to ridicule the white-man's charter of freedom—the declaration that "all men are created free and equal."[24]

The first political leader to speak in this way had been John C. Calhoun. He was also the first to not merely defend slavery as a necessary evil, as Clay had, but actually to justify it as a positive good. He argued that it was the best way for whites and blacks to live together, mitigating the exploitation that was inherent in any relationship between the strong and the weak, as could be seen in the northern capitalist economy. He propounded his theory as a counter to the attacks of the Abolitionists, who condemned slavery as a moral evil. Between the two camps—one demanding slavery's immediate eradication, the other advocating its perpetuation if not universalization—Lincoln could clearly see the other conflicts that slavery could engender. Perhaps he was not really in retirement, but only biding his time.

The first of these conflicts came in 1854, when Stephen Douglas, as chairman of the Senate Committee on Territories, reported out a bill to organize the area north of Missouri and west of Iowa as the Nebraska Territory, later divided into Kansas and Nebraska. To secure the support of southerners, he proposed that it be organized on the basis of popular sovereignty, ignoring the Missouri Compromise prohibition on slavery in the area. This was not sufficient, so he added a provision explicitly repealing the Missouri Compromise. It was declared "inoperative and void," as "inconsistent with the principle of non-intervention by Congress with slaves in the States and Territories" established in the Compromise of 1850. The "true intent and meaning" of the bill was "not to legislate slavery into any Territory or State, nor to exclude it therefrom, but to leave the people thereof perfectly free to form and regulate their domestic institutions in their own way, subject only to the Constitution of the United States."

The Kansas-Nebraska bill ignited a storm of protest, but it eventually passed. It divided the Democratic Party, with half the northern Democrats in the House voting against it, and destroyed the Whig Party, which split irreparably along sectional lines. In the congressional elections of 1854, many Northern supporters of the act were defeated by an anti-Nebraska coalition of former Whigs, dissident Democrats, and free-soilers. By 1856 these groups had organized themselves into the new Republican Party, with the purpose of restoring the Missouri Compromise. In the meantime, virtual civil war had broken out in Kansas between pro- and anti-slavery factions. Rival territorial governments were established, and a pro-slavery mob sacked the anti-slavery capital of Lawrence. John Brown and a group of his followers then murdered five pro-slavery settlers, which led to revenge murders of anti-slavery settlers. Soon the territory was known as "Bleeding Kansas."

The Kansas-Nebraska bill gave Lincoln both a cause and an opportunity to return to active politics. He gave a number of speeches in Peoria and other Illinois cities against it and its author Douglas, who represented the state in the Senate. This gave him enough of a following to make him a candidate for the Senate in 1855, as a Whig. When the balloting started in the legislature, Lincoln had the most votes, but he eventually lost the race. He joined the Republican Party in time to campaign for John C. Fremont in the presidential election of 1856. What Lincoln objected to in the Kansas-Nebraska bill was the repeal of the Missouri Compromise.[25] He emphasized that he was not out to do away with slavery where it existed. He claimed that if all power were given to him, he would not know what to do with it. Every possible solution—emancipation and expatriation, emancipation and segregation, or emancipation with social and political equality—presented great if not insurmountable difficulties. He did think that some kind of plan for gradual emancipation might be adopted and might work. In the meantime, he was even willing to support a stronger fugitive slave law, as long as it would not "be more likely to carry a free man into slavery, than our ordinary criminal laws are to hang an innocent one."

Lincoln insisted, however, that the problem of doing away with slavery where it already existed was no justification for making the problem worse by allowing it to spread into new territories, any more than for reviving the slave trade with Africa, which had been banned in 1808. The moral principle on which the Missouri Compromise was based was indistinguishable from that on which the ban on the African slave trade rested. That principle was not changed by the adoption of popular sovereignty in the Compromise of 1850, the only principle of which was the "system of equivalents" between the North and the South. The Kansas-Nebraska Act was wrong in its "direct effect," to allow slavery into the two territories, but even more in its "prospective principle," to allow it to spread to every part of the wide world, where men can be found inclined to take it. Its *"declared* indifference" was thus in fact a "covert *real* zeal" for slavery's spread.[26]

The essential evil of popular sovereignty, which implied indifference about the spread of slavery, was that it forced "so many really good men amongst ourselves into an open war with the very fundamental principles of civil liberty—criticizing the Declaration of Independence, and insisting that there is no right principle of action but *self-interest.*" The argument that equal justice to the South required allowing slavery to go into the territories—that is, that "inasmuch as you do not object to my taking my hog to Nebraska, therefore I must not object to you taking your slave"—could only be supported by claiming that "there is no difference between hogs and negroes," something that even the laws and social institutions of the South, which treated slaves as fundamentally different from other kinds of property, did not admit. There were hundreds of thousands of free blacks in the southern states and throughout the nation, while there were no free horses or cattle, implying that there was something different about the blacks. It was nothing but a "sense of justice, and human sympathy" acknowledging that "the poor negro has some natural right to himself."[27] The strongest argument Douglas made for the repeal of the Missouri Compromise was that it violated the "sacred right of self-government."

Lincoln agreed that the "doctrine of self-government is right—absolutely and eternally right," but denied that it had any "just application as here attempted." He argued, however, that "When the white man governs himself, that is self-government; but when he governs himself, and also governs *another* man, that is *more* than self-government—that is despotism." No man was "good enough to govern another man, *without that other's consent*, which was "the leading principle—the sheet anchor of American republicanism."[28] The consequences of the adoption of popular sovereignty thus went well beyond opening the territories to slavery. "Is there no danger to liberty itself," Lincoln asked, "in discarding the earliest practice, and first precept of our ancient faith? In our greedy chase to make profit of the negro, let us beware, lest we 'cancel and tear to pieces' even the white man's charter of freedom." The nation's "old faith," represented by the Declaration of Independence, was rapidly being replaced by a "new faith," represented by the Kansas-Nebraska bill. The new faith, "that for SOME men to enslave OTHERS is a 'sacred right of self-government,'" was really the same as the "old argument for the 'Divine Right of Kings.'" The restoration of the Missouri Compromise was, then, nothing less than a readoption of the principles of the Declaration, which would be required if Americans were to save the Union and "to make, and to keep it, forever worthy of the saving."[29]

SLAVERY AND THE CONSTITUTION

The next great conflict came shortly after the 1856 presidential election, which was won by Democrat James Buchanan, when the Supreme Court handed down its decision in *Dred Scott v. Sandford.*[30] Scott, who was suing for his freedom, had been taken by his owner into Wisconsin Territory, from which slavery had been excluded by the Missouri Compromise, and then taken back into the slave state of Missouri. The issues in the case were the right of Scott to bring suit in the courts of the United States, and the legal status of the congressional ban on slavery in the Louisiana Territory. Buchanan had privately urged members of the court to render a broad decision that would settle once and for all the question of slavery in the territories, and that is what the majority, most of whom were from the South, tried to do in their decision. Chief Justice Roger Taney, writing for the majority, held that Scott as a black man and a slave could not be a citizen of the United States, and so had no right to sue in federal courts; and that Congress had no power under the Constitution to regulate slavery, except to protect the property rights of masters in their slaves, nullifying the Missouri Compromise prohibition.

Blacks, Taney argued, were excluded from the apparently inclusive language of the Declaration of Independence, which declared that "all men are created equal," and of the Constitution, which referred to "We the People of the United States of America." Public opinion at the time of the founding regarded blacks as "beings of an inferior order, and altogether unfit to associate with the white race, either in social or political relations; and so far inferior, that they had no rights which the white man was bound to respect; and that the negro might justly and lawfully be reduced to slavery for his benefit. He was bought and sold, and treated as an ordinary article of merchandise and traffic, whenever a profit could be made by it." Those who wrote and approved the Declaration could not have intended to include blacks, because they did not end slavery, or even free their own slaves. The "right of property in a slave," Taney argued, was "distinctly and expressly affirmed in the Constitution," and the "right to traffic in it, like an ordinary article of merchandise and property, was guarantied to the citizens of the United States," and "no word" could be "found in the Constitution which gives Congress a greater power over slave property, or which entitles property of that kind to less protection than property of any other description."

Instead of calming the conflict over slavery, the *Dred Scott* decision intensified it. Some political leaders, even in the North, supported it. Before the decision was handed down Buchanan pledged in his inaugural address to "cheerfully submit" to the decision, "whatever it may be." Douglas embraced it, even though by holding that slave owners had a right to carry their property into any territory, it seemed to invalidate popular sovereignty. The settlers in a territory could not prohibit slavery until they formed a state government, and then it might be too late. The Republicans, in contrast, hotly rejected the decision. Not only did it further open the way for slavery, raising the question whether there was any means to keep it out of any territory, but it in effect declared the Republican Party, the chief platform plank of which was the restoration of the Missouri Compromise, unconstitutional.

The Republicans charged that the decision was the result of a conspiracy among Buchanan, Taney, Douglas, and former President Franklin Pierce, who in his last message to Congress had argued that the Missouri Compromise was unconstitutional. It was a means for the Democrats to destroy their political opposition, at the cost of giving slavery advocates everything they could possibly hope for. The Republicans warned that the effect of the decision, if it were fully and finally accepted by the American people, would be to open the free states to slavery, since the same argument that prohibited Congress from interfering with the practice in the territories would prohibit the state legislatures from interfering with it in the states. All that was required was another decision by the Supreme Court, which would come just as soon as public opinion would allow it.[31] Douglas and the Democrats vehemently denied that there was any conspiracy, and even more that there would be another decision opening the free states to slavery, but they never could give a persuasive argument why such a decision was not possible.

Lincoln understood the *Dred Scott* decision as the logical extension of the Kansas-Nebraska Act's repeal of the Missouri Compromise, and criticized it from this point of view.[32] Douglas attacked Lincoln and others who questioned the decision as enemies of the Constitution and the rule of law. Lincoln retorted that Douglas, as a Democrat, supported President Andrew Jackson's veto of the bill rechartering the national bank, even though the bank had previously been found constitutional. Supreme Court decisions, he argued, established precedents when they were unanimous, without bias, supported by the practice of the other branches of government, affirmed and reaffirmed in a series of cases, and not based on false claims of historical fact.[33] Not one of these circumstances was met in the *Dred Scott* case, however.

The decision was egregiously mistaken in its historical analysis of the meaning of the Declaration of Independence and the Constitution. Taney was simply wrong in claiming that the founding generation had excluded all blacks from the political community, and hence that there had been an improvement in blacks' situation over the years. The reality was exactly the reverse. Blacks were losing the right to vote where they previously had it. Laws were being passed by state legislatures that made it impossible for masters to emancipate their slaves. The laws of Congress prohibiting the spread of slavery were being repealed and overturned by the Supreme Court. Most important, in the early days "our Declaration of Independence was held sacred by all, and thought to include all; but now, to aid in making the bondage of the negro universal and eternal, it is assailed, and sneered at, and construed, and hawked at, and torn, till, if its framers could rise from their graves, they could not at all recognize it." The situation of the black person was fast becoming hopeless: "Mammon is after him; ambition follows, and the Theology of the day is fast joining the cry."[34]

Lincoln particularly objected to Taney's argument, echoed by Douglas, that the founders could not have meant to include blacks in the Declaration's assertion that "all men are created equal" because they did not free their own slaves and make them their social and political equals. It meant nothing more, Douglas claimed, than that British subjects living in America should have the same rights as British subjects living in Great Britain. Lincoln ridiculed Douglas with the observation, "I had thought the Declaration promised something better than the condition of British subjects; but no, it only meant that we should be *equal* to them in their own oppressed and *unequal* condition. According to that, it gave no promise that having kicked off the King and Lords of Great Britain, we should not at once be saddled with a King and Lords of our own."[35] He refuted Taney's argument by pointing out that the founders "did not at once, *or ever afterwards*, actually place all white people on an equality with one another."

To defend the founders' intellectual and moral integrity, Lincoln gave his own explanation of their intentions:

> I think the authors of that notable instrument intended to include *all* men, but they did not intend to declare all men equal *in all respects*. They did not mean to say all were equal in color, size, intellect, moral development, or social capacity. They defined with tolerable distinctness, in what respects they did consider all men created equal—equal in "certain inalienable rights, among which are life, liberty, and the pursuit of happiness." This they said, and this they meant. They did not mean to assert the obvious untruth, that all were then actually enjoying that equality, nor yet, that they were about to confer such boon. They meant simply to declare the *right*, so that the *enforcement* of it might follow as fast as circumstances should permit. They meant to set up a standard maxim for free society, which should be familiar to all, and revered by all; constantly looked up to, constantly labored for, and even though never perfectly attained, constantly approximated, and thereby constantly spreading and deepening its influence, and augmenting the happiness and value of life to all people of all colors everywhere. The assertion that "all men are created equal" was of no practical use in effecting our separation from Great Britain; and it was placed in the Declaration, not for that, but for future use. Its authors meant it to be, thank God, it is now proving itself, a stumbling block to those who in after times might seek to turn a free people back into the hateful paths of despotism. They knew the proneness of prosperity to breed tyrants, and they meant when such should reappear in this fair land and commence their vocation they should find at least one hard nut to crack.[36]

Democrats like Douglas who supported the *Dred Scott* decision, and complimented themselves as "Union-savers" for doing so, merely served to illustrate a very important truth: "The plainest print cannot be read through a gold eagle."[37]

THE CRISIS OF THE HOUSE DIVIDED

Even as the debate over *Dred Scott* continued, a new source of conflict was developing in Kansas. Pro-slavery settlers, a small minority of the whole population, rigged and gerrymandered elections to a territorial constitutional convention, to be held at Lecompton, the pro-slavery capital. Anti-slavery settlers boycotted the election, so the convention was dominated by pro-slavery delegates who drafted a pro-slavery constitution. Knowing that the anti-slavery majority of the territory would vote down the proposed constitution, but also knowing that Congress would not accept it unless it was submitted to the people in some kind of referendum, the delegates devised a clever to plan to insure that it would be approved. They called for a vote, not on the constitution as a whole, but only on the slavery provision, and then only on whether to allow a future prohibition on the importation of slaves. Since there was no way to vote against the constitution as a whole, anti-slavery settlers boycotted the referendum, which was approved by the pro-slavery minority that participated. Anti-slavery representatives later gained control of the legislature and authorized a referendum on the constitution itself. This time, pro-slavery settlers boycotted the election, and the constitution was rejected.

Nevertheless, the Lecompton constitution, labeled the "Lecompton Fraud" by its opponents, was considered by Congress. The Buchanan administration, to placate the South, supported it. The Republicans, of course, opposed it. Also opposing it was Douglas, who saw it as a violation of popular sovereignty, and worked hard to defeat it. The debate was so intense that it provoked fist fights among members of Congress. After narrowly passing in the Senate, the constitution was defeated in the House. A face-saving compromise was then worked out, which allowed for another referendum. In that vote, the constitution was defeated overwhelmingly, and Kansas became, instead of a slave state, a free-soil territory. Douglas lost virtually all support among southern Democrats, who abandoned popular sovereignty and began to demand a congressional slave code for the territories as the only way to secure what the Supreme Court in the *Dred Scott* decision had said were their rights. As Douglas lost popularity among Democrats, however, he gained popularity with some Republicans, who saw him as the leader in the successful fight to keep slavery out of Kansas. Some spoke of Douglas becoming a Republican. At the very least, they called on Republicans in Illinois not to oppose Douglas in his bid for reelection in 1858.

Lincoln decided to run against Douglas, however, and explained why in his "House Divided" speech, with which he began his campaign.[38] He repeated the themes of that speech in a series of debates with Douglas, meetings considered to be so important that they were reported all over the nation, turning Lincoln into one of the principal leaders of the Republican Party. The speech and the campaign that followed it were significant not because they led to his winning a Senate seat—Lincoln won the popular vote, but Douglas was elected by the legislature, which was controlled by Democrats—but because they kept the Republicans from embracing Douglas, and with him popular sovereignty. They also helped to divide Douglas from the South, although that, from Lincoln's point of view, was a secondary consequence. Douglas, as far as Lincoln was concerned, had lost all Southern support because of his opposition to Lecompton.[39]

To be sure, Lincoln did what he could to deepen the divide between Douglas and the South, in particular when he posed his famous question in the Freeport debate: "Can the people of a United States Territory, in any lawful way, against the wish of any citizen of the United States, exclude slavery from its limits prior to the formation of a State Constitution?"[40] Douglas answered that question in the only way he could and still maintain support in the North: they could keep slavery out by refusing to pass legislation that would be necessary to protect it. That answer was fatal to him in the South, however, because, as Lincoln pointed out in the last joint debate, the fugitive slave clause could be treated in the same way: the Constitution might provide that "persons held to labor in one State . . . escaping into another . . . shall be delivered up," but Congress could render the provision nugatory by simply refusing to pass implementing legislation. "I defy any man," he declared, "to make an argument that will justify unfriendly legislation to deprive a slaveholder of his right to hold his slave in a Territory, that will not equally, in all its length, breadth and thickness furnish an argument for nullifying the fugitive slave law. Why, there is not such an Abolitionist in the nation as Douglas, after all."[41]

Lincoln criticized Douglas as one of the authors of a slavery policy that had brought the United States to a great crisis. It was now a "house divided against itself," half slave and half free, and as the Bible warned, "a house divided against itself cannot stand." Lincoln did not think that it would fall—that the Union would be dissolved. But he believed that it would cease to be divided—it would become all one or the other: "Either the *opponents* of slavery, will arrest the further spread of it, and place it where the public mind shall rest in the belief that it is course of ultimate extinction; or its *advocates* will push it forward, till it shall become alike lawful in *all* the States, *old* as well as *new*—*North* as well as *South*."[42] In this situation, Lincoln argued, those who would oppose the spread and finally the universalization of slavery could not turn to Douglas as their champion, in spite of his actions in helping turn back the Lecompton Fraud.

Douglas did not really oppose the spread of slavery, but only how it had been attempted in Kansas. Many times he had declared that he did not care "whether slavery be voted *down* or voted *up*." He could not be counted on to be on the right side in any future slavery dispute, for example, over the reopening of the African slave trade. Having labored for years to "prove it a *sacred right* of white men to take negro slaves into new territories," would he be able—or would he even desire—to "show that it is *less* a sacred right to *buy* them where they can be bought cheapest?" For him, the issue was all a matter of the "mere right of property." Lincoln summed up the problem with Douglas in another proverb: "a *living dog* is better than a *dead lion*." For the work of opposing the spread of slavery, if Douglas was not a "*dead* lion," he was certainly a "*caged* and *toothless* one." Not only did he not care about the matter, "His avowed *mission is impressing* the 'public heart' to *care* nothing about it."[43] What the anti-slavery cause needed, Lincoln argued, was someone who stood against the spread of slavery as a matter of principle, not merely as a matter of circumstance—regardless of whether the vote to allow it into a territory was legitimate. And so far, Douglas had never given the slightest indication that he opposed slavery on principle.[44]

By opposing Douglas in the election of 1858, Lincoln did much to bring to a head what he called the "crisis of the house divided." When the campaign was over, Douglas was unacceptable as a political leader to both northern Republicans and southern Democrats. This was significant because he had sought to position himself, and had been seen by many, as the only individual able to unite the country after the slavery conflicts of the 1850s. He had developed his theory of popular sovereignty to appeal to both northerners and southerners. He had demonstrated his commitment to popular sovereignty by taking on first northern free-soilers, when he pushed through the Kansas-Nebraska Act, and then southern fire-eaters, when he opposed the Lecompton Fraud. If he had had the solid support of the North going into the presidential election year of 1860, he might have been able to repair his relations with the South, perhaps by promising new territorial acquisitions in the Caribbean or Central America, where slavery would have been much easier to introduce than Kansas or Nebraska. He was at least as much a partisan of Manifest Destiny as he was of popular sovereignty. Then he could have been elected president, and perhaps have kept the country together.

Lincoln was accused of opposing Douglas simply to clear his own way to the presidency. What he did was certainly necessary to win for himself the Republican nomination and then the presidency in 1860. If the accusation was correct, then he was guilty of exactly the kind of overweening ambition that many years before, in the Lyceum speech, he had warned was the typical cause of the destruction of democratic governments. Lincoln's justification for his action was that Douglas could not actually unite the country. Popular sovereignty was a primary cause of the conflicts over slavery; it could not, therefore, be the solution to them. Its implementation required the American people not to care about matters—slavery and freedom—that they could not but care deeply about. What Lincoln meant by the "crisis of the house divided" was not, as Douglas claimed in the debates, simply that the United States was divided between free and slave states. That had been the situation since the founding, and as far as Lincoln was concerned, it could continue well into the future, until the people of the slave states could find a safe, just, and honorable way to end slavery. The crisis, which he blamed primarily on Douglas and his doctrine of popular sovereignty, was something much deeper: a struggle over the very principles of American government and society.

The problem with popular sovereignty, for Lincoln, was that it exposed and exacerbated contradictions among the principles of equality, natural rights, and government by consent of the governed, as these related to the practice of slavery. Most obviously, slavery set in opposition the rights of life and liberty. For white slaveholders, who feared slave revolts and revenge killings, it was a necessity for physical security; for black slaves, who belonged completely to their masters, it was the deprivation of all freedom. It did the same thing, on a more fundamental level, with the right of self-government and the principle of human equality, the ultimate basis of that right. The American people had created a government that allowed slavery; in doing so, however, they had acted as if white and black people were essentially unequal, with one group born to rule and the other born to be ruled—rather like the idea of the divine right of kings, which they had opposed in the Revolution.

These contradictions were incorporated in the Constitution, which treated slaves both as persons—for purposes of representation and taxation, in Article II—and as property—in the fugitive slave clause of Article IV. They had not been causes of political conflict because of the general consensus, reflected in the Northwest Ordinance and the Missouri Compromise, that slavery was an evil on its way to eventual extinction. That consensus had been undone, however, by Douglas's repeal of the Missouri Compromise. With slavery free to spread and flourish, instead of dying out, the contradictions it caused were becoming issues of immediate political concern. The people were dividing into warring factions, with each thinking itself the true defender of democracy and constitutional right, defined by its own favored principle. Lincoln believed that the conflict would continue until one side or the other emerged victorious and the United States became all free or all slave, or perhaps until the Union was dissolved. He confronted Douglas in the senatorial election of 1858 in order to allay the conflict, by defeating popular sovereignty and beginning to restore the old national consensus on slavery. If that was not possible, and the conflict should continue to intensify, he wanted to insure that the forces contending for a free society would have a more dedicated and effective champion than Douglas.

THE NEW BIRTH OF FREEDOM

Lincoln was nominated by the Republicans in 1860 as a moderate who could carry Illinois and some other northern swing states. He won the election with less than 40 percent of the national vote, but with 54 percent of the vote in the northern states, where he gained a solid majority in the Electoral College. His election was seen as a disaster by southerners who understood exactly what it meant: an anti-slavery majority in the North could control the presidency for the foreseeable future, which meant no new slave states, regardless of the Kansas-Nebraska Act or the *Dred Scott* decision. Soon seven states of the deep South had seceded and formed the Confederate States of America. Lincoln made no public statements on the secession crisis, while President Buchanan dithered, claiming that secession was unconstitutional but that he had no authority to stop it. Behind the scenes, Lincoln killed a proposal that would have extended the Missouri Compromise line to the Pacific, as a way to placate the South. He instructed his allies in Congress to make no accommodations on the extension of slavery, lest everything the Republicans had fought for be lost.[45] At the same time, he wrote to southern leaders assuring them that he would do nothing to interfere with slavery in the states.[46]

Lincoln stated his position publicly in his Inaugural Address. He did not threaten southerners but sought to persuade them to reconsider their action in seceding. The only alternatives to the rule of the majority, properly restrained by constitutional checks, he argued, were anarchy or despotism. He pointed out that, since the sections could not physically separate, a political division would not resolve their differences, but would actually exacerbate them. He declared that he would support a constitutional amendment expressly prohibiting the federal government from interfering in the domestic institutions of the states. He closed with a moving appeal for unity: "We are not enemies, but friends. We must not become enemies. Though passion may have strained, it must not break our bonds of affection. The mystic chords of memory, stretching from every battle-field, and patriot grave, to every living heart and hearthstone, all over this broad land, will yet swell the chorus of the Union, when again touched, as surely they will be, by the better angels of our nature."[47] His attempt to reassure the South did not succeed, however, and after he ordered the resupply of Fort Sumter in Charleston harbor, southern forces fired the first shorts of the war. Lincoln then called up state militias to suppress the rebellion, which led to the secession of four more states in the upper South.

Once the war began, Lincoln found himself, as he stated later, more controlled by events than controlling them. In part this was because his position, as he understood it, did not allow him to take the initiative. He had taken an oath to preserve, protect, and defend the Constitution, which meant that he could not consent to the dissolution of the Union. But he also took it to mean that he could not go outside of the limits of the Constitution to save it, unless compelled as a matter of indispensable necessity. He could not act to free the slaves until he was "driven to the alternative of either surrendering the Union, and with it, the Constitution, or of laying strong hand upon the colored element."[48] He justified the suspension of habeas corpus in the same way.[49] The most important contribution Lincoln made to military victory was holding together the coalition of forces in the Republican Party, which would have to sustain the war effort in the government and the nation. This meant bringing into his cabinet the party's principal leaders, some of whom thought they were better able to be lead the country than he, and were thus quite difficult to manage. Not only the cabinet, but also the Congress interfered with his conduct of the war. In addition, Congress opposed his lenient plans for reconstruction.

Lincoln could have lost the war at any time by simply giving up the fight; he could do little directly to win it, however. For years, he sought the right commanders to use the superior resources of the North to defeat the South. One after another his generals failed, especially in the East, where the Union suffered a series of terrible defeats—Bull Run, Second Bull Run, Fredericksburg, and Chancellorsville. The North was victorious at Antietam, but at the cost of horrific casualties, and other victories did not follow in the South. The war went better in the West, but the losses were high, in particular at Shiloh. In the summer of 1864, well after the great victories at Gettysburg and Vicksburg, which later would be seen as the turning points in the war, Lincoln was convinced that he would not be reelected. With Union armies bogged down around Richmond and outside Atlanta, he decided that he would have to do whatever he possibly could to save the Union between the election and the inauguration. He believed that the new president would have been elected on a platform that would prevent him from saving the Union afterward.[50] Thanks in part to the capture of Atlanta, Lincoln was reelected, but the war still continued, most notably in the trenches around Petersburg. By this point he had come to see the war as a force in its own right—a force with a providential purpose perhaps that neither he nor anyone else could really control.[51]

Military victory and the post-war reconstruction of the South were only a means to Lincoln's great objective as president, which, as he said many times was to save the Union. For this, something more was required: the reconstitution of the United States as a moral and political community. American society was not, like most (if not all) other societies, based on intrinsic realities such as religion, language, nationality, or culture, but rather on universal principles—the self-evident truths of the Declaration of Independence. What held Americans together, in spite of their many differences, was acceptance of these principles. Lincoln understood the fundamental importance of public opinion in American politics. "Our government rests on public opinion," he claimed. "Whoever can change public opinion, can change the government, practically so much. Public opinion, on any subject, always has a 'central idea' from which all its minor thoughts radiate. That 'central idea' in our political public opinion, at the beginning was, and until recently has continued to be, 'the equality of men.'"[52] Similarly, he argued, "In this and like communities, public sentiment is everything. With public sentiment, nothing can fail; without it nothing can succeed. Consequently he who moulds public sentiment goes deeper than he who enacts statutes or pronounces decisions. He makes statutes and decisions possible or impossible to be executed."[53] The conflict over slavery, he argued, could never be settled except on "some philosophical basis. No policy that does not rest upon some philosophical public opinion can be permanently maintained."[54]

As a consequence of the pre-war conflicts over slavery, and even more of the war itself, that consensus—what Lincoln had called the "old faith"—was breaking down, if it had not already been destroyed. If there were to be a lasting peace after the war, the national community would have to be reconstituted, but not exactly as it had been before the war. Americans' understanding of their political principles would have to take into account the experience of the war itself. What this would mean was not immediately clear. In his first important statement on the war, a message to a special session of Congress convened on July 4, 1861, Lincoln portrayed the struggle as a test of an essentially political question, arising out of the practice of democratic government. "It presents the question," he declared, "whether discontented individuals, too few in numbers to control administration . . . can always . . . break up their Government, and thus practically put an end to free government upon the earth. It forces us to ask: 'Is there, in all republics, this inherent and fatal weakness?' 'Must a government, of necessity, be too *strong* for the liberties of its own people, or too *weak* to maintain its own existence?'" The argument of secessionists from Calhoun on—that states had a constitutional right to leave the Union without the consent of the Union or of the other states—was a "sophism" by which "rebellion" was "sugar-coated." The war was thus fought to demonstrate that "when ballots have fairly, and constitutionally, decided, there can be no successful appeal, back to bullets."[55]

As the war continued and its cost in lives and national wealth mounted ever higher, however, that explanation came to appear insufficient to Lincoln. The war engaged concerns that were clearly deeper than the forms of democratic government. So many men would not have died simply to oppose or defend the right of secession and the doctrine of states rights on which it was based. The real issues were the principles of freedom and equality, on which the right of self-government rested. These are not only democracy's fundamental principles, but the most powerful attachments of democratic peoples. For southerners, freedom meant being able to preserve their peculiar institution of slavery and the culture that it supported. Freedom thus understood was in tension with equality, at least between whites and blacks. Freedom and equality of whites was based on their inequality with blacks. For northerners, freedom meant opposing slavery, which debased free labor and through its expansion threatened to deprive free people of the opportunity to move wherever they wanted to improve their conditions. How did slavery's expansion prevent free people from going where they wanted? Freedom thus understood, in spite of northerners' racial prejudices, required the recognition of universal human equality.

The war in effect elevated freedom and equality into urgent political questions or problems. Lincoln captured that reality in the Emancipation Proclamation, which he issued in January 1863. He tried to explain it later that year in his Gettysburg Address delivered as part of the dedication of the military cemetery on the site of the great battle. In the speech, Lincoln portrayed the United States as "a new nation, conceived in Liberty, and dedicated to the proposition that all men are created equal." Freedom, not equality as in the Declaration of Independence, was the founding principle of American society. And equality, instead of being a self-evident truth, was a proposition—a theorem that had to be proved by the action of the American people. In calling equality a proposition, Lincoln echoed what he had said earlier, in his criticism of the *Dred Scott* decision—that it was a "standard maxim for free society, which should be familiar to all, and revered by all; constantly looked up to, constantly labored for, and even though never perfectly attained, constantly approximated, and thereby constantly spreading and deepening its influence, and augmenting the happiness and value of life to all people of all colors everywhere."[56] Lincoln concluded by summoning the American people to rededicate themselves to the war, "that this nation, under God, shall have a new birth of freedom—and that government of the people, by the people, for the people, shall not perish from the earth."[57]

Lincoln's call for a new birth of freedom—not a "rebirth" of freedom—implied that there was something defective about the first. The war itself, and everything that had led to it, showed that something had been problematic about the founding, and it was not, as Lincoln himself said, the mere presence of slavery in the United States. Slavery had not been chosen by Americans, but had been imposed on them by their former colonial rulers, who had opened the slave trade and then prohibited the colonists from ending it. It was not even the dilatoriness of Americans to do away with slavery. As Lincoln admitted, the problems attendant on emancipation—security for the former masters and a decent economic, social, and political situation for the former slaves—were extremely difficult if not impossible, to solve. A peaceful and humane end to slavery would certainly take a long time. The problem with the founding was that it allowed slavery to regenerate under the new democratic government. Slavery in the early years had seemed to be dying out, but the invention of the cotton gin and the opening of new lands for cotton cultivation had made it extremely profitable, and contributed to its resurgence. In the debates Lincoln had criticized Douglas's argument that slavery would go where it was profitable and be excluded from where it was not, charging that Douglas was putting slavery "on the cotton gin basis."[58] Douglas was only avowing openly, however, what had actually occurred in American society. The problem Lincoln pointed to lay deeper, in the principles of American government, which justified action in accordance with interest.

Self-interest is the primary moral teaching of the Declaration of Independence. From what it calls the "self-evident truth" that "all men are created equal," springs the principle that human beings by nature have rights that they may assert against one another—but no duties that they owe to one another. The situation of rights but no duties is what Jefferson's teachers, the early modern philosophers, call the "state of nature," in which human life is "full of inconveniences," if not "nasty, poor, brutish, and short." In it, self-interest is the only rule of conduct.[59] The remedy to the dangers inherent in the state of nature is government, which human beings must create for themselves by consenting together, because nature does not create it for them by distinguishing between rulers and ruled. In entering into the social contract, human beings take upon themselves obligations to each other and to their society. With those who are not parties to the contract, however, they remain in the state of nature. They may—and indeed must—deal with them as their own interest dictates. They may even kill those who threaten them, and if they may kill them, they may also enslave them.[60] From this point of view, the institution of slavery is a kind of importation of the state of nature into civil society, which, depending on circumstances, might be expedient and even necessary. Lincoln, in effect, accepted this rationale when he refused to call for the abolition of slavery in the states where it existed, but supported the constitutional rights of the people of the states to deal with it as they saw fit.

The fundamental problem with the Declaration is its treatment of equality: the founders considered it a self-evident truth, a fact of nature, and as such, not a moral principle. Human beings simply are equal. Equality thus understood is the ground of morality, but itself makes no moral demands. It implies no obligation to recognize or respect the equality of others. Lincoln's new birth of freedom was essentially an attempt to redefine equality as a moral principle instead of a natural reality. Lincoln did not deny the self-evident truth of human equality, but he emphasized another kind of equality, that of equal justice. He looked for guidance not so much to the beginning of society as to its end, or purpose. For Lincoln, justice meant treating people equally in those respects in which they were equal, and unequally in those respects in which they were unequal. Equality thus understood was a difficult if not quite impossible goal to achieve, something that individuals as well as societies could dedicate themselves to, and make the most sustained efforts to achieve. In extreme circumstances, such as the Civil War, it was a supreme cause that could elicit the greatest sacrifices, and unite the living who devoted themselves to it with the dead who gave their last full measure of devotion to it. Equality understood in this way was a counter to, rather than a justification for, self-interest. As such, it was a better defense against social and political evils such as slavery. Self-interest could be summoned to oppose slavery, but it could not be counted on to be effective. From this point of view, his new birth of freedom appears as a practical application of his understanding, set forth in the Lyceum speech, that reason had to supplant passion as the foundation for democratic government.

Lincoln returned to themes of the Gettysburg Address in his last major speech, the second Inaugural Address. In it, he portrayed the war as an act of divine justice visited on both North and South as punishment for the sin of slavery, in which both were implicated:

> "Woe unto the world because of offences! For it must needs be that offences come; but woe to that man by whom they come." If we shall suppose that American Slavery is one of those offences which, in the Providence of God, must needs come, but which, having continued through His appointed time, He now wills to remove, and that He gives to both North and South, this terrible war, as the woe due to those by whom the offence came, shall we discern therein any departure from those divine attributes which the believers in a Living God always ascribe to Him? Fondly do we hope—fervently do we pray—that this mighty scourge of war may speedily pass away. Yet if God wills that it continue, until all the wealth piled up by the bond-man's two hundred and fifty years of unrequited toil shall be sunk, and until every drop of blood drawn with the lash, shall be paid by another drawn with the sword, as was said three thousand years ago, so still it must be said, "the judgments of the Lord, are true and righteous altogether."[61]

The biblical quotations, one from the Old Testament and one from the New, indicate how distant Lincoln's new birth of freedom was in spirit from Jefferson's original.

Lincoln did not get a chance to implement his moral and political reforms. He was assassinated only a few days after the end of the war. Those who succeeded him in positions of political leadership were either incapable of, or uninterested in, following the course he indicated. Perhaps as a result, the post-war reconstruction was a tragedy of recrimination, revenge, power-seeking, and plunder that left a nation divided, between sections and between races. Still, Lincoln's impact was significant. "Four score and seven years ago" and "With malice toward none; with charity for all" are at least as well known as "We hold these truths to be self-evident," or "We the people of the United States of America." Lincoln introduced into American politics the idea of equality as a transcendent goal that—beginning with the Progressives in the late nineteenth and early twentieth centuries—profoundly influenced and even dominated American politics. For this reason, Lincoln can be considered the father of the big government of modern America. A government devoted to insuring the equality of its citizens has to be large and powerful. By elevating equality to the preeminent value in American life, Lincoln began a process that made the many insensible to the weaknesses of democracy—the government of equals—and at the same time encouraged them to demand that the government rectify every social inequity. That is another thing that Lincoln is now criticized for, in addition to all those he was criticized for in his day. In his own defense, he might have said that if the choice is between a small government that allows such evils as slavery and a big government that prohibits it, it is reasonable to choose the latter.

NOTES

1. "Speech on the Kansas-Nebraska Act at Peoria, Illinois," October 16, 1854, *Abraham Lincoln: Speeches and Writings* (New York: The Library of America, 1989), vol. I: 1838-1858, vol. II: 1859-1865; I: 309.
2. To Henry L. Pierce and Others, April 6, 1859, *Speeches and Writings* II: 19.
3. "Annual Message to Congress, Dec. 1, 1862," *Speeches and Writings* II: 407-408. In 1865 Lincoln was still seeking a way to compensate the southern states for the emancipation of their slaves. See the draft of a proposed Joint Resolution, February 5, 1865, *Speeches and Writings* II: 671-672.
4. "Address on Colonization to a Committee of Colored Men," *Speeches and Writings* II: 353-357. Jefferson's plan for emancipation and colonization is found in Query XIV of the *Notes on the State of Virginia*.
5. "First Inaugural Address," *Speeches and Writings* II: 215.
6. Letter to Horace Greeley, August 22, 1862, *Speeches and Writings* II: 358.
7. See letter to Gen. John C. Fremont requiring him to modify his emancipation order, September 11, 1861, and proclamation revoking the emancipation order of Gen. David Hunter, May 19, 1862, *Speeches and Writings*, II: 266-267, 318-319.
8. "Preliminary Emancipation Proclamation," *Speeches and Writings* II: 368.
9. The text of the Emancipation Proclamation, *Speeches and Writings* II: 424-425.
10. "Address to the Young Men's Lyceum of Springfield, Illinois," *Speeches and Writings* I: 28-36.
11. Ibid., 31.
12. Ibid., 28-29.
13. Ibid., 29, 31.
14. Ibid., 34.
15. Ibid., 32.
16. Ibid., 34.
17. Ibid., 36.
18. "Address to the Washington Temperance Society of Springfield, Illinois," February 22, 1842, *Speeches and Writings* I: 81-90.
19. Ibid., 90.
20. Ibid., 84-85.
21. Ibid., 82-83.
22. Ibid., 85-86.
23. "Address at Cooper Institute, New York City," *Speeches and Writings* II: 125.
24. "Eulogy on Henry Clay at Springfield, Illinois," July 6, 1852, *Speeches and Writings* I: 271.
25. "Speech on the Kansas-Nebraska Act at Peoria, Illinois," October 16, 1854, *Speeches and Writings* I: 307-348.
26. Ibid., 315-317, 320-321.
27. Ibid., 315, 325-327.
28. Ibid., 328.

29. Ibid, 339, 340, 342.

30. *Dred Scott v. Sandford* 60 U.S. 393.

31. See Lincoln's "House Divided Speech," *Speeches and Writings* I: 432.

32. "Speech on the Dred Scott Decision," June 26, 1857, *Speeches and Writings* I: 390-403.

33. Ibid., 393.

34. Ibid., 396.

35. Ibid., 399-400.

36. Ibid., 398-399.

37. Ibid., 402-403.

38. "House Divided Speech at Springfield, Illinois," June 6, 1858, *Speeches and Writings* I: 426-434.

39. Letter to Henry Asbury, July 31, 1858, *Abraham Lincoln: Speeches and Writings* I: 483.

40. "Second Lincoln-Douglas Debate, at Freeport, Illinois," *Abraham Lincoln: Speeches and Writings* I: 537-580, 541-542.

41. "Seventh Lincoln-Douglas Debate, Alton, Illinois," October 15, 1858, *Speeches and Writings* I: 814.

42. "House Divided Speech," *Speeches and Writings* I: 426.

43. Ibid., 432-433.

44. Ibid., 434.

45. See letter to Lyman Trumball, December 11, 1860, *Speeches and Writings* II: 190.

46. See letter to Alexander H. Stevens, December 22, 1860, *Speeches and Writings* II: 194.

47. "First Inaugural Address," March 4, 1861, *Speeches and Writings* II: 220-222, 225.

48. Letter to Albert G. Hodges, April 4, 1865, *Speeches and Writings* II: 585-586.

49. See "Proclamation Suspending the Writ of Habeas Corpus," September 24, 1862, *Speeches and Writings* II: 371; and "Proclamation Suspending the Writ of Habeas Corpus," September 15, 1863, *Speeches and Writings* II, 511-512.

50. Memorandum on Probable Failure of Re-election, August 23, 1864, *Speeches and Writings* II: 624.

51. See letter to Albert G. Hodges, *Speeches and Writings* II: 586.

52. "Portion of a Speech at Republican Banquet Chicago, Illinois," December 10, 1856, *Speeches and Writings* I: 385-386.

53. "First Lincoln-Douglas Debate, Ottawa, Illinois," August 21, 1858, *Speeches and Writings* I: 524-525.

54. "Speech at New Haven, Connecticut," March 6, 1860, *Speeches and Writings* II: 136.

55. "Message to Congress Special Session," July 4, 1861, *Speeches and Writings* II: 250, 255, 260.

56. "Speech on the *Dred Scott* Decision at Springfield, Illinois," June 26, 1857, *Speeches and Writings* I: 398.

57. "Address at Gettysburg, Pennsylvania," November 19, 1863, *Speeches and Writings* II: 536.

58. "Seventh Lincoln-Douglas Debate, Alton, Illinois," October 15, 1858, *Speeches and Writings* I: 811-812.

59. On the idea of the state of nature, see Thomas Hobbes, *Leviathan*, ch. 13; Benedict Spinoza, *Tractatus Theologico-Politicus*, ch. 16; and John Locke, *Second Treatise of Government*, ch. 2.

60. On slavery as the continuation of the state of nature, or rather the state of war in the state of nature, see Locke, *Second Treatise of Government*, ch. 4.

61. "Second Inaugural Address," March 4, 1865, *Speeches and Writings* II: 687.

CHAPTER 3

WOODROW WILSON'S PROGRESSIVE CONSTITUTION

Woodrow Wilson saw himself as a constitutionalist. Yet to the extent that we judge political action by its results rather than its intentions, the nature of Wilson's constitutionalism presents difficult problems. No one has pointed to the essential problem inherent in Wilson's constitutionalism better than James Ceaser, who notes, "Wilson believed that nothing less than a complete transformation of the political system could save representative government in America. As a first step in the transformation, it was necessary to undermine the reverence Americans felt for the Constitution and the Founders."[1] It should be disconcerting for all of us to imagine that saving representation depended on undermining people's reverence for the founding document of American representation. But, the record of Wilson's thought and his political career indicate that he was less concerned with reverence for a document than with adherence to a more innovative and organic constitution. The literary constitution needed to be undermined to save the organic constitution.

The curious situation we face today is that the assault on constitutionalism launched by Wilson for short-term effect seems to have been too successful. America verges on viewing representative government as too confining. The electronic revolution permits us to leap the natural bounds that made representation not only desirable but also necessary. Classical democracy seems within our grasp, and passionate democrats would have us become modern by imitating the ancients. Others may not consider the representative principle actually in jeopardy, but they do complain that the separation of powers and the practical campaign realities which accompany representation are irresponsible and corrupt. Thanks to the transformation in America's understanding of its political structure initiated by Wilson, most people now see in the Constitution the "promise of American democracy" and look forward to the progressive fulfillment of that pledge. In order to oblige the Constitution to fulfill its democratic promise some would modify it, minimally by suppressing the separation of powers and maximally by jettisoning representation altogether. In short, the Constitution has come to represent (even for those who are not reformers) the essence of the modern democratic principle in spite of the fact that its language and structure enshrine the representative—not the democratic—principle. It would seem that

Wilson's attack on the formal allocation of authority in the Constitution in the name of Progressive principles has borne odd fruit in the modern era. The legitimacy of representation has been called into question without really undermining reverence for the Constitution.

Wilson intended to introduce a new American understanding of constitutionalism. His writings leave little doubt that he did not accept what he considered the mechanistic assumptions of the founding generation. Of course Wilson is best known for the fundamental changes he helped initiate to political parties and to the way the president is selected.[2] But those electoral changes were part of a more fundamental critique of the American polity that aimed at a reconfiguration of the constitutional system.

In what ways and why was Wilson a constitutional innovator? Wilson was concerned with both perceived and real corruption of the body politic which had been inherited from the nineteenth century. There were two interrelated problems: trusts and bossism. Wilson saw the trust and boss phenomena as emblematic of deep-seated problems in the constitutional order itself. The deeper problems of the Constitution were threefold: the constitutional framework could not require political accountability from government officials, and without a way to ensure that accountability, the Constitution offered no means for Americans to act collectively to express themselves. Finally, with no coherence at the center, America could not long maintain genuine self-government. To complete the circle, it was little wonder that in Wilson's view, corruption was ubiquitous, for there was no national standard by which to judge policy initiatives; the moving force of legislation was its ability to satisfy the self-interest of congressional committee chairmen.

It is perhaps best to begin analyzing Wilson's constitutional vision at the surface, examining the immediate political problem facing America at the turn of the century. As America moved into the twentieth century, trusts held sway at the pinnacles of economic power, and bosses held sway at the pinnacles of political power. The election of 1912 secured one fundamental policy response to what Wilson considered an interconnected set of problems, but it was not the only possible response that was discussed at the time. A brief historical review will be helpful in putting this problem in perspective.

THE RISE OF AN INDUSTRIAL ECONOMY

By the end of the nineteenth century, America had undergone significant changes with which students of history are perfectly familiar. The country had become continental, and all, or nearly all, parts of the country between the coasts had been brought under control of people of European decent. Railroads had made transcontinental travel relatively fast, safe, interesting and easy. The telegraph had made transcontinental communication nearly instantaneous. Great, nation-building industries had grown up in steel, packing, clothing, and so forth, with the advent of mass-produced automobiles and the rise of air travel on the horizon. These new industries had transformed an essentially agricultural nation into an essentially urban nation in under fifty years. So expansive was the turn to industry that millions of immigrants could come to America with the expectation of earning a living. The population of the country grew 35.2 million in 1865 to 98.8 million in 1915.

It cannot be said that all was absolute prosperity. Many who left the farm and most who left the Old World faced only slightly better living conditions than they had left behind. By any contemporary standard, they endured horrific challenges, both in the workplace and in their homes. Most of the arable land was claimed by 1900, and the agricultural economy did not really provide a living for most farmers. It must have appeared to many people that their future—or perhaps more accurately their children's future—depended on leaving the land and submitting to the discipline of the industrial workplace.

Unlike the debate of the 1930s, the Progressive movement had not decided that it was the national government's responsibility to eliminate fear—or in the words of Franklin Roosevelt guarantee all citizens freedom from want. Social justice was not ignored, but the Progressives sought mostly minimal economic regulation of such areas as working conditions and public health standards. Laborers found it difficult to band together to secure higher wages, while business enjoyed substantially greater opportunities to consolidate. Understandably, the socialist movement sought to organize labor in order to make it more powerful. But, beyond labor's grievances, and for a substantial part of the nation, it was the emergence of big business, and particularly the great trusts, that created the most serious political problems at the turn of the century.

How should the nation deal with these heretofore unknown entities? The railroads had led the way, government subsidized as they were. It was true, of course, that by 1887 the government had begun to regulate rail fees. Other industries, such as steel and oil, had also come under some legislative control. Thus, the political debate during the Progressive era centered not on how the community was to provide for the needs of its citizens, but on the ability of the government to restrain the power of business. The primary activity of the Progressive Era was to redefine the government's role in establishing a more equitable relationship between average citizens and large industrial conglomerates.[3]

POLITICAL PARTIES AND THE CORRUPTION OF DEMOCRACY

The specifically political issue that came to a head during the Progressive Era was the workings of the political party system. Because the political party had become the primary vehicle for entry into and promotion within the government, control of patronage was at stake at the state, local, and national level. That is, political parties controlled electoral politics. It is generally true that the organization of political parties and electoral campaigns has much do to with how parties and politicians behave. It ought not be surprising that the complexity of the federal government and electoral system in general led to a Byzantine organization of the party system. What concerned Progressives was the manner in which politicians responded to the incentives of the system. The American political system seemed to be dominated by regional or state bosses who ran politics in the states and not only set the terms of political debate locally, but because they controlled patronage, nationally as well.. This situation became known as boss-ism. At one level it could not be circumvented since even those who contended against the bosses needed help from the bosses to secure nominations.

The boss system was so widespread that it seemed to compromise the role of the average voter. Once in power, corrupt bosses used patronage, took graft, and granted favors. Far from citizens controlling the political agenda, it appeared that a political class had taken command of states, localities, and even the national government. This political class seemed to govern mostly for self-promotion, not for the general good. Citizens of good will had few means to fight the corruption of the machine. Not surprisingly, reforming the party and boss system became the primary goal of the Progressive Era which promoted such changes as the Australian (state printed) ballot, primaries, and party clubs.

Two basic issues thus dominated the Progressive Era. The first was the new power of nation-encompassing business. The second was the corruption, or at least increasing dissatisfaction with the corruption, of the relationship between citizens and government. Though he was hardly alone in arguing that the political corruption and economic concentration were linked, Wilson's first presidential campaign focused on that linkage and made it a key part of Progressive reformism. From Wilson's perspective, the bosses—and politicians in general—had become beholden to trusts, those great economic combinations that controlled the national economy. Wilson believed that attacking political corruption was the key to breaking the link.[4]

WILSON'S PROGRESSIVE AGENDA

Wilson identified American government with congressional government and congressional government with committee government—or more accurately, government by those who controlled the committees. He was not fond of government by congressional committees, for there could be no coherent national policy developed by a multiplicity of committees. Whatever policy consistency there might be was organized not through the formal institutions, but by political parties, an extra-constitutional addition to the American system.[5] Yet, as he later came to argue, those who controlled committees were dependant, either directly or indirectly, on state party organizations that funded their election. The party organizations themselves, according to Wilson, received campaign contributions from powerful monopolies and trusts, entities greatly mistrusted by the average citizen. Wilson argued that the chief payoff for these trusts was a high external tariff.[6] But why the high tariff? Wilson seemed to accept that corporations might acquire a monopoly domestically, but, he argued, as long as imports were possible the market was more likely to remain competitive. Wilson complained that trusts not only organized production within the country, but they used high tariffs to insulate themselves and their profits from international competition. Trusts used tariffs to pay for the extensive premiums that had accompanied their market consolidation. Wilson did not mind an enterprising man getting rich through innovation, but he objected to political means—government power and authority—being used to subsidize the concentration of important sectors of the economy in the hands of a few. It seemed to Wilson that the captains of industry held power over jobs, access to goods, and political power.[7]

The two most worrisome developments left over from the nineteenth century—business trusts and political bosses—had been fused, creating, in Wilson's opinion, an unseemly model of corruption for American democracy at precisely the time when national politics and priorities should have come into their own. Wilson's response was not without problems, however. Theodore Roosevelt offered an alternative to Wilson's anti-trust policies, arguing that the best way to deal with trusts was not to break them up, but to put them under the control of the government. For all intents and purposes, Roosevelt spoke in the name of what we now call corporatism. Government would define the conditions under which trusts operated. Government would regulate trusts both with respect to their action in society and with respect to treatment of workers. In many respects, Roosevelt was something of an early New Dealer, only perhaps more so. He felt that economic logic spoke for consolidation. He also maintained that consolidation required government regulation. People who had lost power over their lives because of the tremendous resources wielded by modern business could reassert their authority if politics were cleaned up and if government managed and regulated the great combines of industry in the public interest. It might be noted that in the wake of the outbreak of war in Europe, Wilson's actual policies toward tariffs and trusts came to mirror Roosevelt's, but it is impossible to know to what extent this policy was dictated by the need to strengthen American industry during the crisis of war. Suffice to say that by 1916 Wilson believed that the relationship among government, parties, politicians, and business engendered pervasive corruption for which no one and everyone seemed responsible. Not only was reform of policy necessary, America needed a transformation of its basic political structure as well.[8]

As staunch as Wilson's stand against corruption was, it is only one of the many profound changes he sought. It does not explain fully why Wilson was so insistent on introducing and supporting a new political organization and a new understanding of the Constitution. It is true that he wished to clean up politics so that the bosses would no longer serve the will of corporate masters—that is, use politics to benefit those who bankrolled parties. But his anti-corruption agenda was much more expansive because he envisioned much more far-reaching change in the nature of American politics. One may say, without pressing the truth too hard, that the role of the trusts and bosses was, for Wilson, only a symptom of the deeper problem faced by the American republic. American government was open to bossism because the view of politics at the founding had been defective. For Wilson, the original Constitution, even as amended, made it too difficult to assign responsibility.

America is among those countries that laid out their understanding of justice in a written document. It is not clear, however, whether a written constitution actually fashions a community or is a reflection of life within that community. The founders of the American polity believed they had in some measure *constructed* a community with their experiment in self-government, a fact which made the Constitution a novelty in the political world. Wilson, on the other hand, thought the founders had done no more than *discover* a political community and its form that already existed; they merely gave language to that discovery in the Constitution. Moreover, Wilson held that all constitutions were essentially unwritten products of social and political development. In the American context, this meant that the Constitution was in reality a reflection of the political development of Anglo-Saxons, or we might say, Anglo-Americans. In his academic study *The State*, Wilson left no stone unturned to demonstrate the historical continuity of American constitutional development and the Constitution's roots in the political practice of the English race.[9] His more popular book, *Constitutional Government in the United States*, even developed a four-stage schematic defining the phases of political growth from subjection to self-consciousness (self-mastery and self-control). As a community develops, its constitution or fundamental mode of community life grows and matures.[10]

Wilson emphasized that constitutionalism should not imply fidelity to a reified, formal (written) political order, but rather, "A constitutional government is one whose powers have been adapted to the interests of its people and to the maintenance of individual liberty."[11] More specifically, a proper constitutionalism, Wilson suggested, will

> bring the active and planning will of each part of the government into accord with the prevailing popular thought and need and thus make it an impartial instrument of symmetrical national development . . . give to the law thus formulated under the influence of opinion and adjusted to the general interest both stability and an incorruptible efficacy . . .and, put into the hands of every individual . . . the means of enforcing the understandings of the law . . . and . . . the means of challenging every illegal act that touches him.[12]

Wilson's formulation of constitutionalism appears to be neither exactly the understanding of the founders—a compact removing human beings from the state of nature for purposes of securing natural rights—nor a direct replication of the pre-natural right understanding—the distribution of offices and the way of life of a community. It was in some sense a composite of the two views. Wilsonian constitutionalism identified both a way of life and a progressive self-mastery that accommodates fundamental individual interests and citizens' liberties to the common good. For Wilson, modern constitutionalism must be a product of social development, but that social development must also point politics in a particular direction. Thus, says Wilson, the forms of constitutional government will almost invariably reflect:

> A more or less complete and particular formulation of the rights of individual liberty. . . . An assembly, representative of the community or of the people, and not of the government: a body set to criticize, restrain, and control the govern-

ment; a government or executive subject to the laws, and . . . A judiciary with
substantial and independent powers, secure against all corrupting or perverting
influences.[13]

The Wilsonian ends of constitutionalism, then, were individual interests and
the protection of liberties. In order to secure these goals, the political system
should promote symmetrical national development, stable and efficacious law,
and the means for individuals to protect themselves against illegal or arbitrary
government. Such constitutional government requires that people know and understand their specific rights, and that they have representation that controls the
government, an executive who is not arbitrary, and a strong and independent
judicial system. Wilson's constitutionalism was demanding, as was his hope that
the final stage of political development would entail self-mastery and an active
sense of self-government. When Wilson applied this vision to America, he ac-
knowledged that our constitutional development met most of his criteria, but he
concluded that America's final realization of self-mastery had been nearly, but
not definitively, arrested by the provisions of the written Constitution.

To understand this point better it is useful to look at what Wilson regarded
as the definitive model for constitutional government: Walter Bagehot's account
of the English constitution. Wilson seems, from early in his career, to have been
taken with Bagehot's analysis of English political life. While he learned from
Edmund Burke—and perhaps from the Germans—that politics was inherently
organic or developmental, Wilson thought that he had learned from Bagehot
where the weak points of American political development had manifested themselves. "You would go to Burke," he says, "not Bagehot, for education in the
infinite tasks of self-government; though you would, if you were wise, go to
Bagehot, rather than Burke if you wished to realize just what were the practical
daily conditions under which those tasks were to be worked out."[14]

It is in some ways unfortunate that Wilson learned the wrong lessons from
Bagehot. To see why, a point of comparison in the work of Bagehot himself is
necessary. According to Bagehot, the English constitution was not what it
seemed to the casual observer. Where an untutored spectator might see the separation of powers manifested in the spectacle of the King in Parliament, the reality was substantially different. The King and the House of Lords played important roles in British politics, but not the roles most people thought. Bagehot
considered that the King performed a legitimating function for Britain—he lent
dignity to the government and served as a source of popular affection and attachment. The efficient part of the government, that part responsible for actually
governing the nation, was the confluence in the Cabinet of the legislative authority of the Parliament and the executive authority of the Prime Minister and other
ministers. The lynchpin of the British constitution was cabinet government, and,
according to Bagehot, cabinet government is superior to American presidentialism.[15]

Bagehot argued for British superiority on several grounds. First, he reasoned that cabinet government joins administrative responsibility with legisla-

tive power in an accountable way. Administrators know how much needs to be spent to do their job, and in British politics they get what they need because the administrators or cabinet are the same people who control the parliament (or at least the House of Commons). Second, Bagehot contended that cabinet government does a better job than presidential government of educating and informing the politically active classes on the fundamental policy alternatives facing the nation. The fact that a government may fail makes the work of the parliament a matter of daily interest to the nation. Serious people pay attention to politics when a government may dissolve, making debates necessarily fluent affairs. Newspapers educate the population by publishing serious journalism, and informed opinion within and outside parliament determines the fate of legislation. The political fate of the government rests on its capacity to inform and convince and ultimately on its ability to win in a new election.

Third, Bagehot argued that cabinet government produces better leadership. First, since Parliament is a select body, its members are the most politically competent in the nation to determine who should lead the government. The House of Commons therefore functions as a real Electoral College, not a sham institution such as the American Electoral College. Neither provincialism nor demagoguery will work in Parliament. Second, cabinet government permits the electoral system to choose the right man for the right time. In a sense, Bagehot predicted that Britain would be able to exchange Neville Chamberlain for Winston Churchill without an election. As he noted, a wartime prime minister might have substantially different virtues than a peacetime prime minister.[16]

For Bagehot it was the mix of good qualities that made cabinet government better than presidentialism. But, Bagehot qualified his allegiance. The Lords remained a potent factor in British politics and social life. In particular, he credited the Lords with elevating public taste above crass acquisitiveness.[17] The monarchy really was necessary as a distraction and as entertainment for the lower classes. Perhaps most important, the franchise was limited. Bagehot saw few benefits to expanding the franchise,[18] a point for which Wilson chided him.[19] What Bagehot did not dispute was that Americans tended to be somewhat better educated as a response to the democratic condition of the franchise. Still, it was no surprise to Bagehot that American politics was reducible to crude, materialist party politics. The many, he thought, were not up to sophisticated and subtle political distinctions. (Nor would it have surprised him that British parties became much more doctrinaire and disciplined as it became necessary to tailor and simplify messages to appeal to a broader audience. In fact, he predicted it.)

What Wilson learned from Bagehot was not that a restricted franchise is good. Rather, Wilson admired that British government was subject to a point of governing responsibility or accountability which America was not. In his discussion of the relationship between budget and taxes in cabinet government, Bagehot had shown Wilson that Britain was a community and could act as a whole, or, put differently, that Britain was self-directing (self-mastering) in a way that America could not be. As early as "Cabinet Government in the United States" and his subsequent book, *Congressional Government*, Wilson, following Bage hot's cue, argued that American politics had developed under the theory of checks and balances into a system where a responsible party government was not possible and where the real responsibility for government agencies lay in the hands of Congressional committees and the Speaker of the House (institutions that were not able to see or understand the needs of governance and administration).[20] Wilson recommended in "Cabinet Government" that Cabinet members be nominated from the ranks of Congress and forced to resign if their policies could not win majorities in the legislature. The American Constitution would then mirror the virtues of the English government. He stepped back from this advice in *Congressional Government*, merely pointing to the defects of checks and balances rather than offering a definite alternative.

But, the issue was ever before him. Wilson ultimately turned his search for governmental responsibility to an alternative that would not require changes in the documentary Constitution. Whether because he thought an amendment would fail or because an organic adjustment better fit his constitutional conception, by the time Wilson wrote *Constitutional Government* he had found his instrument. Wilson concluded that the President was positioned to assume the mantle of responsibility on the basis of rhetoric. But the essential feature of Wilson's critique of American politics remained the same. American politics was not living up to constitutional hopes because of the defects inherent in its origins. It was not possible under the theory of checks and balances "to bring the active and planning will of each part of the government into accord with the prevailing popular thought and need, in order that government may be the impartial instrument of a symmetrical national development."[21] But presidential leadership, he concluded, could do so. The demands on the central government had grown too dramatically not to develop beyond the theories of the founders.

Wilson would have preferred British parliamentary government to congressional and probably to presidential government (which is what Bagehot said we had). Wilson preferred parliamentarism because he accepted almost completely Bagehot's view that British government was more responsible, had better leaders, and educated the political classes more completely than did American politics. In Britain, power and responsibility were united. The opposing parties critiqued administration, but the legislature did not try to rule outright; in fact, it was ruled except for the brief moment it voted on a ministry. It performed the role of "a body set to criticize, restrain and control the government" with superior proficiency. Congress, on the other hand, kept trying to *be* the government. It tried to perform tasks for which representative assemblies were unsuited and failed its primary function.[22] Moreover, in England men of talent were drawn to politics because the stakes and opportunities were high, and their talents were rewarded. The connection between ministries and parliament meant that debate and rhetoric mattered. The nation was there to be persuaded. Through the contest among talented men in parliament, the British people could engage in genuine self-direction. To the contrary, in the American Congress most politics was carried on behind closed doors in committee rooms, caucus rooms, and the Speaker's office. Only the parties offered anything like real responsibility on the

British model, but the complexity of the American system dramatically reduced their ability to offer coherent choices. Moreover, party government in America led inevitably to extensive corruption and reliance on party bosses and machine politics. Wilson's recasting of the presidency into the center of responsibility was intended to reopen possibilities of self-government and limit the possibilities of corrupt backroom politics. A powerful presidency might also draw men of talent and ambition into political life. Responsible presidential government would raise the bar of political performance.

Did Wilson really learn the right lessons from Bagehot? Did Bagehot teach the right lesson? Did Wilson see correctly how to cure America on the basis of what Bagehot had diagnosed? First one can consider Bagehot's argument itself. He never explained how or in what way the political history of Britain had been superior to that of the United States. He was at pains to show that there was greater public accountability in Britain. He was at further pains to show that in Britain public offices attract superior leaders. The essence of his argument was that Britain was better run than the United States, but he was not really able to give concrete examples of the ways British statesmanship had been superior over the long term. Was British society more just? Did Britain offer better protection from foreign enemies? Did Britain create more wealth or establish more outlets for empire? Was Britain better suited to world power and more successful at acquiring and protecting it than the United States?

At the time Bagehot wrote, it would have been difficult to claim that Britains enjoyed a more just society; though the issue is not clear-cut. Britain had deep class divisions, but America had only recently emerged from slavery. European-Americans probably found more justice in America whereas African-Americans would probably have envied, at some level, the life of the British working classes. Britain was, however, much more powerful internationally than the United States in 1867. Britain was still the economic giant of Europe. It had been secure from threats from the Continent for 800 years, and Englishmen had been masters of the Celts for 250 years. Britain governed a huge, multinational empire that spanned the globe and held it together with a powerful navy. In 1867, America was only beginning its imperial forays.

A curious point emerges when one develops this argument further. In *Congressional Government*, Wilson contended that British political development had made a positive advance when the Civil Service became primarily responsible to the Cabinet: it had stopped serving two masters, Crown and Parliament, and begun serving the nation.[23] The nation could now express and govern itself coherently through the Cabinet. As Wilson also notes, the extension of the franchise had made the government responsible to the nation as a whole. Interestingly enough, between 1850 and 1900, British global power had begun its gradual but steady decline, while America was beginning its steady, long-term ascent to superpower status. Is it possible that Bagehot's, and thereby Wilson's, judgment was premature? Perhaps something in the submission of all British political life to the will of the Cabinet, responsible in turn to the electoral judgment of the nation, bore some relation to the gradual decay of Britain's global position

Perhaps private energies could be given scope when the Lords still influenced the Commons and the Monarch had some say in administration. Perhaps separation of powers among King, Lords, and Commons made for a more dynamic society even if at the same time for a less rational or purposeful government. Perhaps when the British nation was forced to speak, even—or particularly—in normal times, with one voice, important alternatives were left out. Or perhaps the demise of the separation of powers which went hand in hand with democratization in Britain left the government too dependent on the many for its own good. While it should be admitted that there is nothing in America to refine the gold-digging ethos in the same way that the presence of an aristocracy refined British manners, it is also true that in America the commercial sense of the business classes has never been as deprecated as were the British commercial classes in the twentieth century (until the emergence of Thatcherism). One may thus wonder if Bagehot was teaching the right lesson.

Assuming that Bagehot had an important point to make about American governance and political responsibility, is it the case that Wilson learned either to recognize the appropriate symptom or to administer the correct cure for the ills he diagnosed in America's Whiggish politics? In *Congressional Government*, Wilson suggested that changes to the system through constitutional amendments might be possible and useful. By the time he wrote *Constitutional Government*, Wilson had changed his mind. Any necessary changes need not involve changing the constitutional document. Wilson was always skeptical about the written Constitution anyway. He thought that communities grew and developed in ways related to, but not fully dictated by, written constitutions. America had changed significantly since the founding. Some of the changes had been marked by formal amendments, while other, fundamental changes, such as the rise of political parties, had developed outside the bounds of the Constitution. Wilson thought that in some cases the written document had necessitated certain outcomes that were bad for the community but which had been foreseeable given the nature of the document. Party corruption and committee government fell into such a category. But Wilson hoped that political development could, in the end, work its way around the Constitution. He looked forward to the time when those parts of the Constitution that prevented America from basing public policy on the opinions and needs of the people, would be replaced by working institutions. This change did not require formal amendment; it just required political growth. The American Constitution may have laid down a blueprint, but if the resulting structure failed to meet the needs of the people, it was the right and duty of the community to perfect it.

The presidency of William McKinley had shown that the executive could be remade, or at least refined, in such a way as to challenge the supremacy of Congress. The president could become the voice of the entire nation, teaching and elevating the public with rhetoric. The president could govern by circumventing Congress and making use of his central position and singleness of vision. Good men could be recruited to governing and administering if the presidency were elevated beyond the second-rate status assigned to it in the nineteenth century. A powerful presidency offered both the challenges and rewards sought by ambitious people.[24] However, if the presidency were to serve as the focal point of American government, it would have to be perceived so by all or most Americans. Wilson anticipated that the new demands on the national government in the twentieth century, particularly in foreign policy, would go some way to creating a new image of the presidency in the eyes of the populace. Wilson employed his entire rhetorical arsenal, in speeches, in action, and in writing, to redefine the role of the presidency. His goal was to reform political campaigns and to subordinate the party system to the candidate. By doing so he would force those who followed him to emulate the active rhetorical role he assumed throughout his presidency.

Wilson insisted that the exigencies of the times demanded more coherent government than America had stumbled along with in its first century. Technology had solved the problem of distance, but the subsequent increase of immigration required that more intensive efforts be made to homogenize foreign-born citizens into the population and give them for American and Anglo-Saxon character. The nation was becoming more unified economically, but its political capacity to deal with that unity had not adjusted accordingly. The party system, itself a fundamental but informal constitutional amendment and an adaptation of the Founders' structure, had, at best, located government in the hands of an economic elite. For Wilson, at the surface, a new approach to securing the interests of the public, a new way to nationalize political debate, was necessary. Below the surface, and just as important, a new way of conceptualizing the Constitution was required.

It can hardly be doubted that Wilson saw himself as the model for the new president, one who demands responsibility and speaks with the voice of the nation. He believed that his model was "constitutional" in the large sense. American society needed a means to be able to place responsibility on those who made policy. The President could be that means. Congress could critique and refine the work of the executive (on the order of the British Parliament), but it needed to be checked drastically when it undertook to govern. Nothing, he thought, could ultimately dispossess Congress of its constitutional power as bestowed in the document, but he foresaw that a powerful president could go far to redefine the executive-legislative relationship. For Wilson, legislation was much closer to administration than it appeared to be in the Founders' minds. Administrators should makes the rules because it is the administrators who really understand how things get done. Wilson's appreciation for British politics made him see the parliamentary assemblies less as legislators and more as authorizers, criticizers, and caretakers. Proper legislation should proceed from the voice of the nation— the President—as the entity directly responsible to the nation.

Wilson's presidentialism thus dovetailed perfectly with his reading of the English Constitution. Cabinet government gave England a single line of policy responsibility and effective administration. There were no base backroom politicians in England. The English governed in the light of day. Policy was subjected to criticism. Citizens were taught the essentials of the great issues of the day an were then prepared to make a judgment on the success of a governing ministry. It remained always the case that in America, terms of office were fixed. But Wilson hoped that a much enhanced presidency would attract people talented enough to render fixed term less destructive. A sufficiently active president could lead his party, the nation, and Congress, and with a strong leader at the helm, the nation could be considered organically self-governing, for it would chose, and be able to hold responsible, the reconfigured embodiment of American self-mastery—the President. Thus, Wilson pursued political reform not because of a momentary concern for the corrupt politics of trusts and bosses, but as a means to a higher end. The Wilsonian president was meant to enhance statesmanship while at the same time providing the American public with the information and context necessary to judge that statesmanship intelligently.[25]

The great flaw in his plan stems from his misunderstanding of British politics. It was the opportunity and necessity to make and unmake ministries, not just ministers, that gave British politics its depth and seriousness. Wilson wrongly did not accept Bagehot at face value. Perhaps a similar critique could also be made of Wilson's downplaying the effects on British politics of the extension of the franchise. But, institutionally at least, Wilson perhaps should have seen that only a president subject to resignation, or a vote of no confidence, and only a Congress whose every vote determined the fate of the government, could truly be considered responsible in the same way as the British cabinet. Moreover, the challenge of leading a body of seasoned politicians attracted highly talented and ambitious leaders to positions of power in England. America could only, if even then, attract such talent by granting the President the authority to make rational decisions based on the needs of the nation as a whole. Making campaigns more popular and expecting the President to more fully utilize the rhetorical opportunities of the office are inadequate inducements to that high-minded, responsible statesmanship, which unites responsibility and power in a sober accord between rulers and ruled, desired by Wilson.

Today people are probably as ill informed about the specifics of government policy as they were a century ago. Most real decisions are still made in Congress and there is little respect for, or attention given to, great debates on the issues of the day. The only difference between the present and Wilson's day is that Presidents are now held accountable for everything that happens in the nation and subject to nearly unbearable pressure to persuade people that they should be satisfied with their lives. Such persuasion, it should be noted, almost never coincides with presidential ability to effect genuine governmental action. Moreover, once rhetoric becomes the standard of governance, the accountability of that rhetoric itself requires attention from the unwritten constitution. Trusting almost completely in the maturity of the citizenry, Wilson inflated popular expectations of the President without articulating a way (such as a parliamentary electoral college) by which the nation could differentiate spurious demagoguery from genuine leadership.[26] Bagehot previewed such a critique when he criticized the extension of the franchise to the working classes.

It is not clear, therefore, that Wilson correctly understood Bagehot's advice for America, nor is it clear that Bagehot's advice was correct. In trying to overcome the defects of America's "Whig Constitution," Wilson necessarily devalued the views of those founding American Whigs who had been careful to limit the effects of factionalism in politics. Wilson considered the founding generation too distrustful and too imbued with Newtonian physics to see clearly that the only way to secure good government was to trust the government to get things done. He had no sympathy for the proposition that America benefits from the representation of diverse interests in the various branches of government—an arrangement that makes lawmaking more deliberative and moderate.

Has the case for Newtonian checks and balances lost its force because of the demands of the modern world? As Publius showed in *Federalist* #51, the method of selecting government officials is intended to be unique to each branch. In fact, each of the popular branches (House, Senate, President) represents a different collection of the American voting citizenry and, as such, makes possible the claim by each institution to a kind of universality. It is this claim that infuses the institution with power. In Great Britain, the upper house, the Lords, can be charged with partiality. It represents but a segment of the British population. In America, no such charge can be leveled against the Senate. Prior to passage of the Seventeenth Amendment, the Senate represented state legislatures, which in turn represented state voting populations. After passage of the Seventeenth Amendment, the Senate was chosen by direct popular elections in the states. It is the claim of a popular mandate—and the desire and need to resecure that mandate in elections—that serve to gratify ambition in American politics. The system works, as Madison informed us, by making the members of each institution protective of the rights and prestige of that institution over and against the others. Elections connect pride of place to the interest of the officer. Nor is it clear that the system is one exclusively of checks. The branches are to cooperate when possible and defer action when not possible.[27] In the nineteenth century, the government showed that, if called upon, it could act. But it also refrained from much action. When no action was taken, the people were free to engage in direct, personal self-mastery.

One could suggest that after eighty years of lambasting rather than substantively revising the separation of powers, Americans have reached an all time high in political skepticism and an all time low in political participation. When parties and bosses ran the government, people participated in politics more often and were no more cynical about its policies than today. One is tempted to say that Wilson's effort to change the way people think about the presidency and his effort to make parties instruments of national politics ended only in corrupting the appeals of presidential candidates to the American people and encouraging irresponsibility. His goal could only have been accomplished by the creation of a genuine cabinet, and this depended on eliminating fixed terms of office and on making the executive directly responsible to Congress

Why then did Wilson not make substantive reform of the documentary Constitution a central part of his campaign? Wilson wanted American government t be as responsible as British government. He wanted American government to be able to speak for a unified community. Perhaps he thought that documentary reform would ultimately make it impossible for the South to protect Jim Crow laws. Britain had a unitary government, and Parliament governed all of Great Britain in all aspects (though this was not entirely true of the empire). Or perhaps Wilson despaired of persuading America of its serious defects, for to do so may have cost him the presidential election. Perhaps he also thought that his proposed, non-formal amendment of the separation of powers was even more legitimate than an amendment.

According to Wilson, Anglo-American political life inevitably moved away from checks and balances toward unified responsibility. Britain had led the way, but America was ultimately an Anglo-Saxon polity and would eventually follow. The Anglo-American experiment in government pointed toward responsible government that could be fairly judged by a democratic population. On that score the Anglo-American side of that experiment still had some way to go. How fully this was an Anglo-American issue for Wilson is difficult to judge, but it is important to keep in mind his constant concern for homogenizing immigrants into the American way of life and his willingness to exclude African-Americans from political responsibility and even political and social rights. Or, as he noted on the end of Reconstruction, "natural legal conditions once more prevailed. Negro rule under unscrupulous adventurers had been finally put to an end in the South, and the natural, inevitable ascendancy of the whites, the responsible class, established."[28] But if the real constitution is in the practice, not in the document, Wilson's reformed conception of the presidency was not de-constitutionalizing but constitution-fulfilling.

At one level, Wilson was making a constitution, for he led Americans to believe in the organic, developmental character of the Constitution. He was not alone in his faith in pragmatism and organic politics, but his was the most powerful, or at least most public and persuasive, voice championing that conviction. Wilson, though always considered an idealist—and in some ways he was—asserted that he brought a profoundly conservative understanding to the American Constitution. He portrayed himself as a good Burkean, looking to the life of the community, not to the textual letter of a constitutional document, when evaluating constitutional development. Every generation assigns its own needs to the mechanism and freedoms of a working constitution.[29] Perhaps to Wilson, informally amending the Constitution (and showing people how to do it self-consciously) was the way for America to remain constitutional.

There can be little doubt that Wilson undermined reverence for the formal Constitution in his pursuit of a new constitutionalism. There can be equally little doubt that Wilson's informal amendments created a new place for the popular arts in American politics. On the surface he made those changes to rescue America from an entrenched political and economic cronyism that stifled individual initiative while at the same time leaving Americans with little sense that they could govern themselves or craft a decent political community. Clearly, he also thought the century demanded more of American political leadership. But his work seems to go even deeper than this. Lincoln had said during the Lincoln-Douglas debates that "with public opinion everything is possible, without it nothing is possible."[30] Following Lincoln's lead, Wilson undertook to change at the most fundamental level public opinion about the character of the Constitution. One is tempted to say that Wilson discredited America's narrow constitutionalism as both a conservative and life-giving gesture. But it might also be said that he failed to create the tools for the nation to manage its new constitutional dispensation. The new system requires more of its leaders without providing either a way to secure statesmen at the helm (in the way that Bagehot argued the parliamentary "electoral college" did) or a way to hold them responsible. Constitutionalism now assumes the wisdom of those at the helm, and in some ways is even dependent on it. There is, however, no greater assurance than there was in 1912—or 1787—that wisdom will be present. In the meantime, the document that purports to show us how to govern ourselves even when statesmen are not at the helm is celebrated more for its vision than its literal text.

NOTES

1. James Ceaser, *Presidential Selection: Theory and Development* (Princeton, NJ: Princeton University Press, 1979), 171.

2. James Ceaser, Glen Thurow, Jeffrey Tulis, and Joseph Bessette, "The Rise of the Rhetorical Presidency," *Presidential Studies Quarterly* 11 (Spring 1981): 223-251.

3. Consider here Richard Hofstadter, ed., *The Progressive Movement: 1900-1915* (Englewood Cliffs, NJ: Prentice-Hall, Inc., 1963) for a short but solid documentary review of the opinions of the times. There are any number of other solid histories of the progressive movement.

4. See particularly Woodrow Wilson, *The New Freedom* (New York: Doubleday, Page & Co., 1919) particularly 136-191. A solid, readable account of Wilson's approach to the campaign of 1912 can be found in Arthur S. Link *Woodrow Wilson and the Progressive Era: 1910-1917* (New York: Harper & Row, 1954).

5. Wilson continued to develop this thesis in virtually all of his popular and more general academic work. The first statement of this train of thought appeared from Wilson while he was in college at Princeton. It was printed in the *International Review*, vol. VI, August 1879 46-153. It is reprinted in Woodrow Wilson, "Cabinet Government in the United States" in *Selected Literary and Political Papers and Addresses of Woodrow Wilson* (New York: Grosset and Dunlap, 1925), vol. 1: 1-30.

6. *New Freedom*, 138.

7. *New Freedom*, 189.

8. He indicated this obliquely also in Woodrow Wilson, *Constitutional Government in the United States* (New York: Columbia University Press, 1908), 103-104.

9. Woodrow Wilson, *The State: Elements of Historical and Practical Politics* (New York: D.C. Heath, Inc. 1908), 267-386.

10. Wilson, *Constitutional Government*, 25-53.

11. Ibid., 2.

12. Ibid., 23-24.

13. Ibid., 24.

14. Consider here also the entire comparison in Woodrow Wilson, "Mere Literature and other Essays," in *Selected Literary and Political Papers* (New York: Grosset & Dunlap, 1926-27), vol. 3: 99. He also wrote a separate appreciation of Burke in the same set of essays. 104-160.

15. Walter Bagehot. *The English Constitution* (Ithaca, NY: Cornell University Press 1867, 1915, 1963), 59-82.

16. Ibid.

17. Ibid., 122-23.

18. Ibid., 176.

19. Wilson, *Selected Literary and Political Papers*. vol. 3: 99-100.

20. Compare Wilson, "Cabinet Government in the United States," in *Selected Literary and Political Papers*, vol. 1: 1-30 and Woodrow Wilson, *Congressional Government: A Study in American Politics*, intro. Walter Lippmann (Gloucester, MA: Peter Smith 1885, 1956, 1973), 25-57.

21. Wilson, *Constitutional Government*, 23-24.

22. Ibid. 86-87.

23. Wilson, *Congressional Government*, 188-89.

24. Wilson, *Constitutional Government*, 54-81.

25. See further on this point James Ceaser's argument concerning the intentions of Wilson's reformism. Ceaser, *Presidential Selection*, 207-212.

26. Ibid., 188-197.

27. *Federalist* #51.

28. Woodrow Wilson, "Division and Reunion: 1829-1889," in *Epochs of American History* (New York: Longmans, Green and Co., 1893, 1898, 1902), 273.

29. Wilson, *Constitutional Government*, 4.

30. "Portion of a Speech at Republican Banquet in Chicago, Illinois," December 10, 1856, *Speeches and Writings* I: 385-386.

CHAPTER 4

FRANKLIN ROOSEVELT, THE GREAT DEPRESSION, AND THE RISE OF INTEREST-GROUP GOVERNMENT

Franklin Roosevelt began his presidency by quieting the nation's alarm. "So first of all, let me assert my firm belief that the only thing we have to fear is fear itself," he professed to an audience made anxious by the worst economic cataclysm since the rise of the industrial age. A less well-known, but perhaps more controversial, element of his first inaugural declared that "I shall ask the Congress for the one remaining instrument to meet the crisis—broad Executive power to wage a war against the emergency, as great as the power that would be given to me if we were in fact invaded by a foreign foe."[1] The remark made even his wife Eleanor fearful "because when Franklin got to that part of his speech when he said it might become necessary for him to assume powers ordinarily granted to a president in wartime, he received his biggest demonstration."[2]

To many, Roosevelt's statement and his later assertion of executive power during the New Deal marked a turning point in the stature of the presidency and in the transformation of the Constitution. Prior to Roosevelt, it is argued by scholars such as James Sterling Young, the presidency was weak and subordinate; except in times of military crisis, presidents were hardly more than errand-boys for the law-making branch. The Constitution granted few actual powers to the chief executive. When a president had to act quickly and decisively without a congressional mandate, he did so solely on the strength of his personality.[3] Roosevelt's years in office changed all that. His "extraordinary leadership in expanding the federal government to meet the demands of . . . the Great Depression and . . . the Second World War," created the "modern presidency."[4]

David Nichols insists that the modern presidency is mostly a myth. According to Nichols, all of the elements of what is called the modern presidency were present at the creation of the office, including initiating and forwarding legislation in Congress, overseeing the administration of government, directing the nation in foreign relations, and acting as the people's representative—the so-called rhetorical presidency. What changed under Roosevelt, Nichols maintains, was the responsibility of the national government. He writes, "The truth behind the myth of the modern Presidency is that recent Presidents do more than previous Presidents, but that is traceable to the simple fact that modern American

government as a whole does more. It is the broader change in the extent of government action, not a change in the constitutional balance of power among the
branches, that provides some legitimacy to the myth of the modern Presidency."[5]

Both proponents and detractors of the modern presidency thesis agree that
Roosevelt altered the role of the national government. Why did Roosevelt wish
to overhaul our constitutional system and to bring about a massive shift in the
function of government? Roosevelt hardly understood himself to be an enemy of
the Constitution. Quite the contrary, he believed that he was its savior. But the
Constitution had to function within the economic environment created by free-
market capitalism, and Roosevelt was dubious about that system's viability. We
cannot fully understand the New Deal and the long-lasting transformation of
government it brought about unless we comprehend what Roosevelt thought
caused the Great Depression.

Roosevelt is often cast as a moderate who took a pragmatic approach to
reform. As Roosevelt himself said when asked about his political philosophy,
"Philosophy? I am a Christian and a Democrat—that is all."[6] Arthur M. Schlesinger's three-volume biography goes to great lengths to show that although
Roosevelt was a reformer and a pragmatist, he had no clear-cut vision of what
actions to take in order to stem the downward economic spiral.[7] For example,
during the 1932 campaign, the Democratic platform insisted on a balanced federal budget rather than the lavish government expenditures later adopted under
the tutelage of John Maynard Keynes.[8] As one commentator explains, "Roosevelt's search for measures to bring about recovery from the depression was not
very successful. By the spring of 1932 he had not worked anything more than a
few general ideas. . . . One thing was certain, however: a workable recovery plan
would have start with stimulation of consumption . . . while underlying his
whole attitude was a willingness to experiment with any proposals that seemed
sensible."[9] However, while it is true that Roosevelt undertook "bold, persistent
experimentation" because he was uncertain about how to cure the Depression, it
is also clear that Roosevelt had a well-defined understanding of the causes of the
collapse.[10] He believed that the very strength of the free-market was the source
of its malaise. Like some giant, cresting wave, capitalism had crashed under its
own inner dynamic, and Roosevelt feared that it would sweep away freedom and
democracy in its rushing undertow.

CAUSES OF THE GREAT DEPRESSION

For most of its history the United States accepted what is generally called free-
market capitalism. The role of the government was to apply the rule of law so
that the competing business and labor interests could interact on a more or less
equal footing. "The business of America" really was "business," as Calvin Coo-
lidge expressed it. Indeed, prior to the Great Depression, and even after it of
course, the "American success story" was attributed to the ability of individuals
to invent, invest, buy, sell, own, and labor without interference from the government. Since the New Deal, it has become somewhat customary to portray

defenders of the market system as hard-hearted capitalists, oblivious to the cares of the common man. But as the overwhelming victories at the polls of the pro-business Republican party attest, the majority of Americans believed that they benefited from economic liberty as much as from civil and religious freedom. It is important to realize that Republicans also wanted increased wealth and individual prosperity; the debate over the proper arrangement of the economy has always been a fight over the best means to achieve those ends. Of course, there were dissenters. The Progressive movement attacked the corruption and greed of the newly developing urban and industrial life. To the Progressives, the most egregious example of the perversion of American ideals was the rise of monopolies. Progressives wanted to break up the monopolies and, despite their name, return to a model of small business competition.

Prior to the Depression, Roosevelt too had been a Progressive. In a speech comparing his hero, Thomas Jefferson, to his political mentor, Woodrow Wilson, Roosevelt echoed the principal fear of the Progressives: the perversion of individual liberty through the concentration of economic power. FDR explained that "Woodrow Wilson, elected in 1912, saw the situation more clearly. Where Jefferson had feared the encroachment of political power on the lives of individuals, Wilson knew that the new power was financial."[11] But the Great Depression made Roosevelt rethink his position. Nothing like it had ever been seen—a worldwide economic panic with millions of people unable to find work. Roosevelt still saw the concentration of economic power as dangerous, but he distrusted competition as well. He doubted whether market forces, left untended, could actually sustain prosperity. "This attitude toward our economic machine requires not only greater stoicism," he explained, "but greater faith in immutable economic laws and less faith in the ability of man to control what he has created than I, for one, have."[12]

In 1932 Roosevelt continued to criticize monopolistic business, complaining that: "if the process of concentration goes on at the same rate, at the end of another century we shall have all American industry controlled by a dozen corporations, and run by perhaps a hundred men, but plainly we are steering a steady course toward economic oligarchy, if we are not there already."[13] Like the Progressives of an earlier age, Roosevelt thought that monopolies squeezed out the little man.

A glance at the situation today only too clearly indicates that equality of opportunity as we have known it no longer exists. . . . Just as freedom to farm has ceased, so also has the opportunity in business has narrowed. It still is true that men can start small enterprises, trusting to native shrewdness and ability to keep abreast of competitors; but area after area has been preempted altogether by the great corporations, and even in the fields which still have no great concerns, the small man can starts under a handicap.[14]

However, Roosevelt came to doubt the efficacy of an economy made up of small entrepreneurs and businesses. Such a system allowed the little man to compete, but that competition itself turned out to be socially harmful.

> In the same we cannot review carefully the history of our industrial advance without being struck with its haphazardness, the gigantic waste with which it has been accomplished, the superfluous duplication of productive facilities, the continual scrapping of still useful equipment, the tremendous mortality in industrial and commercial undertakings, the thousands of dead-end trails into which enterprise has been lured, the profligate waste of natural resources. Much of the waste is the inevitable by-product of progress in a society which values individual endeavor and which is susceptible to the changing tastes and customs of the people of which it is composed. But much of it, I believe, could have been prevented by greater foresight and by a larger measure of social planning.[15]

Just after Roosevelt's election in 1932, his "brain trust" released a statement which reflected this new thinking on competition. It rejected

> the traditional Wilson-Brandeis philosophy that if America could once more become a nation of small proprietors, of corner grocers smithies under spreading chestnut trees, we could solve the problems of American life. We agreed that the heart of our difficulty was the anarchy of concentrated economic power. . . . We believed that any attempt to atomize big business must destroy . . . a higher standard of living. . . .Competition, as such was not inherently virtuous . . . competition created as many abuses as it prevented.[16]

Rather than commending the entrepreneurial spirit that had been the hallmark of the expansion of the American economy, Roosevelt saw overly eager industrialists as outlaws who had effectively brought the law of the jungle into civilized society. He explained, "Whenever in the pursuit of this objective the lone wolf, the unethical competitor, the reckless promoter . . . declines to join in achieving an end recognized as being for the public welfare, and threatens to drag industry back to a state of anarchy, the Government may properly be asked to supply restraint."[17] Liberty had turned into license, or at least license of the few who were denying freedom to all the rest.

Not only did economic centralization close the door to economic opportunity, according to Roosevelt, more important it created a mal-distribution of wealth. The rich had too much money, even to spend on luxuries; the poor had too little, even to purchase necessities. The result was not just inequity, but an odd economic condition in which consumers could not consume what they produced. Supply outstripped demand. Furthermore, since the rich had an overabundance of money, they continued to invest their profits in plants which only served to create more excess. Roosevelt explained,

> In the years before 1929 we know that this country had completed a vast business cycle of building and inflation . . . expanding far beyond our natural and

normal growth. [T]here was little or no drop in the prices consumers had to pay
. . . although . . . the cost of production fell very greatly; corporate profit . . .
was enormous. The consumer was forgotten . . . the worker was forgotten . . .
the stock-holder was forgotten.

What was the result? Enormous corporate surpluses. . . . Where did the surpluses go? [I]nto new and unnecessary plants which now sit stark and idle; and
into the call-money market of Wall Street.[18]

For Roosevelt, the Great Depression was merely a symptom of the general
failure of capitalism. Capitalism collapsed not because it had strayed from its
optimal path, but rather because its very strengths caused its weakness. In fulfilling it highest or best course, capitalism produced goods quickly, cheaply, and
efficiently. This was so because corporations were compelled to compete with
their rivals. In order to produce more goods at a lower cost, the owners introduced ever-more complex technologies and simultaneously kept wages flat. The
result was a market glutted with too many goods. When companies could not
sell their merchandise, they warehoused inventory, then lowered prices, and
finally laid-off employees. As people became unemployed, the demand for
goods dropped even further, resulting in more layoffs, more plant closings, and,
of course, less demand for what was being produced. There was a tumbling effect in the economy that eventually led to collapse. Although, in Roosevelt's
words, "plenty is at our doorstep," most could not afford to purchase it.

The primary cause of the Great Depression for Roosevelt was overproduc-
tion. The most powerful impulse of free market capitalism was to produce more,
always more. Therefore, it was necessary to rethink the very foundations of the
free-market system.

Clearly, all this calls for a reappraisal of values. A mere builder of more industrial plants, a creator of more railroad systems, an organizer of corporations, is
as likely to be as a danger as a help. The day of the great promoter or the financial Titan, to whom we granted anything if only he would build, or develop, is
over. Our task now is not discovery or exploitation of natural resources, or necessarily producing more goods. It is the soberer, less dramatic business of administering resources and plants already in hand, of seeking to reestablish foreign markets for our surplus production, of meeting the problems of undercon-
sumption, of adjusting production to consumption, of distributing wealth and
products more equitably, of adapting existing economic organizations to the
service of the people. The day of the enlightened administration has come.[19]

Market forces could not be counted on to correct the ills of the nation, for competition would result in more speculation, more investment, more productive
capacity, and more unemployment.[20]

CURES FOR THE GREAT DEPRESSION

At the beginning of the twentieth century, most people in the West accepted that
civilization was at the dawn of a more prosperous and enlightened age. Europ

and the United States had enjoyed a relatively long period of peace, and it appeared as if the scourge of war had retreated in the face a more humane and tolerant attitude toward mankind. New scientific discoveries were announced nearly every day. New technologies revolutionized the way people lived. The opportunity for economic advancement seemed unlimited. While the shock and horrors of World War I dampened much of this optimism, many people were still hopeful that the war had been a temporary deviation from the road of progress; for them, the 1920s were a return to normalcy.

The Great Depression was more than just an economic crisis. It was a challenge to the belief in progress, prosperity, individual effort as a means to advancement, and free democratic government. Indeed, as Arnold Toynbee wrote at the time, there was real doubt whether Western civilization would survive. "In 1931, men and women all over the world were seriously considering and frankly discussing the possibility that the Western system of society might break down and cease to exist."[21] Furthermore, the liberal democratic governments appeared less capable of dealing with economic dislocation than were the communist regime in the Soviet Union, the fascist dictatorship in Italy and later Germany, or the autocratic states in Latin America. Although we know now that their prosperity was as much propaganda as successful policy, many in the public believed that freedom and democracy might be overwhelmed. Even in the United States people talked openly of revolution and what to do if one occurred. Some thought that the "Reds will run the country—or maybe the Fascists. Unless, of course, Roosevelt does something." Reinhold Niebuhr wrote that "capitalism was dying," and that "it ought to die."[22] Father Charles Coughlin exclaimed to a congressional committee, "I think by 1933, unless something is done, you will see a revolution in this country." Huey Long, the other great populist leader of the Depression years, wanted to share the nation's wealth through a radical policy of redistribution that would make "ev'ry man a king."[23]

Roosevelt's first act upon taking office was to call for a "bank holiday," a measure taken to forestall a run on depository reserves. The new president closed the banks under his executive authority and sent a bill to Congress asking for legislative approval. So potent was the fear engendered by the Depression that the usually deliberative House passed the measure in less than an hour and the Senate took less than half a day. "Vote! Vote!" echoed from the floor during the brief debate. "The House is burning down," said the impatient Bertrand H. Snell, Republican floor leader, "and the President of the United States says this is the way to put out the fire."[24]

With fear, desperation, and talk of revolution looming in the background, Roosevelt reasoned that only a major shift in government's relationship to the economy could salvage the American way of life. Government could "obviate revolution" by acting more vigorously to forestall the root causes of misery. "We have got beyond the point in modern civilization of merely trying to fight the epidemic of disease by taking care of the victims after they are stricken. . . . We seek to prevent it; and the attack on poverty is not very unlike the attack on disease."[25] "I believe," the President maintained, "that we are at the threshold of a fundamental change in our popular economic thought, that in the future we are going to think less about the producer and more about the consumer."[26] "A small group had concentrated into their own hands an almost complete control over other people's property, other people's money, other people's labor—other people's lives. . . . Against economic tyranny such as this, the American citizen could appeal only to the organized power of government."[27]

At first, Roosevelt attempted to coordinate production, distribution, and consumption through the voluntary "agreements" of the National Recovery Act (NRA). Then the act was ruled unconstitutional by the Supreme Court. Despite his attack on the Nine Old Men, Roosevelt had lost confidence in the NRA by the time the Court ruled. When businesses acted in unison under the provisions of the bill, they in effect became a trust, limiting competition and pocketing high profits. Although Roosevelt had believed that high prices were necessary to invigorate industry, thereby restoring jobs and wages, he saw that this "bold experiment" had resulted in price fixing. By 1938 he had lost faith in industrial cooperation as a viable policy. He reverted to the Progressive notion that competition was good because it insured lower prices.[28] On the other hand, he worried that low prices could lead to more business closures. The principle of adjusting production to consumption remained active in the New Deal's agriculture programs, where subsidies and price supports were instituted to support the family farm. One critic said of Roosevelt's wavering on this issue that the "basic faults in the congeries of the administration's economic policies sprang from Roosevelt's refusal to make a choice between the philosophy of Concentration and Control and the philosophy of Enforced Atomization."[29]

Much more successful and long-lasting was Roosevelt's graduated income tax. He favored this course not simply for reasons of equity. He did argue that the rich benefited more from society and therefore ought to bear a greater share of the burden. But, the most important reason for redistributing wealth, according to Roosevelt, was to take money out of the speculators' hands, thereby decreasing production, and to enlarge the buying power of the populace, thereby increasing demand. "No, our basic trouble was not an insufficiency of capital. It was an insufficient distribution of buying power coupled with an over sufficient speculation in production."[30] Roosevelt believed in demand-side economics. He might have accepted that a rising tide lifted all the ships, but he was not certain that the free market, left to itself, would move in the direction of shore. The government had to ensure that citizens could afford to buy what their labor produced. "We know, now, that these economic units cannot exist unless prosperity is uniform, that is, unless purchasing power is well distributed throughout every group in the nation."[31]

Limits of space make it impossible to discuss Roosevelt's halting acceptance of Keynesian economic theory. Whether Roosevelt ever fully understood Keynes's principles is unclear, but he came to the conclusion, perhaps by trial and error, that deficit spending and expanding the money supply, the primary tools of Keynes's macro-economics, could serve to increase demand by putting money in people's hands. Moreover, deficit spending was used for governme jobs programs, such as the Civilian Conservation Corps (CCC) and the Works Projects Administration (WPA), which could be steered toward helping the most needy citizens.

None of Roosevelt's policies seemed to have much of an effect. Well into his second term, the Depression continued only somewhat abated. Although he remained personally popular, his policies were losing much of their support. The pragmatist in Roosevelt understood that his agenda might be abandoned for lack of results if it did not get a firm hold in the minds of the people. Moreover, Roosevelt dismissed the idea of adopting a more radical solution to the nation's economic plight because any "paternalistic system which tries to provide for security for everybody from above only calls for an impossible task," and because the regimentation such a program would entail was "utterly uncongenial to the spirit of our people." It was late in the 1930s that he began to emphasis what was arguably his boldest and most far-reaching strategy. He attempted to rise above disputes concerning policy and emphasize something on which virtually all Americans could agree. Although "we cherish the elective form of democratic government," he explained, "progress under it can be retarded by disagreements that relate to method and to detail rather than broad objectives upon which we are agreed." [32]

On what do most Americans agree? They agree on the protection of their rights. In order to advance his program for recovery, Roosevelt changed the definition of rights. "The task of statesmanship has always been the re-definition of these rights in terms of a changing and growing social order. New conditions impose new requirements upon Government and those who conduct Government," [33] he wrote. To the freedom *of* speech and the freedom *of* religion he added the *from* want and the *from* fear. [34] The new rights were not specific in their content, as were religion and speech. They were to be defined by the ever-changing desires of the people for well-being. The new rights could be forwarded by individuals as claims or demands on the government. The new rights made the government responsible not just for the safety of the nation, or even for the health of the economy, but also for the security of every citizen. Roosevelt foresaw that he could promote his cure for capitalism's ills without having to become too specific about details. He could create an expectation in the people that the government must stand as a bulwark against economic disaster and personal failure. It must establish and maintain a social safety net—the welfare state.

The best way for the government to satisfy people's needs was, ironically, not to follow their every wish. Rather, the people would supply the ends by dictating to the rulers what they desired, and the government would contrive the means to satisfy those ends. It would employ experts who would administer the programs based on the latest scientific and technological knowledge. It would be government of the people and for the people, but not necessarily by the people.

The presidency too would have to change. Although Roosevelt is famous for putting together a winning electoral coalition, he did not think that the executive needed to play off the various factions against one another. As the Brownlow Commission Report suggests, the New Deal was dependent on centralization of decision-making in the White House both as a mechanism for formulating policy and for carrying it out. Perhaps Nichols is correct to argue that all of Roosevelt's actions had precedents in earlier presidents, but surely Roosevelt greatly increased the scope of those actions. It is an axiom that differences in degree become differences in kind. Moreover, Roosevelt also changed the expectation of what a president should be. We might say that prior to Roosevelt, presidents served to preserve and protect the nation, and after Roosevelt, they undertook to preserve and provide for the people.

CONCLUSION

Franklin Roosevelt believed that the economic disaster of the Great Depression was an inevitable outgrowth of capitalism. Capitalism could not be reformed by restoring it to its proper workings. Exactly when it was working properly, the drive to compete inherent in the free market could not help but squander resources, concentrate wealth, restrict opportunity, and overproduce goods. If strong actions were not taken to overcome the depression and forestall future crises, free and democratic government would vanish. The cure was for the government to take on the role of manager. Its power over the whole society had to be increased in order to administer the nation's riches in a manner which would not lead once again to the economic anarchy that had precipitated the Depression. In this Roosevelt acted as founder of sorts, for he saw "the task of Government in its relations to business is to assist the development of an economic declaration of rights, an economic constitutional order."[35] While he was unsure exactly what might be called for in the new order, he did perceive clearly that the structure of the government had to change, and along with it the responsibilities, authority, and expectations placed on the presidency.

John Kenneth Galbraith argued that Roosevelt's policies have been responsible for creating the extensive middle class in the United States. New Deal measures boosted the buying power of many groups in the nation, especially wage earners and farmers. By distributing wealth, the welfare state corrected the imbalance inherent in free-market capitalism.[36] Yet, it is more persuasive that the large middle class in America is the result of economic expansion. Since the Great Depression, the Gross Domestic Product in the United States has grown nearly 1,000 percent. New factories, new industries, and new technologies have increased the productivity of workers without economic disaster. Wholly new inventions, such as the computer, have changed the way we live. It is difficult not to conclude, with the wisdom of hindsight, that Roosevelt was wrong about the causes of the Depression. The free market had not reached the outer limits of its useful productive capacity. No politician and few experts or citizens would argue in the 1990s as Roosevelt did in the 1930s that, "we may build more factories, but the fact remains that we have enough now to supply all of our domestic needs, and more, if they are used."[37] We are more likely now to agree with Herbert Hoover's criticism of Roosevelt than with Roosevelt's assessment of o' economic plight. Hoover "challenged the whole idea that we have ended the advance of America, that this country has reached the zenith of its power, the height of its development." He argued that progress is "due to the scientific research, the opening of new inventions, new flashes of light from the intelligence of our people." He predicted that there "are a thousand inventions for comfort in the lockers of science and invention which has not come to light."[38] Moreover, liberal democracy is triumphant. It is not threatened as Roosevelt believed it was. Partly due to his leadership, it has defeated all serious challenges to its way of life. Even the worst despots pay lip service to its tenets. It has prevailed in part because of its ability to satisfy the material needs of its citizens.

If Roosevelt was incorrect about the origins of the Great Depression, why has the welfare state survived? First, Roosevelt was successful in changing people's expectations of government. Government became not the enemy of liberty, but the guarantor of people's economic rights. When problems arise, many expect the government to solve them. Second, the very wealth created by the free-market system makes overt poverty in any segment of society unacceptable to most Americans. There is a broad consensus that providing some sort of a social safety net is a fundamental obligation of government. Finally, as Theodore Lowi has argued, once a program is initiated, it develops its own constituency, making its elimination extremely difficult. Roosevelt helped establish a system whereby government programs are supported by interest groups who benefit from the government programs that create and sustain them. Indeed, each of the factions that Madison had imagined would bargain with one another to reach some kind of common consensus on policy now demand their own share of the public treasury. Instead of balancing one another, as Madison had predicted, the groups conspire to trade individually tailored benefits. Advocates for the young, the old, labor, business, the environment, the gun lobby, the anti-gun lobby, just to name a few, demand that the government sustain some program that aids their group. The interest-group government may be the most important legacy of the Roosevelt presidency. Even a Congress dominated by Republicans who had been swept into office promising a contract that would break the power of special interest groups had little success in dampening the desire for government programs. After 1996, Republicans quickly fell into the pattern established by all post-New Deal Congresses; members log-rolled government benefits to groups that supported their reelection.

Despite having been proved wrong about the weakness of the free market, Roosevelt would no doubt be pleased to look back on the years since the Great Depression. Democracy has flourished, and there is no "paternalistic system" guiding the economy. Yet, the harsher aspects of capitalism have been softened. Few citizens are ill clothed, ill housed, or ill fed. The government is much stronger than it once was and therefore more able to meet any future crises that might befall the nation. And the presidency that Roosevelt helped establish is the center of the country's political life within a constitutional system that has been transformed in ways that he would have thought helped the average man.

NOTES

1. Franklin D. Roosevelt, "First Inaugural" (March 1932), in *The Public Papers and Addresses of Franklin D. Roosevelt* (New York: Random House, 1938), vol. II, 15. See also Arthur M. Schlesinger, *The Crisis of the Old Order* (Boston: Houghton Mifflin, 1957), 8 and Thomas H. Greer, *What Roosevelt Thought: The Social and Political Ideas of Franklin Roosevelt* (East Lansing: Michigan State University Press, 1958).

2. Quoted in Arthur M. Schlesinger Jr., *The Coming of the New Deal* (Boston: Houghton Mifflin, 1958), 1.

3. James Sterling Young, *The Washington Community* (New York: Columbia University Press, 1966).

4. Sidney M. Milkis and Michael Nelson, *The American Presidency: Origins and Development, 1776-1990* (Washington, DC: Congressional Quarterly Press, 1990), 259. See also Philip Abbot, *The Exemplary Presidency* (Amherst: University of Massachusetts Press, 1990).

5. David K. Nichols, *The Myth of the Modern Presidency* (University Park: Pennsylvania State University Press, 1994), 7.

6. Quoted in Schlesinger, *The Coming of the New Deal*, 585.

7. Arthur M. Schlesinger Jr., *The Politics of Upheaval* (Boston: Houghton Mifflin, 1960), 647-659. See also Ted Morgan, *FDR: A Biography* (New York: Simon & Schuster, 1985), 413-441.

8. Although Roosevelt knew Keynes, evidently he never fully appreciated the finer points of the economist's theories. Still, Roosevelt agreed with the "demand-side" principles espoused by Keynes. These ideas became the backbone of welfare state economics until the 1980s. See Howard Zinn, ed., *New Deal Thought* (Indianapolis: Bobbs-Merrill, 1966), 403-404.

9. Daniel Fusfeld, *The Economic Thought of Franklin D. Roosevelt and the Origins of the New Deal* (New York: Columbia University Press, 1956), 206.

10. "Address at Oglethorpe University," *Public Papers and Addresses*, I: 646.

11. "Commonwealth Club Address," *Public Papers and Addresses*, I: 749.

12. "Address at Oglethorpe University," *Public Papers and Addresses*, I: 643.

13. "Commonwealth Club Address," *Public Papers and Addresses*, I: 751.

14. Ibid., 750-751.

15. "Address at Oglethorpe University," *Public Papers and Addresses*, I: 642.

16. Raymond Moley, *After Seven Years* (New York: Harper and Brothers, 1939), 23-24.

17. "Commonwealth Club Address," *Public Papers and Addresses*, I: 755.

18. "A New Deal for the American People," *Public Papers and Addresses*, I: 650-651.

19. "Commonwealth Club Address," *Public Papers and Addresses*, I: 751-752.

20. Schlesinger explains, that the

tenets of the First New Deal were that the technological revolution had rendered bigness inevitable; that competition could no longer be relied on to protect social interests; that large units were an opportunity to be seized rather than a danger to be fought; and that the formula for stability in the new society must be combination and cooperation under enlarged federal authority. This meant the creation of new institutions, public and private, to do what competition had once done (or was supposed to have done) in the way of balancing the economy—institutions which might well alter the existing pattern of individual economic decision, especially on investment, production, and price. . . . The depression introduced special elements . . . a sobering sense that the age of economic expansion had come to an end. The First New Deal thus tended to see the problem of institutional reorganization not in the context of economic growth which the New Nationalism [of Theodore Roosevelt] had carelessly assumed but in the context of what became known as 'economic maturity.' Schlesinger, *The Coming of the New Deal*, 179-180.

21. Arnold J. Toynbee, *Survey of International Affairs: 1931* (London: Oxford University Press, 1932), 1.

22. Schlesinger, *The Crisis of the Old Order*, 4-5.

23. Schlesinger, *The Politics of Upheaval*, 17, 66.

24. James MacGregor Burns, *Roosevelt: The Lion and the Fox* (New York: Harcourt Brace Jovanovich: 1956), 167.

25. "The Philosophy of Social Justice through Social Action," *Public Papers and Addresses*, I: 773; Schlesinger, *The Politics of Upheaval*, 648.

26. "Address at Oglethorpe University," *Public Papers and Addresses*, I: 645.

27. "Acceptance of the Renomination for the Presidency, (1936), *Public Papers and Addresses*, V: 231.

28. "Recommendation to Congress to Curb Monopolies and the Concentration of Economic Power," *Public Papers and Addresses*, VII: 305-332.

29. Raymond Moley, *After Seven Years* (New York: Harper & Brothers, 1939), 367.

30. "Address at Oglethorpe University," *Public Papers and Addresses*, I: 645.

31. "Commonwealth Club Address," *Public Papers and Addresses*, I: 752.

32. "Address to the Young Democratic Clubs of America," *Public Papers and Addresses*, IV: 343.

33. "Commonwealth Club Address," *Public Papers and Addresses*, I: 753.

34. "Address to International Student Assembly," *Public Papers and Addresses*, XI: 354.

35. "Commonwealth Club Address," *Public Papers and Addresses*, I: 752.

36. John Kenneth Galbraith, *American Capitalism* (Boston: Houghton Mifflin, 1952).

37. "Address at Oglethorpe University," *Public Papers and Addresses*, I: 645.

38. Herbert Hoover, *The Memoirs of Herbert Hoover* (New York: Macmillan Co., 1952), 252.

CHAPTER 5

CONGRESS:
INCREASED POWER AND INSTITUTIONAL WEAKNESS

Of the institutions of American government defined in the Constitution, Congress has undergone the greatest formal and informal change over the past two centuries. But there is an inherent difficulty in discovering signs "deconstitutionalization" in Congress. In essence, we must recognize that the major Progressive thinkers, and most notably Woodrow Wilson, argued that the problem with Congress was that it *already* had been deconstitutionalized. We have to take seriously the Progressives' charge that political developments between the time of the framing of the Constitution and the reforms of the Progressives had caused Congress to evolve into an institutional form very different from that envisioned in the Constitution—and that this evolution had produced many unintentional and adverse consequences.

Wilson thought that the misapplication of the rigid formalism in the "literary" constitution had undermined our access to the true, "organic" constitution, the evolving Anglo-American commitment toward a responsible system of democratic politics in which the people ruled through representatives. In relation to Congress in particular, Wilson and the other Progressives argued that the growth in importance of political parties, the consolidation of power in committee chairmen, and the rise of commercial interests with significant influence over congressional campaigns and the legislative process had corrupted the original plans for a deliberative body that would provide a "refined and enlarged view" of the public good capable of giving voice to the true will of the people. Therefore, Wilson and some other Progressives could argue that their intention was to make Congress live up to its true potential instead of being retarded by a written constitution that thwarted the natural development of the legislative body on this side of the Atlantic. Approached with this in mind, some of Wilson's writings might lead us to ask whether Congress was deconstitutionalized or reconstitutionalized by the many progressive reforms applied to it during the past century.

THE ORIGINS OF CONGRESS

The essential elements of the framers' approach to Congress can be summarize by discussing two important characteristics of their design for the legislative branch of government: *bicameralism* and *enumerated powers.* Their decision to stress these two characteristics was informed by their previous difficulties with representative government. On the one hand, they had seen the Congress formed by the Articles of Confederation rendered powerless by the super-majorities required for passing major legislation. The executive's inability to enforce Congress' laws when the governments of the several states opposed them was an added problem. Every attempt by the Articles of Confederation Congress to carry out its own laws failed because its legislative committees lacked the necessary enforcement powers. Each committee meeting inevitably devolved into arguments about the "true" meaning of the legislation and effectively re-opened all the debates that had taken place during the making of the law. No legislative disagreement was ever definitively settled.[1]

On the other hand, the framers had the experience of their colonial history under the rule of Great Britain that had shown them the dangers posed by a powerful but irresponsible legislature. Although the Declaration of Independence clearly addressed wrongs committed by King George III, Jefferson's *Summary View of the Rights of British America*, the closest intellectual ancestor of the Declaration, shows that the American colonists associated many of their problems with the tyranny of the British Parliament. "Taxation without representation" was but one example of Parliament's oppression of the colonists. While it is true that the early Americans were aggrieved because they were denied representatives in Parliament, the lack of representation was only half the problem. The colonists' more pressing complaint was that Parliament claimed plenipotentiary legislative powers, the ability to pass laws without any limits, "binding them in all cases whatsoever." Even though they suffered from Congress's inability to enforce its laws from 1776 to 1787, the framers knew that once they created a Congress as a coordinate branch capable of enforcing the laws, legislative tyranny would be an imminent possibility.[2]

Therefore, when the framers gathered in Philadelphia in 1787, they intended to address two problems with their national legislature. They needed to make it effective, and once they made it effective, they had to make it safe. Any view of Congress that fails to take into account the framers' very real fears that an effective legislature might become tyrannical misses one of their most important concerns. As Madison wrote in *Federalist* #47, "The accumulation of all powers, legislative, executive, and judiciary, in the same hands, whether of one, a few, or many, and whether hereditary, self-appointed, or elective, may justly be pronounced the very definition of tyranny." Only one essay later, he added "[t]he legislative department is everywhere extending the sphere of its activity and drawing *all power* into its impetuous vortex."[3] The Madisonian constitutional system was designed to prevent the legislature from seizing and exercising "all power," and both bicameralism and enumerated powers were considered indispensable mechanisms for controlling Congress.

It is a common error to assume that the Senate was created as part of the Connecticut Compromise that aimed to reconcile the so-called small state delegates to the creation of a strong national government. Bicameralism, however, was included in the Madisonian plan for the new government from the very beginning of the constitutional convention and may be traced to English practice as well as to many theoretical writings on liberal republicanism, most notably Montesquieu's *Spirit of the Laws*.[4] The Connecticut Compromise did not represent the *origin* of the commitment to bicameralism so much as a regrettable but necessary modification of Madison's ideal bicameralism. The so-called Virginia Plan, prepared by Madison and presented by Governor Edmund Randolph at the beginning of the convention, included two houses of Congress, in both of which states were to be represented according to their population.[5] Even as it became increasingly clear that equal representation for all states in the Senate was likely to be necessary in order to win assent for any constitution creating a strong national government, Madison resisted the move. In the spirited debates on the Connecticut Compromise from June 28 through July, he argued that any plan that reduced more populous states to legislative equality with less populous states would violate the fundamental republican principles that each individual should be equally represented in government.[6] This charge against the Senate has recurred throughout our constitutional history.[7]

It is unclear whether or not Madison was truly reconciled to the constitutional design of the Senate. Discussions about Congress in the *Federalist Papers* are overwhelmingly concerned with defending and explaining the importance of the Senate and the advantages of its form. In *Federalist #51*, which may be understood as forming the key transition from a discussion of the general principles of government to those reflections explicitly devoted to Congress, Madison explains his rationale for creating the Senate by stressing that "in a republican government the legislative power necessarily predominates" and therefore that the "remedy for this inconveniency" is "to divide the legislature into different branches; and to render them by different modes of election, and different principles of action, *as little connected to each other as their common functions will admit.*"[8] According to this standard, the difference in the relation between population and representation may prove to be a useful additional method to render the two branches "little connected" and therefore guarantee that they will not be inclined to act in concert.

While Madison considered equal representation in the Senate to be the reasonable result of necessary compromise, he devoted a considerable portion of the discussion on Congress to a detailed examination of the advantages the Senate brings to the government proposed by the Constitution. The Senate provides a useful check on the House because it is unlikely that they would both agree on any "schemes of usurpation or perfidy," thus protecting the people against some temporary but dangerous conspiracy in the lower chamber. Most such schemes are, according to Madison, the result of a demagogue's success in exciting the members of a legislative body to act in a manner that they themselves would soon regret, and Madison notes that insofar as the Senate is less numerous, it is less vulnerable to being misled by the type of public speaking more commonly used before multitudes.[9] The Senate will, he argues, be more likely to be co posed of experienced statesmen with significant practical knowledge about the workings of government—men with a "due acquaintance with the objects and principles of legislation." In this regard, Madison thinks that the Senate will be inclined to preserve stability in the law: they will not be inclined to pass too many laws or repeal laws already enacted. While one assembly like the House might be inclined to adjust the law frequently, the Senate will be inclined to preserve the existing laws and therefore will help assure the regularity and predictability of the law.[10]

Madison insisted that the Senate's stability and experience will be of great value in dealing with foreign nations.[11] He also argued that the Senate will make it possible for the people to hold the legislature responsible for its actions. Because complex and long-term policies may require longer than two years to take effect, it is possible that the members of the House will be occasionally cashiered for the perceived defects of policies that appear effective in theory only. Madison contended that only by having a branch with a term of office long enough to be judged correctly on the actual success or failure of major policies can the people hold legislators accountable for what they have actually done.[12] Finally, he provided an extended historical argument against the common Antifederalist charge that the Senate was so situated that it might take over the government and rule as a permanent aristocracy.[13]

While much is made about their decision to create the Senate, it is difficult to overestimate the importance of the framers' decision to grant Congress only certain enumerated powers. As Alexander Hamilton demonstrates in *Federalist* #78, circumscribing the legislative authority is the key element in forming a constitutionalized government: "By a limited constitution, I understand one which includes certain specified exceptions to the legislative authority." While this passage demonstrates the significance of limiting the legislative authority, there is a distinction here between a constitution that "specifies exceptions" and one that "enumerates powers." The former would represent the people transferring *all* sovereignty to their government *except* in certain specified cases. The latter, which may be combined with the former but should not be confused with it, would represent the people transferring only *some* sovereign authority to their government. In *Federalist* #39, Madison clearly states that the American Constitution is to be of the latter sort, and the language of Article I, Sections 1 and 8 as well as the Tenth Amendment testifies to this fact. The Articles of Confederation had protected American citizens against federal oppression by guaranteeing that the government was too weak to oppress them, but those who wrote the Constitution, still smarting from the embarrassments of the weak government under the Articles, intended to create a legislature whose laws would be enforced. To do so, they had to ensure that laws that should not be enforced would not be passed. Their solution was to limit the authority of the legislature.

The theory of enumerated legislative authority lies at the very core of the founders' liberal political philosophy. In fact, the enumeration of legislative powers, more than any other part of the Constitution, reveals the fundamental connection between the Constitution and the Declaration, two documents that are sometimes thought to be in conflict. The Declaration insisted that all legiti-mate political power was derived from the consent of the governed and was based on the need for government of all human beings wishing to protect their fundamental rights. Therefore, the people, as the source of all sovereign author-ity, were free to create as much or as little government as they felt necessary to preserve their rights. According to the Declaration, no government could claim unlimited sovereignty, because all sovereignty ultimately was retained by the people, and the government acted merely as a delegate charged with using only as much sovereignty as the people gave it. The framers understood that the Con-stitution gave Congress only those powers necessary for performance of the tasks the people considered appropriate to government. All other powers, being unrelated to government's legitimate ends, would be retained by the people. This supposition was confirmed by the ratification of the Tenth Amendment. Therefore, the Constitution's treatment of the question of enumerated powers was appropriate to any constitution based on liberal political principles, and it expressed in writing what was already present in theory, namely that the people were responsible for spelling out what powers they wished to give government and what powers they wished to retain for themselves. It was not willful misin-terpretation that led Jefferson and other thoughtful Americans to assume that in doubtful cases, the constitutional design implied that we should assume that any power not granted is denied rather than that any power not denied is granted. The very first line of the First Article of the Constitution underscores this inter-pretation by declaring that Congress possesses only those legislative powers "herein granted."

Before leaving our discussion of the origins and essence of what we could call "the constitutional conception of Congress," we must note that it is an error to assume that bicameralism and enumerated powers were stressed *only* because they were needed to place restraints on Congress's power. While bicameralism was intended to check the excesses of the House, Madison's defense of the dis-tinctive character of the Senate also stresses the positive advantages derived from structuring a legislative body in this way. The particular structure of each house serves both as a check on the defective actions of the other house and a source of positive benefits that it alone can provide. Without the Senate, we would not have a legislative body to look at the long-term consequences of pro-posed laws. Without the House, we might endure unnecessary evils in the short term in pursuit of uncertain and hypothetical long-term goods. Each and every legislature, whether real or imagined, has biases. It will see some problems and overlook others, be designed to confront some issues and dodge others, or be institutionally capable of meeting some challenges and institutionally incapable of meeting others. By requiring the concurrence of two very different legisla-tures, each of which can be said to represent "the people of the United States" yet each with particular tendencies, biases, inclinations, and limitations, the framers tried to ensure that the fewest possible public policy dilemmas would go unrecognized or unsolved. Bicameralism's benefits are at least as important as its drawbacks.

As discussed in chapter 1, Madison and the framers conceived the extended republic as one in which various and conflicting interests were locked in a ceaseless struggle for power or wealth. They thought that this struggle would create circumstances in which reason could exercise its greatest possible political influence. If reason itself could prevail in politics through the all-knowing actions of a philosophical statesman, then such a ruler would determine the proper balance between short-term and long-term interests and between national and local interests with informed objectivity. But given that "enlightened statesmen" are rare and even more rarely in control of the reins of government, constitutionalized bicameralism gives different types of interests institutional advocates whose bargaining, which will be necessary to reach a single consensus, may approximate the rule of reason in the legislature.

Finally, it is important to note that insofar as the "constitutional" character of the Congress can be distinguished by bicameralism and enumerated powers, in this respect it differs sharply from the parliamentary legislatures of most other major democracies. For our purposes and within the context defined by the American framers, constitutional legislatures and parliamentary legislatures are mutually exclusive. Parliamentary legislatures are in theory endowed with plenipotentiary legislative powers, but in practice often become rubber stamps for policies dictated by their executive committees or cabinets.[14] Just as bicameralism has both negative and positive functions—preventing the tyranny of half of the legislature and providing two legislatures with distinctive complementing strengths and abilities—the same can be said for enumerated powers. While the relatively clear and explicit enumeration of Congress's powers in Article I, Section 8 serves to prevent Congress from overstepping its authority, it also *protects* Congress's authority by making it clear which powers it *does have*. In *Federalist* #17, Hamilton pointed out that many factors—including the historical importance of the states and the state governments' daily involvement in those public affairs that the people care most about—created some danger that the states would usurp the prerogatives of the national government. While this may no longer be perceived as a serious threat, its importance at the time of the founding should not be discounted. Furthermore, it is clear that removal of the states as threats does not necessarily mean that crossing the line between enumerated and plenipotentiary power works to Congress's advantage. When the lines separating Congress's enumerated powers from all other powers are erased, the net result may be that Congress gives up powers rather than gaining them.

THE REORGANIZATION OF POWER IN THE HOUSE AND SENATE

As explained in chapter 3, Progressive thinkers sought to realize a more democratic union, a union in which the will of the majority of the American people, taken as a whole, was not prevented from exercising "unobstructed sweep and ascendancy." When this criterion is applied to Congress, it seems to require that Congress be democratized, but democratizing Congress is not as straightforward a proposition as it might first appear. The Progressive call for the removal of "institutional impediments to democracy" so that "public opinion" can serve as the dominant motive in the halls of Congress can take at least two very different forms. Therefore, it is necessary to distinguish between reforms intended to increase democracy *within* the institution of Congress and those designed to make Congress more responsive *to democratic forces outside the institution*. In making this division, it is important to recognize that insofar as progressive-inspired reforms have attempted to accomplish both these goals—a more democratic institution within and an institution more responsive to democratic impulses from without—Progressive political thought has often found itself at cross purposes within Congress. The Progressive reforms that have made Congress internally more democratic have more often than not made Congress less responsible to national majorities, and those reforms that have made Congress more responsible to national majorities have often made it less internally democratic.

For instance, the congressional reforms that gave more power to subcommittees and therefore to more junior members in the 1970s essentially necessitated the re-invigoration of the powers of the Speaker in the 1980s. While the reform Congress was internally democratic, it proved almost incapable of any sort of coordinated action, and progressive government requires action. After all, Wilson thought that effective leadership was the key to making Congress democratically responsible to the people, and he argued that the best seat for this leadership lay outside Congress itself in the presidency.[15] His argument would, in many crucial respects, de-democratize Congress internally by laying out a more institutionalized hierarchy of authority both over and within Congress. The scheme would significantly limit the role that most members could play in the legislature by raising some members to positions of institutional authority and relegating others to the backbench. As Congress moves in fits and starts to respond to demands that it democratize itself, junior members of Congress have a considerable personal stake in trying to make internally democratic changes that open up spaces in which they can have influence, make policy, and perform deeds of honor and importance. But as the public increasingly demands that Congress answer to an identifiable popular majority of the people, Congress is driven to establish more effective and hierarchical mechanisms for orchestrating cohesive policies. It is a dilemma that is virtually impossible to resolve within the current framework.

CHANGES IN THE SEPARATE CHARACTERS OF THE HOUSE AND THE SENATE

Of all the major changes in the framers' Constitution, the changes in the mode of selecting the officers of government probably appear most striking. There have been major shifts in the methods by which the President is selected, but Congress, because it is a branch with two parts, presents a different situation. The House of Representatives is selected much as it was more than two centuries ago in the first federal election. Each House member is elected by the peo ple in an open election within a single-member district designed, within certain limits, by the state legislature. Although the single-member-district mode of organization is not expressly called for in the Constitution, it seems to have been largely assumed and was adopted by most states immediately. The Congressional Organization Act of 1842 mandated that each state elect members of the House through single-member districts, and in spite of some modern attempts to question the legitimacy or desirability of such districts, it is unlikely that this practice will change in the foreseeable future.

On the other hand, the mode of electing senators has changed drastically since the framing. The initial plan called for senators to be selected by the state legislatures. Madison, who had opposed the plan to give the state legislatures direct control of the election of any institution of the national government, admitted that this mode of election gives "the State governments such an agency in the formation of the federal government as must secure the authority of the former" and therefore serves as "a recognition of that portion of sovereignty remaining in the individual states and an instrument for preserving that residual sovereignty."[16] The means by which state legislatures made their selection were left up to the individual states and varied quite widely in the first decades of the republic. But what does appear to be clear is that the state legislatures never were able to compel senators to act as agents of the state government in the national government. As Elaine Swift has demonstrated, senators were very quick to express their independence from the state legislatures and to cultivate popular constituencies, even serving as the "heads of tickets" for their parties' candidates for the state legislatures.[17] The most obvious example of this trend of national politics dictating state elections as opposed to state concerns dictating national ones was the Lincoln-Douglas Senate race in 1858.

The calls for direct election to the U.S. Senate began as early as 1826. Any reform requiring a constitutional amendment faces an uphill battle, and this reform faced some particularly difficult challenges. First, it required that two-thirds of the Senators agree to change the means by which they were elected. Second, in the absence of a call for special state ratifying conventions, it required that state legislatures vote away their own ability to elect those senators. Finally, it must be remembered that up until the Civil War, the Senate was in many regards the most important branch of government because it was nearly evenly divided between the slave-holding and non-slave-holding states.[18] The key turned out to be revelation of the corruption that held together some cabals in the state legislatures and the widespread ascendancy of Progressive thought in the early twentieth century. Woodrow Wilson identified the adoption of a constitutional amendment authorizing direct election of senators as a core principle of the Progressive platform on which he was running for president. He insisted that such a measure would root out a persistent source of corruption in our political institutions and better realize democracy's desire that all representatives should speak directly for the people.[19]

One might argue that the adoption of the Seventeenth Amendment in 1913 served only to constitutionalize practices that had been developing for some time. Nevertheless, it would be misleading to suggest that the transformation of informal and indirect popular elections for the Senate into outright, statewide popular elections was of little consequence. To give only one simple example, even though more votes were cast for Republican candidates in the Illinois Senate race of 1858, more Democrats were elected to the legislature, and Douglas, not Lincoln, was sent to the Senate. Over time, this shift could only mean that different types of candidates would win election to the Senate. Contrary to what Woodrow Wilson argued in his speeches on the topic, it was not just the corrupt and the inept who had to fear being turned out of office with the change in voting patterns. Madison thought the Senate would serve as a repository of political experience and accumulated knowledge, and, in fact, state legislatures proved to be inclined to send "senior statesmen" to the upper chamber. More recently, we have seen that statewide popular elections sometimes tend to produce successful candidates who have *no* political experience but who are good speakers or are extremely wealthy. Republican (Fred Thompson and Bill Frist) and Democratic (John Edwards and John Corzine) examples are easily cited. In fact, the states, being larger than House districts and not drawn to partisan design in the political redistricting process, are ideal venue for mass media campaigns based on emotional national issues. In many respects, the Senate, not the House, is being transformed into the Wilsonian house of Congress.

It should not be assumed that the election of first-time candidates is the only or most important change in the character of the Senate in the wake of adoption of the Seventeenth Amendment. In *Federalist* 51, Madison noted that the key to making bicameralism a means to ensure legislative checks and balances was to "render them [the House and Senate], by different *modes of election* and different principles of action, as little connected with each other as the nature of their common dependence on society will admit."[20] Popular election of the Senate makes the "modes of election" much more similar than they had previously been, and according to Madison's logic, the homogenization of the House and the Senate makes the latter progressively less likely to check the former. Furthermore, as the two houses become more likely to share a similar character, they also lose their peculiar talents, and therefore the legislative branch as a whole becomes less versatile. If each house is increasingly like the other and therefore interested in the same problems and disposed toward the same types of solutions, less useful and less deliberate legislation is likely to result.

Even though the Progressives have found bicameralism—and particularly the Senate, insofar as that body is distinct from and an impediment to the progress of popular legislation through the House—to be defects of our system of government, Woodrow Wilson certainly admired the Senate as the venue in which the best public debates on the people's issues took place.[21] It is certainly true that the Senate has always been the chamber more open to displays of public oratory on great questions of the day, and that this difference with the House was entirely anticipated by the framers of the U.S. Constitution. But this reliance on rhetoric, which might have made the Senate more susceptible to demagog ery, was countered by the Senate's long terms in office and sophisticated constituencies in the state legislatures.[22] Those limits have now been removed, and senators regularly use their higher visibility to present speeches designed to appeal to public audiences—often far beyond their state boundaries—as they position themselves as national leaders with presidential aspirations. Although governors have had greater electoral success, the Senate has become the source of the greatest number of would-be presidents.

In the numerous House, by contrast, the framers predicted that many decisions would of necessity be delegated to committees and leaders and that many of the negotiations that produced those decisions would be held in select groups of members meeting in private sessions. In the Senate, a more distinguished and select group of statesmen might be expected to engage in great public discussions in which each carried sufficient political stature and public experience to guarantee that the body could not be swept away by the blandishments of a single demagogue.[23] The Senate has indeed been the site of debates from the golden age of Daniel Webster, Henry Clay, and John C. Calhoun to the present.

Progressivism clearly envisioned the possibility that such great debates might become the normal means for governing and might take place in the House and in the Senate. Progressive thinkers believed that institution of a more parliamentary government would encourage such debates and that the American people would take more of an interest in these debates than they had hitherto shown in the actions of the legislature. Wilson and others argued in effect that the only reason the American people did not take, or only occasionally took, such an interest was that they could not see or understand the secret committee machinations by which legislation was negotiated. In a more parliamentary system, these debates would move to the floor and be more open to and interesting for the public to watch. Furthermore, this open forum would attract the most capable debaters and potential statesmen to high political office and therefore raise the quality of the debates. Having been enlightened by the debates about pressing issues of the day, the people would therefore become more capable of managing their own affairs.

In this regard, the Progressives have had a dubious and problematic, but somewhat successful impact on the character of congressional debate. On the one hand, progressive reforms, including the passage of sunshine laws in the early 1970s and the creation of C-Span and C-Span 2, have made speaking on the floor of both chambers of Congress more common and more useful for representatives interested in arguing issues important to their constituents, but it is less clear that the growth of congressional speech-making has resulted in improved deliberation on pending legislation, has educated the American public about important issues, or has made Congress, whether considered collectively or individually, more accountable to their constituents. Croly and Wilson both assumed that when great speeches took place on the floor of the House and Senate in clear view of the public, the public would be inclined to pay attention and take sides, but such has not been the result. Croly insisted that as soon as the debates in Congress about important issues were readily available to the public, private outlets would find that there were many citizens eager to pay a reasonable price for the most precise and up-to-date reporting on the actions of government. On the contrary, C-Span broadcasts to a very small audience, consisting only of the most active and interested citizens and professional lobbyists and advocates who have vested interests in the outcome of legislation. Any hope that making coverage of the debates widely available would decrease or eliminate control of legislation by special interests has been dashed by evidence that broadcasting Senate debates has increased rather than decreased the role of powerful, well-funded organizations in shaping legislation.

In his time, Woodrow Wilson worried that members of Congress, and particularly the House, were not accountable to their particular constituents or to the nation, and he sought to open the workings of the legislative branch so they could be more adequately controlled. He argued that Congress needed to respond more efficiently and effectively to the will of the people, as much as that will can be ascertained at particular moments in time. Today, we face the remarkable possibility that our representatives, in thrall to the poll numbers that they take to be "the will of the people," are afraid to govern. Ironically, Wilson lamented that the U.S. government was paralyzed because it had not kept up with the movement of the European democracies in a great world-historical march toward greater democratic accountability. But in a recent article in the *Atlantic Monthly*, Antony King has pointed out that in none of the European democracies are there so many elections and is so much attention paid to polls. Contrary to Wilson's expectations, King argues that our legislative leaders have become so dependent on day-to-day public support that they cannot effectively govern.[24]

THE EXPANSION OF CONGRESSIONAL POWER

The very essence of American constitutionalism is the ability of the constitution's apportionment of powers to restrain political leaders and to prevent institutions from gathering "all powers, legislative, executive, and judiciary, [into] the same hands, whether of one, a few, or many, and whether hereditary, self-appointed, or elective." The very meaning of "constitutionalized" government in the American context must be associated with "limited" government. The key limit on congressional powers, according to the *Federalist*, is the fact that Congress is given only the "legislative powers herein granted." In this sense, we can say that Congress is "constitutionalized" only so long as it is limited to those powers contained in or fairly inferred from the constitution. One need not necessarily decide between the strict constructionist approach of Jefferson and the more pragmatic and permissive loose constructionist position of Hamilton to declare that when Congress *clearly* reaches beyond the enumerated powers, it slips its constitutional moorings and therefore might be said to be "deconstitutionalized."

Given this formulation of Congress's proper powers, it is very difficult to argue that Congress today operates within the bounds allotted to it by the con tutional framework. There is ample evidence that Congress acts far beyond the enumerated powers that it received from Article I, Section 8 of the Constitution of 1787 and that many of the new powers that it has since exercised since 1787 bear no connection to the subsequent amendments that might have been read as enlarging Congress's power in some identifiable field of activity.[25]

In the earliest Congresses, debates over such issues as whether the President had the power to remove executive officers, whether the Senate had a role in determining if a treaty was still in force, and whether the national government had the power to charter a bank quickly sparked legislative disagreements about the nature of the enumeration in Article I, Section 8. One group, generally led by those associated with Jefferson, insisted that Congress had only those powers explicitly granted, and that all other powers, no matter how necessary they might seem, were not delegated.[26] Another group, commonly considered the ongoing embodiment of the Federalist Party that sponsored the ratification of the Constitution, insisted that there was considerable latitude in the powers of Congress because of the "necessary and proper clause."

Congress, reacting to the many demands of its constituencies, has always shown some willingness to expand its sphere of authority. During the administration of Andrew Jackson, Democrats in Congress prevailed in insisting that the institution had the power to build and maintain "internal improvements" such as canals, turnpikes, and railroads. In the latter half of the nineteenth and early years of the twentieth century, in spite of some temporizing interference by the courts, Congress slowly succeeded in claiming authority over many new areas of economic activity by expanding the reach of its power to regulate interstate commerce. The Progressives, of both the Theodore Roosevelt and Woodrow Wilson schools, increasingly relied on claims that the changing economic situation, especially the growth of major corporations and the centralization of the nation, necessitated federal regulation of economic matters, even those only tangentially related to Congress's delegated powers to regulate interstate commerce. In fact, contrary to Hamilton's assertions that judicial review would serve as the primary means by which Congress would be restricted to its enumerated powers, the expansion of Congress's dominion can be largely traced to the Supreme Court's willingness to read this clause broadly and therefore to allow Congress to exercise broader legislative authority than described in the enumeration of its powers.[27]

The first major case in this regard was *McCullough v. Maryland* (1819), in which the court overruled a Maryland challenge to the constitutionality of the Second Bank of the United States. Although the courts in the post-Civil War era and early twentieth century showed some inclination to restrain Congress from venturing into new legislative arenas, there is good reason to think that these rulings, particularly in the area of economic regulation, were animated more by the Court's support of free-market economic theories and less by the Court's earnest desire to limit Congress to its textually defined authority.[28] By the 1940s, the Court's "switch in time that saved nine" had led to a series of cases that suggested that it now recognized no limits on Congress's legislative powers.[29] By the late twentieth century, the Court seemed exceedingly reluctant to identify any type of law that was beyond Congress's authority to legislate. More recently, Congress has used selective withholding of intergovernmental payments to force states to pass certain regulations in areas of the law where even Congress admits it lacks authority to regulate directly. While this practice would appear to constitute a blatant attempt to evade limits on Congress's legislative authority, it was nevertheless held constitutional in *South Dakota v. Dole* (1997) and has continued to be employed by both Republican and Democratic majorities in Congress.

A surprising series of pro-federalism cases in the 1990s, including *Seminole Tribe of Florida v. Florida* (1996), *City of Boerne v. Flores* (1997), *Alden v. Maine* (1999), and *Board of Trustees of the University of Alabama v. Garrett* (2001), might appear to mark a shift in the direction of limiting Congress to the authority granted it in the Constitution, but this appearance is misleading. In these cases, a five-member majority of the Court struck down Congressional actions based on their supposed violation of a "principle of federalism" that was not literally found in any particular provision of the Constitution but was suggested by certain vague ideas about liberty and federalism that were binding on Congress. In form, these cases are more similar to the substantive due process decisions of the Warren and Burger courts than to the constitutionalism of Marshall. In fact, some of the most outspoken critics of these cases are scholars who have actively asserted, in other contexts, that the courts have erred in allowing Congress to exercise supra-Constitutional plenary powers.[30] Whether the Court's reversal on this principle in *Nevada Department of Social Services v. Hibbs* (2003) marks the ebb of the Court's interest in defending federalism against Congressional encroachments, we should note that even in recent cases the Court has done so on a basis that is less strictly "constitutional" in its impulse than might appear to be the case.

While the expansion of Congress's power has come at times in which Progressive thought has held sway it could be argued that Congress's powers have expanded in nearly every period of our history under both strict constructionists and loose constructionists, even under committed confederalists as well as supporters of a centralized national power. In fact, the history of our federal constitution has seen almost inexorable growth in the range of Congress's legislative authority, and many commentators, as well as many political leaders, have argued that this growth was inevitable because of changing economic circumstances and the increasing interconnection of the various regions of the country. If this reading of Congress's growing legislative authority is accurate, it would appear to be unfair to argue that the influence of Progressive political thought is responsible for the expansion.

However, here we must confront Wilson's own argument based on what he took to be the effective deconstitutionalization of Congress *before* his time. Wilson argues that the doctrine of limited, enumerated legislative powers was a historical artifact of the precise period in time when the constitution was written. Confronted with unlimited powers that were being used against them, the ea

Americans sought to protect themselves by creating institutions with only limited powers. In a rather short time, however, those powers escaped the limiting language intended to constrain them. Wilson argued that as a result we have been led to a most astonishing and dismal position. Legislative powers were limited because the authors of the U.S. Constitution feared giving any individual or group, even a majority, the plenipotentiary power that had been used against them by Great Britain. Therefore, they built their systems of federalism, separation of powers, and enumerated legislative powers to ensure that a dominant majority in society could never exercise such plenipotentiary power. In our short history, those who exercise the most power had progressively overcome the limits on their authority, but they had done so by a series of legislative actions and complementary court decisions not necessarily informed or backed by public consensus. As a result, Wilson claimed, "[t]here could be no more despotic authority wielded under the forms of free government than our national Congress now exercises."[31] Ironically, the limits placed on Congress's legislative authority did not prevent those who wielded power by virtue of their position in Congress, but they did prevent the people from controlling those who used that power.

Wilson had to undermine the claim of constitutional legitimacy to justify his call for changing the constitution. Wilson believed that Congress's power should be based on following the public *forms* of the literary Constitution, such as elections and terms of office, but should abandon the *spirit* of the Constitution written that hoped to limit the powers of government. The natural evolution of American society had compelled Congress to abandon limits of its power: Congress has managed to seize what is essentially unlimited legislative power, rendering appeals to legislative authority grounded in Article I, Section 8 into sophistic formalities rather than necessary appeals. Wilson recommends that we make this virtually unlimited authority *in fact* responsible to the people. We have all the evils of unlimited government and none of the control available through modern democracy. Given that Congress no longer takes its bearings from the enumeration of its powers in the Constitution, we must guarantee that it be regulated by the authoritative voice of contemporary popular opinion. Congress will no longer act as the Constitution instructs; it will act as the people wants dictate. Any decent respect for the principle of democratic accountability requires that this control be guaranteed.

Wilson's argument here makes it appear that we have only two choices—absolute power in a government wholly subservient to public opinion and hence democratic in character, or absolute power in a government subservient to some other force in society and hence undemocratic in character. If these are in fact the choices, Wilson's support for a progressive government controlled by the will of a majority of the people appears almost unarguably correct. But Wilson has created a false dilemma that omits any possibility of limited government. Rhetorically, Wilson and the other Progressives not only denied the desirability of limited and constitutionalized democratic government. They denied that it could exist at all, and thus changed the terms of the debate in a way that made significant institutional change not only more likely but virtually inevitable and unassailable.

The character of modern legislation is, in fact, significantly different from that once passed by Congress. To be precise, Congress has come to legislate about *many more* issues with *less* specificity. To some degree, the increasing lack of specificity or precision is an inevitable result of Congress's growing areas of responsibility. As the fundamental constitutional limit on Congress's power has become largely a pro forma requirement easily evaded by vague references to enumerated powers only tangentially related to the matters at hand, Congress has been increasingly exposed to withering public pressures to deal with a wide range of issues that even the members might be inclined to leave to less centralized institutions. As both Jefferson and Hamilton recognized, Americans have a tendency to meet each perceived public problem with a legislative response. Congress is faced with the problem of dealing with an exponentially increasing range of issues with a relatively fixed amount of time and other resources. When we then consider the increasingly technical nature of regulatory legislation in a very technologically advanced age, we must face the inevitable fact that Congress must provide legislation on more—and more difficult—topics that many members cannot be expected to understand. The result of these converging trends has been that Congress delegates its authority more frequently and more broadly than it ever has before.

But, it might be asked, is this really the result of deconstitutionalization? Could Congress behave otherwise, given the complexity of the nation that it governs? This is, after all, in many respects at the very heart of the Progressive critique of the framers' constitutional political science. Wilson, Croly, and Roosevelt all agree that the requirements of modern political life *require* that Congress adapt as it has adapted. The only alternative might be for Congress to become the bottleneck preventing any effective government in the United States. Nevertheless, we must recognize that attention to the limits on Congress's legislative authority based on even a broad reading of Article I would significantly restrict national lawmaking on a wide variety of issues that are currently handled by the federal government.[32]

CONCLUSION:
CAN CONGRESS GOVERN OUR DECONSTITUTIONALIZED DEMOCRACY?

While this discussion has hardly covered many of the important areas of deconstitutionalizing innovation in the operations of the House and the Senate, it is not too soon to ask the crucial question: Has deconstitutionalization made Congress more or less capable of fulfilling its duties within the American system of government? For better or worse, the evidence suggests that Congress's ability to govern the country has been undermined both by institutional changes that have been promoted by Progressive political thought and perhaps more importantly by the changes in political expectations that accompanied the popularization of some of the Progressives' political ideas. We now expect the type of legislat that might proceed from a Wilsonian form of parliamentary government, and we expect both our Congress and our president to deliver it. The President cannot do so because the office simply does not have, or only rarely and informally has, the necessary institutional powers. Congress, conversely, has the powers, but its design, conceived with other purposes in mind, is ill suited to the task. As a result, members of both the House and the Senate find themselves increasingly under pressure to do what they cannot do, and the requirements of reelection have led them more and more to engage in campaign rhetoric, the harried adoption of vague and incomplete legislation, and symbolic behavior. The campaign rhetoric and symbolic behavior are both aimed at creating the impression that either a particular group within Congress *would* do what is required if only its opponents would agree, or conversely, that Congress *is* doing what it cannot do. As Steven Stark put it: "The public has arrived at new and often contradictory expectations of how Congress should act and what it should do. Until these contradictions are resolved, Congress is doomed to unpopularity and ineffectiveness, no matter who controls it."[33]

In the midst of all of this, the words and actions of particular members of Congress, the hearings and investigations of particular committees in Congress, and the reports of the party conferences on what is often referred to as the "legislative agenda" reflect the same false dictum that has been identified prominently with the rise of the so-called rhetorical presidency: to speak is to govern. While popular election of senators may have been inevitable and certainly has some positive attributes, it must be noted that retaining the power in the state legislatures would have allowed the Senate to counter this tendency in the House. As things currently stand, the more visible Senate is in fact more inclined to this conflation of rhetoric with governing than is its coordinate body. Furthermore, the executive can speak clearly and decisively, but Congress cannot. Congress speaks in many voices, and those voices often speak at cross-purposes. While one of the major purposes of this book is to emphasize that speaking is *not* governing and that deconstitutionalized government is always inclined to obscure this crucial distinction, it is clear that so long as we confuse speaking with governing, the image of Congress will suffer. Debate and deliberation, the modes of speech appropriate to a legislature, are less clear, less lofty, and less programmatic than the speeches of a single executive like the President.[34] Congress can never "control its message" unless the majority party is able to enforce both strict majority rule in both houses and strict party loyalty, and this is in turn likely to happen only if the President exercises dominant leadership in Congress.

Congress has been trapped by its own powers in many regards. While rhetorically Congress has gained legislative responsibility for nearly all of the public problems in this vast and complex nation, Congress has discovered that it can legislate so widely only by handing legislative authority to others. Wilson and the other Progressives argued for the centralization of legislative power in Congress under the leadership of the President because they thought that this would make legislative decisions more directly responsive to public opinion. But given that Congress lacks such leadership and is now seemingly detached from the constitutional principles that would make it work without such leadership, that body has ceded much of its added power to members of the federal bureaucracy who are even less responsible to the American people than were members of standing committees. Individual members of Congress have adopted a strategy of earning credit through non-legislative actions, most notably constituency services, by which they seek to avoid blame for their legislative activities. The net result has been an increasing tendency to pass all major legislation in omnibus packages for which no single member can be given much credit or suffer much blame.[35]

Although Wilson never succeeded in establishing cabinet government in the United States, and even abandoned his insistence that it was necessary, a view of the changes in Congress over the past century certainly bears the mark of the Progressives' recommendations. These reforms have rendered Congress less capable of providing effective, responsive, and responsible government in the United States, and it thus seems inarguable that the incremental adoption of some of Wilson's recommendations may have rendered Congress less effective and responsible than it was in his day. It is perhaps one of the greatest ironies of the deconstitutionalization of America that those who make the most sustained and heartfelt appeals to the forms of constitutionalist government often engineer the most deconstitutionalizing reforms. George W. Bush based his claim to the presidency on the importance of returning dignity to the office of the President and ultimately gained the office through the Electoral College, the institution that may appear to be the most "constitutionalist" (as opposed to "popular") in our contemporary system. His campaign rhetoric appeared to contain a critique of his predecessor's reliance on popular moods, and this reliance on mood is, it can be argued, a result of Wilson's attempts to give the President a handle with which to control Congress in spite of the constitutional impediments intended to prevent him from doing so. But, based on the first two years of the Bush presidency, it is hard to remember any president who has governed in such a parliamentary fashion. President Bush has repeatedly involved himself in Congressional races both by using his personal appeal as the chief executive in a time of crisis and by directing his considerable fund-raising machine to provide money to his favorites. He has tied the Republican Party in the White House more closely to the Republican Party in Congress, particularly the House of Representatives, than has any previous administration, creating what one commentator has called "near-lockstep party loyalty."[36] This result is not surprising given the Hobbesian choice that a deconstitutionalized Congress often faces between unpopularity and impotence. But it is a truth of our times that the study of the "legislative power" is increasingly a study of the presidency.

NOTES

1. See James Madison, "Vices of the Political System of the United States," in *The Writings of James Madison*, ed. Jack N. Rabocov (New York: The Library of America, 1999) especially 72-73. Also see *Federalist #70*.

2. Thomas Jefferson, *A Summary View of the Rights of British America* in *The Portable Thomas Jefferson*, ed. Merrill D. Peterson (New York: Penguin Books USA, Inc., 1975), 3-21. Also see Harry V. Jaffa's detailed discussion of the *Summary View* in *A New Birth of Freedom* (Lanham, MD: Rowman & Littlefield, 2000) 6-30.

3. *Federalist #48*. Emphasis added.

4. See Comte de Montesquieu, *The Spirit of the Laws*, trans. and ed. by Anne M. Cohler, Basia Carolyn Miller, and Harold Samuel Stone (Cambridge: Cambridge University Press, 1989), 155, 160.

5. *Elliot's Debates*, vol. III, ed. James McClellan and M. E. Bradford (Richmond, VA: James River Press, 1989), 32.

6. For Madison's opposition to the plan for the election of senators see his speeches on June 29 and 30. *Elliot's Debates*, vol. III, 207-208, 216-218, and 221. For evidence that this was absolutely necessary, consider Bedford's threat that the small states might call in "a foreign power to take us by the hand and do us justice."

7. For a particularly clearly argued recent example, see Michael Lind, "75 Stars," *Mother Jones*. January/February 1999.

8. *Federalist #51*. Emphasis added.

9. *Federalist #62*.

10. *Federalist #62*.

11. *Federalist #63*.

12. Ibid.

13. Ibid.

14. On the plenipotentiary powers of parliaments, even in the eighteenth century, see again Jaffa on Jefferson's *Summary View* in *A New Birth of Freedom*, 41-42. Examples of legislatures with broad statutory powers and little authority include those in Russia, France, and Japan.

15. Croly and the other major Progressives agreed with this position. See Croly's discussion of the superiority of executive leadership to party leadership in *Progressive Democracy* (New York: The MacMillan Company, 1914), 315-316 and 330 ff.

16. *Federalist #62*.

17. Elaine K. Swift, *The Making of an American Senate: Reconstitutive Change in Congress, 1787-1841* (Ann Arbor: Michigan University Press, 1996).

18. Between the simultaneous invitations to statehood for Maine and Missouri in 1820 and the entrance of California into the union in 1850, a balance between slave state and non-slave state senators was virtually codified by the Missouri Compromises of 1820. This tacit agreement to preserve a sectional balance between the North and South vindicated Madison's statements in the debate on representation in the Senate that the principle differences between the states were those between the free and slave states. *Elliot's Debates*, vol. III, 217.

19. See Wilson's speeches on August 7 and September 25, 1912. *The Papers of Woodrow Wilson*, vol. 25 (Princeton, NJ: Princeton University Press, 1978). 3-18, especially 6 and 15, and 234-257, especially 235-237.

20. *Federalist #51*. Emphasis added.

21. *Congressional Government*, 218-219.

22. On differences in floor debate in the House and Senate today, see Barbara Sinclair, *Unorthodox Lawmaking: New Legislative Processes in the U.S. Congress* (Washington, DC: Congressional Quarterly Press, 1997), 26-31 and 42-50.

23. One example of Madison's predictions about the different types of debate likely to prevail in the House and the Senate may be found in *Federalist #58*.

24. Anthony King, "Running Scared," *Atlantic Monthly*, January 1997: 41-61.

25. By this, we refer predominantly to the enabling clauses attached to some post-Civil War amendments that authorize Congress to make all laws needed to put into effect the forgoing provisions. See especially, Section 2 of the Thirteenth Amendment and Section 5 of the Fourteenth Amendment.

26. See James Madison, "Speech Opposing the National Bank," in *Writings*, 484-488 and "Speech on the Jay Treaty," *Writings*, 565.

27. Contrast *Federalist* 78, *Federalist* 39, and *Brutus* 1.

28. As Justice Holmes claimed in his famous dissent in *Lochner v. New York* (1912), "A constitution is not intended to embody a particular economic theory." It is clear that the Supreme Court in the early twentieth century espoused limited and enumerated powers to protect a particular economic theory of laissez-faire capitalism rather than to preserve a set of constitutionalist limits on Congress's authority.

29. See for instance the position taken on the regulation of intrastate commerce in *Wickard v. Filburn* 317 U.S. 111 (1942).

30. See Ralph Rossum, *Federalism, the Supreme Court, and the Seventeenth Amendment: The Irony of Constitutional Democracy.* (Lanham, MD: Lexington Books, 2001).

31. Woodrow Wilson, "Cabinet Government in the United States."

32. In saying this, we should point out that the most commonly used critique of these limits on national lawmaking authority, namely that such limits on Congress would effectively preclude any meaningful federal role in protecting the rights of minorities, is simply not valid. While it is true that the landmark Civil Rights Act of 1964 was enacted under what can only be called a highly tangential reading of the Commerce Clause [See *Heart of Atlanta Motel v. United States* 379 U.S. 241 (1964) and *Katzenbach v. McClung* 379 U.S. 294 (1964)] this approach was necessitated by the refusal of the Supreme Court to accept the clear expansion of Congressional authority included in Section 5 of the Fourteenth Amendment that effectively expanded the enumeration of Congress's powers in Article I, Section 8. Few members of the Congress that adopted the Fourteenth Amendment doubted that it explicitly gave Congress the legislative authority to pass the very types of civil rights legislation that it enacted under a strained reading of the Commerce Clause nearly 100 years later. This entire problem was effectively created by the untenable "state action doctrine" created by Justice Bradley in the *Civil Rights Cases* 109 U.S. 3 (1883) and thus the courts should be recognized as the *source* of the civil rights problem that Congress faced in the 1950s and 1960s as much as its *solution.*

33. Steven Stark, "Too Representative Government," *Atlantic Monthly.* May, 1995.

34. See again Stark, "Too Representative Government."

35. See Roger Davidson, *The Postreform Congress* (New York: St. Martin's Press, 1991), especially 17-18.

36. E. J. Dionne, "The New Rules of Politics," *The Washington Post*, May 30, 2003, A23.

CHAPTER 6

PRESIDENTIAL LEADERSHIP AND THE TWO PUBLICS

Many aspects of the presidency are conducted with strict adherence to the forms of the Constitution. The President is elected in the manner prescribed by the Constitution. The four-year term of office has not changed since the beginning of the Republic. The President vetoes bills, commands the military, has primary responsibility for conducting foreign policy, and appoints judges, cabinet officers, ambassadors, and other executive officials with the consent of the Senate. The chief executive can ask Congress for legislation, for a treaty, or for a declaration of war, but he is limited in what he can do without the authorization of law.[1] How then is the presidency becoming deconstitutionalized? Before answering this question it is proper to examine the nature of the executive office as it was conceived by those who wrote the Constitution.

ORIGINS OF THE PRESIDENCY

It is clear from James Madison's notes taken at the Constitutional Convention that constructing an executive officer whose powers were consistent with republican government was one of the most vexing tasks facing those gathered in Philadelphia in 1789.[2] The founding generation was faced with contradictory life experiences. On the one hand, the British king and his agents had abused their power. The lesson learned by those who established the state and national governments under the Articles of Confederation was to preserve liberty by restricting the power of government. Fearing especially the abuse of executive power that had been prevalent under colonial governors—or worse, a gradual return to monarchy—they purposely refused to establish powerful domestic institutions. The national government had few powers and no executive. The Continental Congress needed nearly unanimous consent to enact laws and had to requisition—in essence to beg—the states for money to operate and for soldiers to defend the country. Most state governments, with the exception of New York, were equally ineffectual. Governors were feeble or non-existent, judges could easily be removed from office, and legislative elections were held quite often—every six months in Virginia, for instance.

The consequence of the faulty institutional arrangements under the Articles was a system of government that was at once too strong and too weak. The legislatures enacted laws, but when they attempted to carry them out through legislative committees, squabbling broke out among the committee members about how to administer policy. The process was similar to a group project where one person does all the work while others in the group take praise when things go right and criticize when things go awry. Legislative committees were even less effective than other kinds of groups because political ambition and intrigue were added to the mix. Few statutes were actually carried out. Without the effective implementation of law, it is little wonder that problems mounted. Legislatures reacted by doing what comes naturally to legislative bodies when problems arise; they passed more laws. But these decrees also went unexecuted. Since it is in the nature of legislatures to meet crisis by enacting laws, legislators passed edict after edict, all to no avail. James Madison complained at the time that America had produced more laws in eleven years than were needed to govern Rome during the long centuries of its reign.[3] Moreover, since elections were held often, the makeup of the assemblies changed. In an effort to overcome the governing crisis, new representatives passed new and different statutes, but these too went for naught. The multiplicity and variability of the ordinances confused and disheartened citizens, and it was inevitable that people began to take the law into their own hands, as they did during Shay's Rebellion.

When citizens of a country lose faith in the government, they come to doubt the value of the currency. During the Articles, the currency plunged in value. Representatives reacted to the economic suffering of their constituents by establishing trade barriers, printing more money, and enacting statutes that forgave debts owed to private lenders. But these measures served only to create more uncertainty in the economy. Eventually, speculators took advantage of the instability and amassed wealth from the misery of their fellow citizens. Again lawmakers responded to public opinion and enacted ex post facto laws aimed at punishing excessive profiteering. When judges refused to apply these unjust decrees, the legislatures lowered judicial salaries or replaced judges altogether. After even these measures failed to subvert the independence of some judges, the legislative bodies held trials within the legislative chamber itself. In effect, some states experienced a form of legislative tyranny, made all the more oppressive because it had popular support.

The experience of the Articles convinced Madison that a weak executive could be as much a threat to liberty as a strong one. He reasoned that if the powers of government were separated, each branch could more efficiently complete its assigned task. The legislature could deliberate and debate the broad issues of public policy, the executive could administer the laws with a single line of command, and the judiciary could ensure that decrees affected all equally. The separation of powers, then, was not a limitation of institutional authority, but rather a grant of power whereby each branch was able to competently fulfill its duties. The government became stronger, not weaker, as a result of the separation of powers.

What guarantee was there that these greatly strengthened branches of government would not abuse their power? Obviously, the first was that distinct organs check one another. Furthermore, since the powers of each branch were clearly delineated, citizens would have a better perspective from which to hold public officials accountable for their actions. The separation of powers enhanced the powers of the government, but that power was held in check and forced to be responsible.

Still, there was great fear that the executive might become the leader of a faction or a popular leader, more intent on fulfilling the desires of his followers and his own ambition than on following the rule of law. Alexander Hamilton reasoned that since the principle of equality dominates republican regimes, there is little outlet for high ambition. There are, however, always some people not satisfied with everyday lives. "Men of this class," explained Hamilton, "have not scrupled to sacrifice national tranquillity to personal advantage or personal gratification." How best to attain an exalted position in an egalitarian society? Hamilton mapped out one plan for rising to the top as follows: "If I were disposed to promote Monarchy & overthrow State Governments, I would mount the hobby horse of popularity—I would cry usurpation—danger to liberty. . . . I would endeavor to prostrate the National Government—raise a ferment—and then 'ride in the Whirlwind and direct the Storm.'"

The difficulty of managing the quest for glory under republican governments was compounded by the kinds of leaders the popular party tended to throw up. They seemed not to be aware of their own ambition, or if they were, they disguised their true designs from the many. Hamilton speculated that "the Catalines and the Caesars of the community (a description of men to be found in every republic) who, leading the dance to the tune of liberty without law, endeavor to intoxicate the people with delicious but poisonous draughts to render them the easier victims of their rapacious ambition." He calculated that "no wise man" could believe "a Government continually changing hands" could turn into a monarchy. However, the republic could be overthrown if "popular demagogues" excited "confusion" and "civil commotion." "Tired at length of anarchy, or want of government, they may take shelter in the arms of monarchy for repose and security."[4]

The founders saw a clear distinction between popular leadership and effective government. A president who was guided exclusively by public opinion was one of three things. He was pretending to be the people's servant, since the complexity of issues made direct participation in national affairs impossible for the many. He was feigning popularity for more sinister motives of personal ambition, as Hamilton suggested. Or, he was foolish in believing that people were wise in all regards. True statesmanship, on the other hand, required that the President make decisions that were good for the nation, even if they were unpopular at the moment. Hamilton reasoned in *Federalist* #71:

> The republican principle demands that the deliberate sense of the community should govern the conduct of those to whom they entrust the management of

their affairs; but it does not require an unqualified complaisance to every sudden breeze of passion, or to every transient impulse which the people may receive from the arts of men, who flatter their prejudices to betray their interests. It is a just observation, that the people commonly INTEND the PUBLIC GOOD. This often applies to their very errors. But their good sense would despise the adulator who should pretend that they always REASON RIGHT about the MEANS of promoting it. They know from experience that they sometimes err; and the wonder is that they so seldom err as they do, beset, as they continually are, by the wiles of parasites and sycophants, by the snares of the ambitious, the avaricious, the desperate, by the artifices of men who possess their confidence more than they deserve it, and of those who seek to possess rather than to deserve it. When occasions present themselves, in which the interests of the people are at variance with their inclinations, it is the duty of the persons whom they have appointed to be the guardians of those interests, to withstand the temporary delusion, in order to give them time and opportunity for more cool and sedate reflection.[5]

Independence in the executive is an essential element of self-government, Hamilton suggests. At the level of national policymaking, public opinion would either be uninformed or dangerously partisan. A leader who claims to implement the wishes of the people would be deluding himself or his followers. Such a government could not long endure the vagaries of political life, especially in foreign affairs, an arena that gives rise to the most extreme passions of hatred and revenge and is fraught with greatest danger.

MODE OF SELECTION

The founders feared an executive who would be elevated to office at the head of a mass-based political party and who would govern as a factional leader, ignoring the law in order to satisfy his followers and to gratify his ambition. They hoped that the Electoral College would avert the likelihood of demagogic leaders appealing directly to people for their authority and governing without the rule of law. They hoped that the "intermediate body of electors" would "be much less apt to convulse the community with any extraordinary or violent movements, than the choice of ONE who was himself to be the final object of the public wishes."[6] Since the electors were a small body chosen from the public on the basis of their judgment and not political loyalty to a particular candidate, it was thought they would be able to discern the character of potential presidents directly, perhaps through personal acquaintance. Even if electors were bewitched by the alluring rhetoric of a local leader, it was considered unlikely that such a person would be able to command a national audience. Finally, the two votes that each elector cast—one had to be for a person outside the elector's home state—made it likely that a demagogic leader would not be selected for the highest office. It was reasoned that the second vote would go to persons who had gained a reputation through some service for the nation. Having previously performed a sacrifice for the country, such a person would be less likely to trample on its laws when in office.

> The process of election affords a moral certainty, that the office of President will never fall to the lot of any man who is not in an eminent degree endowed with the requisite qualifications. Talents for low intrigue, and the little arts of popularity, may alone suffice to elevate a man to the first honors in a single State; but it will require other talents, and a different kind of merit, to establish him in the esteem and confidence of the whole Union, or of so considerable a portion of it as would be necessary to make him a successful candidate for the distinguished office of President of the United States. It will not be too strong to say, that there will be a constant probability of seeing the station filled by characters pre-eminent for ability and virtue.[7]

The Electoral College never worked as planned. Self-governing people are too concerned about who should rule over them for electors to remain independent. The nation quickly split along party lines. In the election of 1800, the apogee of partisan sentiment, the two top candidates, Thomas Jefferson and Aaron Burr, garnered exactly the same number of electoral votes, forcing the election to be turned over to the House of Representatives for resolution. As a result of the confusion in 1800, the Twelfth Amendment, which limited each elector to one vote for President and one for Vice President, was adopted, thereby silently recognizing prearranged presidential-vice-presidential tickets—and with them political parties—as the mechanism for choosing candidates.

America's two-party system confounded the dire predictions of political disaster. While it was true that presidents chosen from the ranks of party leadership were more likely to be politicians than statesmen, it was also true that the parties were so diverse and amorphous that only moderates—candidates who did not alienate one or the other wing of the coalition—could hope to win the nomination. Since parties consist of so many factions, office holders were rarely beholding to any particular group and could maintain the distance from public pressure necessary to govern effectively. Moreover, under the "closed party system," established primarily by Martin Van Buren, leaders of each party had a long-term interest in the party's future, and served as checks on personal ambition. They knew the potential candidates personally and were reluctant to choose a person for president whose character was not compatible with high office and whose term of service might damage the reputation of the party, resulting in a humiliating loss in the next election.[8]

As a result of the 1968 presidential election, the party system underwent a radical change. Vice President Hubert Humphrey won the Democratic nomination without running in any of the primaries. The "anti-Vietnam War" candidates, Senators Robert Kennedy (who was assassinated after winning the California primary) and Eugene McCarthy competed in all the primaries, but did not garner enough delegates to clinch the nomination. Reformers in the Democratic Party interpreted Humphrey's narrow defeat at the hands of Richard Nixon in the general election as a call for more openness and democratic participation in the nominating process. They claimed that the "closed" system by which party leaders picked the lion's share of delegates to the presidential nominating convention thwarted the popular will and inevitably resulted in abuses of power, such as American involvement in the Vietnam war. The Democrats empowered the McGovern-Fraser Commission to overhaul the nominating process.

The goal of the McGovern-Fraser Commission was to make the nominating process fairer and more democratic. "The cure for the ills of democracy is more democracy," was its motto. Perhaps the direct or "open" method of selecting party nominees for the presidency was inevitable, given the independence from party allegiance that mass communication and increased education have given to the electorate. Yet the reforms made by the McGovern-Fraser Commission marked a critical alteration in America's electoral system. Changes were made first within the Democratic Party, then copied by the Republicans, and ultimately put into law by most state legislatures. The initial reforms themselves went through several transformations, but the consequences were to remove the power of nominating presidential candidates from the party organization and give it to the people as they expressed their will in the state party primaries and caucuses.

This so-called reform party system has been one component in the deconstitutionalization of the presidency. It has resulted in longer, more expensive, more personalized, and more negative campaigns, as well as influencing how presidents understand their role in governing. The message of candidates is no longer filtered through the principles of the party. There is not much permanent party organization to help office seekers with campaigns. Instead, candidates must appeal constantly to public opinion in order to be elected. To win election, office seekers are compelled to become exactly the kind of popular favorite that the founders feared. While no president has yet attempted to govern "informally," or outside the constitutional proscriptions, it is true that those now elected are more likely to be guided in making policy by public opinion polls and less committed to constructing and implementing good policies.[9] The long and arduous campaign for president tends to reward those whose political instinct it is to do what is immediately popular rather than what is wise.

POWERS OF THE PRESIDENT

What exactly were the powers granted to the President under the Constitution? The text of the Constitution dealing with the presidency is short and inconclusive. Does the sentence, "The executive power shall be vested in a president of the United Sates of America," bestow some indeterminate executive power on the President, or is it merely intended to give a name to the executive? Does the President's oath of office confer some special obligation and power in the President to protect the nation when it is in jeopardy, or is it a reminder to the commander in chief to obey the laws that he is in the most favorable position to violate? Does the power to make treaties authorize the President to conduct the day to-day foreign relations of the United States with other nations when no tr exists? These issues have bedeviled politicians and commentators since 1787. The debate began in the first Congress. It concerned the authority of the President to remove inferior executive officials, and continued with the exchange between Madison and Hamilton over whether the President could act on his own authority to proclaim neutrality. President Adams's power to arm merchant vessels was challenged, as was President Jackson's authority to remove U.S. funds from the National Bank. Congressman Abraham Lincoln attacked President Polk for sending troops to Texas without prior congressional approval, but President Lincoln spent money out of the treasury, raised an army, blockaded southern ports, and suspended the writ of habeas corpus in order to counter the secession of Southern states. Lincoln reasoned that the power to preserve the Union was executive in nature, and he therefore undertook these actions without prior Congressional authorization. He feared that Congress worked too slowly for decisive action and encouraged Congress, then home on recess, not to come back into session.

Later presidents, often with Lincoln's actions in mind, have vigorously exercised the foreign affairs power. President Truman seized the steel mills using the executive authority. President Nixon invaded Cambodia without informing Congress. President Clinton sent American troops as peacekeepers to various hot spots around the world, ignoring congressional protests. All of these actions—and many more too numerous to list—have produced cries of unconstitutional usurpation of power.

Although these actions were controversial, it can be argued that they fell within the range of the proper exercise of executive power. Most were undertaken during a crisis, usually in foreign affairs, and it is a reasonable construction of the Constitution that the President's powers increase in order to meet every exigency. As David Nichols argues, the powers of the President were left vague in the Constitution because at the time of the founding many citizens feared that a powerful executive would necessarily evolve into monarchy. The Constitution was written in such a way that the executive powers, though not threatening on the surface, could expand to meet future emergencies.[10] The framers of the Constitution understood that it was impossible and unwise to attempt to limit the president too severely, for such restrictions would probably be ignored if political necessity dictated a different course. Yet, it was exactly because the powers of the executive were both undefined and vast that the framers hoped to check future presidents by making them obedient to the formal stricture of the Constitution. What they feared most were popular leaders who might take advantage of the latitude in the constitutional powers of the executive to elevate themselves above legal limitations. Such leaders might exploit the popular passion, always present within democratic countries, by promising quick and easy solutions to political problems in order to suspend the rule of law and govern on their own authority.

THE EXPANDED ROLE OF THE PRESIDENCY

The twentieth century challenged the nation and its constitutional system. Theodore Roosevelt is often credited with the expansion of executive power. Yet, his "stewardship theory," as broad as it was, still took its bearings from the forms and restrictions in the Constitution. "My belief," he explained,

> was that it was not only his right but his duty to do anything that the needs of the nation demanded, unless such action was forbidden by the Constitution or by the laws. Under this interpretation of executive power I did and caused to be done many things not previously done by the President and the heads of the departments. I did not usurp power, but I did greatly broaden the use of executive power. In other words, I acted for the public welfare, I acted for the common well-being of all our people, whenever and in whatever manner was necessary, unless prevented by direct constitutional or legislative prohibition.[11]

While Roosevelt's position was expansive, it was quite different from that of Woodrow Wilson. Wilson attacked the sagacity of the founders and maintained that their system of checks and balances was too slow and cumbersome, especially in the swiftly changing industrial age. Wilson decried the parochialism and narrow self-interest that Madison's pluralist system had fostered. He worried that the government was not competent to counteract the growing dominance of large corporations. He thought that political parties were corrupt, candidates available to be bought and sold, and democracy little more than a vehicle for gratifying self-interest. His cure for the nation's ills was a stronger, more rational leadership. Only the President, he reasoned, could salvage the system. He explained that

> The nation as a whole has chosen him, and is conscious that it has no other political spokesman. His is the only national voice in affairs. Let him once win the admiration and confidence of the country, and no other single force can withstand him, no combination of forces will easily overpower him. His position takes the imagination of the country. He is the representative of no constituency, but of the whole people. When he speaks in his true character, he speaks for no special interest. If he rightly interpret the national thought and boldly insist upon it, he is irresistible; and the country never feels the zest of action so much as when its President is of such insight and caliber. Its instinct is for unified action, and it craves a single leader. It is for this reason that it will often prefer to choose a man rather than a party.[12]

A strong president could overcome regionalism, factionalism, and parochial self-interest, Wilson believed. A powerful president could propose legislation designed to help the entire nation, not just the most powerful groups. He could coordinate policy at the national level so as to control far-flung corporate enterprises. According to Wilson, the presidency could become more powerful and represent the interests of the entire nation only if the executive drew his power from the people. Wilson argued that true democratic statesmen "lead n reason of legal authority, but by reason of their contact with and amenability to public opinion."[13]

Unlike the founders, Wilson did not fear demagogic rulers employing the authority of the executive office to play one group off against another and then capitalizing on the social unrest to aggrandize themselves. He maintained that there was only one "true" public opinion, and that a forceful leader could both discover and express that view in his rhetoric and policies. He did not fear "rhetorical adroitness, dialectical dexterity, even passionate declamation." According to Wilson, "Charlatans [could] not play statesmen successfully" for long, since "the air is too open for either stupidity or indirection to thrive."[14] The American populace, just as their political system, had grown and changed. The organic nature of that transformation made it impossible for the American public to accept anything less than an authentic democratic leader. At their core, Americans were democrats; the ethos of that form of government was ingrained in their psyche. Not only did the democratic way of life unite them, but it prevented even the most convincing rulers from leading them astray.[15]

While Wilson's theory of executive power was influential, especially in academic circles, he never fully implemented his ideas while president. It can be argued that Franklin Roosevelt's years in the White House were the practical manifestation of Wilson's principles. Roosevelt argued that the Great Depression was evidence of the free market's failure and that if the economic system was not reformed, liberal democracy might be swept aside by popular discontent. Roosevelt had little faith that the "invisible hand" of unrestrained material self-interest could end the Great Depression or provide for the needs of the average citizen. The economy had failed because the free market was too competitive, too efficient at producing unneeded goods, and too likely to concentrate wealth in too few hands. The only road out of the economic calamity was for the government to manage economic activity, ensuring the proper distribution of wealth so that there would be an adequate market for the goods produced. To institute these economic policies, the national government had to be more powerful, taking on responsibilities far beyond those imagined at the time of the founding. Unlike Wilson, Roosevelt did not challenge the wisdom of the founders; he simply ignored the principle of enumerated powers and limited government. Although much of the New Deal legislation was initially struck down by the Supreme Court, Roosevelt's view of an expansive national government prevailed.[16] The new role for government also required a more central status of the presidency. Under the Roosevelt model, the executive would not merely administer the nation's laws; he would foster a national consensus and use it to propose an integrated policy agenda to be presented to Congress. In essence, the President would become the center of political life.

Roosevelt differed from Wilson in one important respect. Although FDR's programs were aimed at helping the majority of Americans, there was no real consensus about who should be the primary beneficiaries of government largess. Therefore, Roosevelt left it up to the American people themselves to decide which programs they should demand from the government. The result was that various interest groups formed, each claiming its share of the federal budget. Government programs spawned their own interest groups, whose primary agenda was to ensure the continuation of policies that aided those interest groups. Rather than unifying public opinion, the legacy of Roosevelt's welfare state was to divide the nation into competing interest groups. Since, as Madison explained, a "connection subsists between . . . reason and . . . self-love," most members of these groups do not see themselves as special interests. Rather they often consider their own programs to *be* the common good and understand themselves to be the *entire* American people.

The Wilson-Roosevelt model of a strong presidency dependent on public opinion became the norm in American politics. Presidents after FDR were expected to be the focal point of the nation's politics. Even conservative presidents such as Ronald Reagan defined themselves as popular leaders. No contemporary presidential candidate would dream of running for office without putting forth a substantial legislative package. A President who merely administers the laws is considered weak and ineffective. The founders' constitutional presidency is held in contempt. Although the elder George Bush's record of achievement was considerable—he presided over the demise of the Soviet Empire, lowered the national debt, resolved the Savings and Loan crisis, and patched together a most extraordinary military alliance in order to defeat Saddam Hussein's forces in Kuwait—a rather minor economic downturn in 1991 led to his electoral defeat.[17] Bush's theory of governance also hurt his chances for reelection. Except in times of crisis, Bush did not believe in a proactive presidency, preferring to allow his subordinates, experts in their fields, to formulate and execute policy. Before his elevation to the presidency, Bush had been the consummate insider, a professional who disdained political rhetoric and favored letting expertise and performance speak for themselves. He had neither the talent nor the disposition to duplicate Reagan's rhetorical feats. Bush was, by his own admission, uncomfortable with "the vision thing." Peggy Noonan, Reagan's most able speech writer, summed up Bush's predicament. "Serious people in public life stand for things and fight for them," she explained. "Mr. Bush seemed embarrassed to believe. It left those who felt sympathy for him embarrassed to support him."[18] President Bill Clinton understood the character of the modern presidency much better than his immediate predecessor, Bush. After some initial missteps, Clinton's finely honed political skills adjusted to public demands. In making policy, he consulted polling and focus group data more than had any previous president. He discovered that the President must actually speak to two public opinions in order to be effective. The first, "Wilsonian" public opinion, encompasses the whole nation and really is "the American people." In media events meant for a broad audience, Clinton captured the public mood of outrage and shock on occasions such as the Oklahoma City bombing, the shooting at Columbine High School, various natural disasters, and other such incidents where there was a deep-rooted national consensus. But normally such unanimity is shallow and brief. Americans usually look out for themselves, and public opinion is fracture among the groups that make up our diverse society. In order to appeal t second, more contentious, opinion that was established as the result of Roosevelt's welfare state, Clinton sponsored "micro-initiatives." "Micro-initiatives" were aimed at localized media coverage, usually at symbolic venues somehow tied to the policy being proposed. They entailed very little federal spending—sometimes only a few million dollars—on the problem or issue at hand. They were meant to satisfy a particular interest group's aspiration to have the government do something for them. For that specific interest group the President was fulfilling his role as leader and delivering on the promise that the government existed to address the needs of the people. Since the monetary sums at hand were small and the media coverage limited, these presidential events stirred little negative reaction from other interest groups, who often see government spending on anything other than their policy agenda as wasteful or even corrupt. Clinton's most successful "triangulation" was not, as the political consultant who coined the word argued, between liberals and conservatives, but rather between public opinion as it expresses itself generally, which it does only occasionally for some important event, and the more narrow special interests that expect the government to fulfill their particular wishes.[19]

Just as the framers had predicted, Clinton's personal popularity tempted him to rule "informally." He skirted senatorial hearings and appointed his designees to official posts during congressional recesses far more often than had any of his predecessors. In the final days of his presidency, he bypassed Congress and significantly altered environmental regulations. He added millions of acres of land to the national parks by executive order. He granted last-minute pardons to hundreds of people, in some cases evidently without even consulting his own Justice Department. While it may be true that each of these decisions can be defended, in total they add up to a clear pattern of neglect or even disrespect for the forms of executive action. Had Clinton exhibited high political ambition instead of a longing for personal acclaim, had he been among "the tribe of the eagle," as Lincoln calls those who thirst for distinction, America's democratic constitution might have been unhinged.

In two areas Clinton exhibited independence of judgment rather than political expediency. After his party's humiliating defeat in the midterm elections of 1994, when Republicans gained control of both houses of Congress for the first time in a generation, he resisted the temptation—always strong among Democrats—to interfere with the economy. He left the free market and the burgeoning global markets to do their work. The result was the fastest and most sustained growth in American history. Clinton also demonstrated independence and judgment in foreign affairs. He intervened militarily in Bosnia and Kosovo in order to forestall further massacre despite polls showing an overwhelming majority opposed American involvement.

It could be argued that George W. Bush's presidency has reversed the trend toward deconstitutionalization. After all, he was elevated to office by the Electoral College, not in the popular election, which he lost by half a million votes. The defining mission of his presidency has been to counter terrorist threats, a task whose urgency became poignantly clear after the attacks of September 11,

2001. As we have seen, the Constitution provides much latitude to presidential action in foreign affairs, and Bush has made full use of the powers granted to the executive. Moreover, the public traditionally rallies behind the President when the security or freedom of the nation is imperiled. Bush was able to combine the popular and the constitutional presidency. But it is not clear whether he can maintain his authority if his foreign policies, especially the war in Iraq, are unsuccessful. After a crisis has passed, the public mood customarily shifts against aggrandizement of the executive. More important, Congress reasserts its power and limits the President. If there are no further terrorist attacks on the United States, it is almost certain that such laws as the Patriot Act, which permits the government to pry into people's private lives, will be reformed or even rescinded.[20]

In one sense, the terrorist menace has been good fortune for Bush. He does not possess the electoral mandate, political deftness, or rhetorical skill necessary to reenact Clinton's triangular politics. Had the attacks on the United States not occurred, Bush would surely have been forced by the expectations placed on the chief executive, as was his predecessor, to govern by creating a popular mandate, not by exercising the authority of his constitutional powers. John Diluilo, Bush's former adviser on faith-based programs for the needy, resigned in August 2001 because pollsters, not policy makers were setting the agenda of the President. We should forget that as the attacks on the Pentagon and World Trade Center were taking place, the President of the United States was promoting his modest educational reforms by reading to a second-grade class.

CONCLUSION

How, then, has the presidency been deconstitutionalized? The presidency has become the figurehead for the hopes and desires of the nation. The President must constantly attempt to use the government to satisfy people's desires, thus depriving them of the ability to solve their own problems. As the President has become the focal point of political life in the nation, many people have come to expect that the national government can solve all social problems. Many responsibilities that were once local in nature have been shifted to the national level. But, it is at the local level where the people can have an actual, rather than merely rhetorical, influence on issues and policies. The presidency imagined by Wilson and constructed by Roosevelt makes people misunderstand their own limitations. It raises the false expectation that the whole people are capable of directing the activities of the national government through the executive. It flatters their worst instincts, making them think that they can do no wrong and encouraging them to believe that their own narrow self-interests should be addressed and satisfied. It deceives them into thinking that their particular will is representative of the American people generally and is an expression of the common good, while everyone else's position is evidence that special interests have taken over the country.

Polls show that the electorate has become cynical and distrustful of the government, since it is impossible for the President and the national government to satisfy all demands made by every interest group. Moreover, the electoral system has made presidents likely to act more like office seekers than office holders. Candidates who are elected under our current system are so sensitive to the public mood that they often let pollsters formulate policies. Our current mode of selecting presidents has also opened the door to ambitious demagogic leaders who might someday pander to the widely held belief that the "system is corrupt" and avoid obeying the forms of the Constitution in order to follow the desire of their followers to achieve quick political solutions.

Franklin Roosevelt once said that the government should use Hamiltonian means to achieve Jeffersonian ends. Although the two founders in question rarely agreed on anything, both would be uneasy with the presidency created by Roosevelt's synthesis. Jefferson would deplore the loss of civic virtue and political responsibility implied by a strong president presiding over a powerful government. He would fear that a government intent on satisfying people's desires would corrupt the citizens by making them docile and ultimately unable to govern their own affairs. Hamilton would decry the loss of responsibility that a president too closely tied to public opinion faces. He would warn us that the executive of a great nation must have the requisite freedom to undertake actions for the public good. He would remind us of lessons learned during the Articles of Confederation when the lack of a strong executive and the preeminence of unrestrained democratic will almost brought the country to ruin. He would argue that although the people intend to do the public good, they have very little knowledge or ability to carry out that impulse at the national level. He would surely remind us that some of the greatest leaders in history have "saved the people from very fatal consequences of their own mistakes," and have "procured lasting monuments of their gratitude" by having "had courage and magnanimity enough to serve them at the peril of their displeasure."[21]

NOTES

1. Since there have not as yet been any women elected president, we have used the masculine pronoun for the sake of brevity.

2. James Madison, *Notes of the Debates of the Federal Convention*, ed. Adrienne Koch (New York: Norton Library, 1968), 45 where Madison notes "a considerable pause ensuing" after a motion was made "that a National Ex. to consist of a single person, be instituted." The elder statesman Benjamin Franklin broke the silence with an observation "that it was a point of great importance" and ought to be debated. See also 46-60, 92-94, 124-125, 182, 310, 324-332, 392-393, 509, 526-528.

3. James Madison, "Vices of the Political System of the United States," *The Writings of James Madison*, ed. Gaillard Hunt (New York: G. Putnam's Sons, 1901), 361-369.

4. *Federalist #6*; Hamilton to Edward Carrington, May 26, 1792, in Harold C. Syrett, ed., *The Papers of Alexander Hamilton*, 26 vols. (New York: Columbia University Press, 1961-1979), vol. 1, 4; hereafter cited as *PH*, 11: 444. Hamilton to George Washington, August 18, 1792, *PH*, 12: 251-252. See also *Vindication No. 1*, *PH*, 11: 462; *Catullus No. III*, *PH*, 12: 500-501; *Publius Letter, II*, *PH*, 1: 569; and *Defense of the President's Neutrality Proclama-*

tion, PH, 14: 503, where Hamilton warned that "The noblest passion of the human soul. . . the zeal for the liberty of mankind. . . . [could become] subservient to this fatal project."

5. *Federalist* #71.

6. *Federalist* #68.

7. Ibid.

8. Ceaser, *Presidential Selection*, 123-69.

9. One wonders whether Ross Perot would have bothered with the rule of law if he had been elected president. His slogan was "Just Do It!" He would have arrived in Washington with high hopes and a good deal of popular fanfare. He would not have had any institutional support in Congress. Neither the leaders of Congress nor the members of political parties who make up the law-making branch would have felt any loyalty to him. Given that members of Congress are under intense political pressure to please their constituents, it is unlikely that they would have followed his lead. What then would Perot have done? Would he have turned to his old ally, polls, in order to push forward his campaign promises? Would he have attempted to put into effect without congressional approval policies which surveys indicated were popular? Would he have tried to govern with polls, but without law?

10. David K. Nichols, *The Myth of the Modern Presidency* (University Park, PA: Pennsylvania State University Press, 1994).

11. *The Autobiography* of *Theodore Roosevelt*, ed. Wayne Andrews (New York: Scribner's, 1958), 197-200.

12. Woodrow Wilson, *Constitutional Government*, 68.

13. Woodrow Wilson, *The New Freedom*, 81.

14. Woodrow Wilson, "Cabinet Government in the United States," 1-30.

15. Woodrow Wilson, *Leaders of Men*, ed. T. H. V. Motter (Princeton: Princeton University Press, 1952), 45. Wilson's easy acceptance of the inevitability of democracy rests on a particular progressive movement of history. Wilson seems to be an early advocate of the "End of History" thesis first proposed by George Hegel.

16. The Court began to interpret the Commerce Clause in such a way as to allow the national government to legislate on any condition that affected interstate commerce.

17. Jonathan Rauch, "Father Superior: Our Greatest Modern President," *The New Republic*, May 22, 2000: 22-25.

18. Peggy Noonan, "Why Bush Failed," *New York Times*, November 5, 1992, A35.

19. For Clinton's use of polling data as a means to govern see John F. Harris, "Policy and Politics by the Numbers," *Washington Post*, December 31, 2000, A1, A10. See also John F. Harris, "Clinton Never Liked the Media: But Don't Ask Him Why," *Washington Post* 31 December 2000, B1, B2.

20. The national debate on the wisdom of the Patriot Act is beginning as this book goes to print. See "Fierce Fight Over Secrecy, Scope of Law," *Washington Post*, September 8, 2003, A1, A12, A13.

21. *Federalist* #71.

CHAPTER 7

THE MODERN JUDICIARY AND PALLIATIVE GOVERNMENT: STILL THE "LEAST DANGEROUS BRANCH"?

Hamilton's declaration in *Federalist* #78 that the federal judiciary would be an institution with neither "force nor will" but only "judgment" has long been treated as either an intentional but noble exercise in deceit or an anachronism in modern constitutional history.[1] It is now common place to refer to the judiciary as merely another political institution and judges as just another class of political actors. The Supreme Court's critical intervention in the election of 2000 cemented that belief in the consciousness of the American people.[2] What is often lost in commentaries on the contemporary judiciary is that there is a cost associated not just with having courts behave as political decision-makers, but with the public perception of the courts as political institutions. Perceptions do matter, and the conviction that judicial officials are also political actors can have undesirable effects on the behavior of citizens. Lingering perceptions of the judiciary as a nonpartisan institution are part of the social and political capital that must be carefully preserved and guarded if the constitutional system is to produce the beneficial results desired by founders such as James Madison.

No jurist has been more critical of the "willfulness" of the modern judiciary than Justice Antonin Scalia. Writing in the most important abortion case of the early 1990s, *Planned Parenthood of Southeastern Pennsylvania v. Casey*, Scalia bluntly declared that the "Imperial Judiciary lives."[3] He chided the Court for embracing a "Nietzschean vision of . . . unelected, life-tenured judges—leading a Volk who will be 'tested by following,' and whose very 'belief in themselves' is mystically bound up in their 'understanding' of a Court that 'speak[s] before all others for their constitutional ideals.'"[4] It is not only activist jurisprudence that provoked Scalia's scathing attack on his colleagues, but the willingness to make policy on the basis of personal convictions about what is good or desirable for society. Scalia's fulminations are a critique not only of the prevailing law school view of the judiciary, but of the general layman's view as well. A large number of scholars and jurists, however, have argued that the situation described by Scalia is not only unavoidable but has proven to be desirable. According to persons of this persuasion, the resolution of disputes by courts of law fits well with the rationalism associated with modern commercial republic—a rationalism that commonly is conceptualized as the pursuit of order and progress through established and knowable rules that are interpreted and enforced by impartial arbiters. The case for an "imperial judiciary" typically is made with reference backward to the role courts have played in addressing social problems such as racial and gender discrimination and in challenging restraints on expression and the pursuit of preferred lifestyles. Accompanying this argument is the claim that the judiciary is the most effective institution for responding to institutional and interest-group gridlock. It is hard to quarrel with these arguments in any public arena, especially in light of general public tolerance of judicial policy making. Rather than bringing closure to this issue, however, the fact that activist policy making engaged in by unelected judges has been accepted as a fact of life by a democratic citizenry warrants careful review precisely for what it tells us about possibly troubling changes in Madison's constitutional republic.

THE MAKING OF THE "COMPREHENSIVE CONSTITUTION" DOCTRINE

The willingness of the Supreme Court to open its doors to more claimants and to make judgments about public policies that regulate sexual practices or lifestyle choices did not appear in the last half of the twentieth century like one of Zeus's famed lightning bolts. The conviction that members of the judiciary have a duty to offer their own assessment of "social utility" in the course of rendering decisions can be traced to the writings and opinions of Progressive and New Deal-era figures such as Benjamin Cardozo. Cardozo's influential treatise, *The Nature of the Judicial Process*, was published shortly after World War I during the period when Justice Oliver Wendell Holmes and Louis Brandeis were faulting their conservative brethren for defeating progressive legislation such as the federal child labor law and a District of Columbia minimum wage law for women. In his treatise, Cardozo championed the view that the "great generalities of the constitution have a content and a significance that vary from age to age."[5] While acknowledging the value of history and precedent as sources of guidance, Cardozo argued that judges might properly take "some compelling sentiment of justice" or a "semi-intuitive apprehension of the pervading spirit of the law" as their guide when deciding "where to go."[6] The unmistakable message of *The Nature of the Judicial Process* is that jurists should be sensitive to the demands of social justice. In a sentence as curt as it is instructive, he observed, "The final cause of law is the welfare of society."[7] The combined advancement of social justice and the welfare of society emerge as the decisive test of whether the judiciary is meeting its high obligations. During his own short tenure on the Supreme Court, Cardozo lent support to the regulatory efforts of the New Dealers by defending an expansive interpretation of governmental powers. Writing in dissent in *Carter v. Carter Coal*, a 1936 commerce power case, he asserted that this power "is as broad as the need that evokes it."[8] The "need" in this case had to do with remedying the social and economic traumas associated with the Depression. With his declaration in *Carter*, Cardozo anticipated the more rel approach to constitutional interpretation that would mark the Court's handling of commerce clause cases—and indeed all economic regulation cases—between 1937 and the 1990s.

The theme that government exists to protect the people from "bitter wrongs" and tragedies that might interfere with comfortable preservation was writ large in New Deal-style liberalism. The attainment of happiness—not merely protection for the pursuit of happiness—by everyone, not just a select few or the "industrial oligarchy," became the measure of the respectability of government. The stated aim was the conquest of domestic problems such as those associated with the Depression. Ideally, fear itself would be eliminated as a significant feature of American life. To this end, New Dealers looked to mobilize public opinion and interest group support behind policies designed to eliminate or conquer all remaining sources of deprivation and intimidation, and thereby raise "the level of happiness" of the people.

It is a short step from Cardozo's reasoning and the work of the New Dealers to the arguments that later liberal jurists like Justice William Brennan would employ when interpreting the powers of the national government and what he called the "majestic generalities" of the Constitution. Brennan, who saw Cardozo as legitimating reliance on passion as well as reason in judicial decision-making, labored over thirty-four terms to advance the aims of the Progressives and New Dealers. What Brennan meant by passion was compassion rooted in the conviction that each person should be able to enjoy the full pleasure of his or her own existence. Only through a compassionate jurisprudence did he believe that law could develop "progressively." For liberal jurists like Brennan, the American legal profession will satisfy its high responsibilities under the Constitution only when it commits itself to the comprehensive protection of all rights and redress for all grievances—what has been dubbed the "comprehensive constitution" doctrine.

The conviction that government exists to protect the people from obstacles to the enjoyment of comfortable preservation, and even from fear itself, was a hallmark of New Deal liberalism. This belief, wedded to the view of Progressives that nation states are organic—hence malleable and historical—entities, provided a great opening for activist governance of the sort associated with Franklin Roosevelt and his "Brain Trust," as well as with activist jurisprudence. New Deal-style coalition politics built on the vision of a progressive democracy that was popularized by Woodrow Wilson. For Wilson, the end of real political history coincides with the appearance of the truly free society that efficiently implements the will of a self-conscious and self-directing people. This messianistic thinking marries political populism with scientific management. Just as Wilson believed that his leadership could serve as the catalyst needed to move the United States to the last stage of historical development, so judges who subscribe to the objectives of the New Deal are convinced that the Court can serve the same function for a post-New Deal America that has not yet made good on the promises of Wilson and Roosevelt. Justice Brennan, for example, shared Wilson's insistence that progress can only be made if the opinions and practices of the people are liberated from historical or traditional standards of legitimacy. Such "liberation" will enable society to address an ever-expanding range of obstacles to social justice and individual authenticity (i.e., hate speech, sexual harassment, etc.).

THE "COMPREHENSIVE CONSTITUTION" DOCTRINE IN PRACTICE

Modern liberal jurisprudence has both procedural and substantive sides. The procedural side has to do with enlarging access to the judicial forum by weakening barriers to standing and shrinking the political questions doctrine. On the substantive side, the objective is to ensure that claimants receive the right treatment from courts, which for jurists like Brennan and William O. Douglas means action that liberates the human will by removing or weakening constraints on the pursuit of preferred lifestyles while compensating those who have been victims of such constraints. Here is the core of Brennan's self-described jurisprudence of "libertarian dignity." What is contained in this jurisprudence is an independent authorization, in the form of the pursuit of libertarian dignity, for judicial decision-making that can be either reflective of current thinking about "the welfare of society" or ahead of prevailing views on this subject. Brennan had no qualms in getting ahead of society whenever he believed that existing practices did not advance the dignity of people, especially disfavored persons or groups.

By the 1960s, liberals on the Court were prepared to challenge arrangements like unequal electoral districts, and later the sovereign immunity doctrine, that they believed were incompatible with an egalitarian, rights-oriented society. No Justice wrote more opinions designed to bring about such a social order than Brennan. He believed that New Deal America had unnecessarily made its peace with practices that were incompatible with Roosevelt's objective of general happiness for the people. He was not alone in this opinion. Nor was Brennan alone in arguing that correction of the remaining deficiencies would necessitate a transfer of power to the courts.

Baker v. Carr, the first major malapportionment case of the 1960s, is one of the more well-known Warren Court rulings that were designed to remove "impurities" from the American political system or eliminate limitations on personal freedoms. In *Baker*, as in a number of other cases, the Warren Court left no doubt about its willingness to open the judicial forum to parties who sought standing—the right to come before the Court—to challenge political or electoral processes.[9] Until *Baker v. Carr*, the federal courts had routinely dismissed attempts to litigate challenges to state districting schemes. Writing in a 1946 Illinois districting case, Justice Felix Frankfurter announced that persons wishing to contest the way electoral districts had been drawn should seek reforms through legislative processes.[10] Frankfurter counseled the judiciary to stay clear of what he saw as a "political thicket." By the time of *Baker* in 1962, the Court had abandoned its cautionary approach in favor of a more generous view of standing that Justices believed was necessary for the United States to make good on the promises of the Progressives and New Dealers. To reach his end, the Court

fined the terms of the political questions doctrine, a long-standing rule of justi-
ciability that could be traced back to Chief Justice John Marshall's observation
in *Marbury v. Madison* that "Questions, in their nature political . . . can never be
made in this court."[11] Brennan, writing for the *Baker* Court, effectively recon-
structed the term "political" to encompass much less than what it had been construed to cover in the century and a half that had elapsed between *Marbury* and
Baker. With the backing of a majority of his colleagues, Brennan matter-of-
factly declared that the Supreme Court alone is responsible for "deciding
whether a matter has in any measure been committed by the Constitution to another branch of government, or whether the action of that branch exceeds whatever authority has been committed."[12] He went on to announce that electoral
districting suits fell well within the jurisdiction of the courts. In many respects, it
was the *Baker* ruling that opened the door to federal judicial review of the con-
tested presidential election of 2000.

That federal courts could take cases that previously were off limits under
the political questions doctrine represented only part of the Warren Court's message in *Baker*. Also emerging out of this case was an unmistakable directive to
lower courts to act whenever possible to protect rights and redress grievances:
"They [the courts] will not stand impotent before an obvious instance of a manifestly unauthorized exercise of power."[13] Judicial oversight not only of state
governance but also of the activities of the coordinate branches of the federal
government would now be a central feature of American constitutional law.
With *Powell v. McCormick*, a 1969 political questions doctrine case that opened
congressional disciplinary procedures to judicial oversight, the Court signaled
that even the internal matters of the "political" branches of the national government were subject to its scrutiny.[14] The Court refused to accept Frankfurter's
argument in his dissent in *Baker* that "there is not under our Constitution a judicial remedy for every political mischief, for every undesirable exercise of legislative power."[15] Appeals to the principles of federalism or to governance
through elected officials were losing their clout by 1962 and would no longer
carry the weight that they had been accorded until the 1960s.

Where the Warren Court expanded judicial oversight of state action in
Baker and in Fourteenth Amendment civil rights cases, the Burger Court declared in 1971 that inferior officers of the legislative and executive branches as
well as the President were fully amenable to the judicial process. Once more it
was Brennan who announced in *Bivens v. Six Unknown Named Federal Narcotics Agents* that the judiciary would open its doors to persons seeking damages
against government employees for abusive practices.[16] Justice Harry Blackmun,
before he joined the liberal bloc that looked to Brennan for guidance, accused
him of engaging in "judicial legislation" since Congress had not decided to
amend the sovereign immunity doctrine to provide for remedies where federal
agents violate Fourth Amendment rights in the course of carrying out their assigned duties. With the judicial oath as well as the "[great] capacity for harm"
enjoyed by government agents in mind, and appealing to the principle that all
injuries should be subject to redress, Brennan defended the unilateral action

taken by the Court on Bivens's behalf. Significantly, in the Watergate Tapes case of the same year, Burger announced that even the President's Oval Office activities are subject to scrutiny by the courts when judicial determinations of guilt or innocence hang in the balance.[17] The judiciary's responsibility for protecting rights and redressing grievances dwarfed Nixon's appeal to institutional responsibilities, including his arguments for preserving the effectiveness of the executive department. As the executive cannot share his veto power with the judiciary, Burger argued that the courts have an unshared responsibility to act as the final interpreters of the Constitution.

The conviction that the Constitution mandates that all rights be protected and all injuries redressed, and empowers courts to implement this mandate, did not disappear with the retirement of William Brennan or the passing of the Warren and Burger Courts. The Rehnquist Court extended the principle of *Bivens* when it required President Clinton to make himself available to respond to sexual harassment charges brought by Paula Jones.[18] The argument that the imposition of this burden on a sitting president might distract him from the effective performance of his official duties carried little weight with the majority. When given this opportunity to immunize a dimension of political life from judicial inquiry, the Court once more allowed an appeal to individual rights and redress for alleged grievances to trump arguments based on what might be called practical politics or the necessities of governance.[19] In another Rehnquist-era decision, although issued this time over the objections of the Chief Justice, the Court announced in a 1999 Georgia case that schoolyard bullying that amounts to sexual harassment can be the basis for a federal cause of action against school officials.[20] All these cases are examples of the Court acting as an agent for the advancement of the social welfare or, to use Cardozo's language, the "welfare of society," defined largely in terms of the satisfaction of the multiplicity of individual and group interests that seek protection at any given moment. The conjunction of rulings like *Clinton v. Jones* with New Deal reasoning that defines the common good in terms of the accumulation of satisfied individual and group claims is unmistakable.

Liberalizing access to the judicial forum by individuals or groups was for justices like Brennan only part of what would be required for America to be a fully legitimate democratic state. It also is necessary that the people be liberated from restrictions and enjoy maximum self-expression and self-determination. In this connection, the Supreme Court has signaled that beyond being hospitable to suits by aggrieved parties, the judiciary should be prepared to return verdicts that expand the realm of freedom of choice and self-construction in a highly egalitarian society.

The Warren Court repeatedly challenged long-standing police power regulations affecting moral conduct during the 1960s. Evidence that the Court was willing to translate expanded access into enlarged rights and reduced governmental powers is not hard to come by. Piggybacking on a 1958 ruling that upheld a right to privacy in association, Justice Douglas defended in a 1965 Connecticut contraceptive case a fully matured right to privacy that came t equated with the right to pursue a preferred lifestyle.[21] He construed a right to privacy from explicit constitutional guarantees such as the right to be free of illegal searches and seizures. The state's appeal to its police powers, and specifically to its interest in discouraging persons from engaging in legally-defined illicit sexual unions, carried insufficient weight to trump the appeal to personal privacy. Once the Court had determined that the Bill of Rights should apply to state action through the Fourteenth Amendment, it was predictable that traditional arguments based on the police powers or on federalism principles would lose much of their clout.

Between *Griswold* and *Roe v. Wade*, the 1973 abortion case, the Court paused to declare in *Stanley v. Georgia* that states have no real interest in the moral well-being of the people.[22] The issue in this case had to do with the private possession and enjoyment of pornographic material. After *Stanley*, it was going to be difficult for states to prevail with arguments based on promoting morality in police powers cases involving restrictions on personal freedom. An interest in the moral well-being of someone like Jane Roe or Stanley would no longer be enough to sustain laws that confined a person's pursuit of a preferred way of life—for example, a life without the burden of caring for a child.[23] Nor would traditional appeals to national security or effectiveness in government or self-preservation be sufficient to protect government agencies or officials against suits intended to expand expressive freedoms or to compensate persons for the costs associated with governance.

In *Brandenburg v. Ohio*, a 1969 criminal syndicalism case, the Warren Court concluded that the states would have to show evidence that organized activities by groups such as the Ku Klux Klan posed an immediate danger of creating irreparable harm to the interests of the people in order to overcome First Amendment objections.[24] The Court took the opportunity to overturn *Whitney v. California*,[25] a 1927 case that sustained a criminal syndicalism law. The message from *Brandenburg* could not have been clearer. The bar was now raised so high that the states effectively were instructed to desist from prosecuting groups for their expressive activities. Two years after *Brandenburg*, the Court emasculated the "fighting words" doctrine in *Cohen v. California* and announced in the Pentagon Papers case that constitutional protection for media publication of stolen classified military documents is considerable.[26] The principle that the government received from the Constitution the authority to preserve not only the institutions of the society but an American way of life had been rendered problematical.

Justice Brennan's reasoning in the Pentagon Papers case is characteristic of the approach of the contemporary Court in cases involving First Amendment clashes with governmental regulations. While few justices have embraced the absolutist position used by Justice Hugo Black in his concurrence, an increasing number of jurists do the next closest thing by adopting Brennan's insistence in *Pentagon Papers* that "only governmental allegation and proof that publication must inevitably, directly and immediately cause the occurrence of an event kindred to imperiling the safety of a transport already at sea can support even the issuance of an interim restraining order."[27] Here is a standard that is about as close as one can get to taking an absolutist position with regard to government restraint of the press without embracing absolutism. This standard, like the standard set out in *Brandenburg v. Ohio*, is calculated to reduce to a minimum (if not to nil) the occasions when the government might legitimately restrain expression. The Court was systematically shrinking the range of actions that the government could take in the name of self-defense or self-preservation while expanding protection for rights and redress for grievances.

It was with the specific aim of attacking the problem of unredressed injuries that the Court in 1971, again with Brennan writing the majority opinion, created a new judicial remedy for people seeking damages against government employees charged with abuses of authority. *Bivens v. Six Unknown Named Federal Narcotics Agents* represented a frontal attack on the sovereign immunity doctrine that historically had protected government agents in the discharge of their formal duties.[28] According to the Court, the costs associated with the sovereign immunity doctrine had become unacceptable and clearly collided with the spirit of the comprehensive constitutional doctrine. Justice Harry Blackmun's charge that his brethren were engaging in "judicial legislation" carried little sting by 1971.[29] Congress's failure to amend the doctrine, as had the failure of the states and the national government to address the problems of school segregation and malapportionment, became in itself a justification for judicial activism in the view of liberal jurists like Brennan.

Contained in decisions like *Bivens*, *Brandenburg*, and *Pentagon Papers* is a willingness to shrink what the government may do in the name of preserving or protecting an "American way of life." The decision of the Court to void flag desecration laws at the end of the 1980s and beginning of the 1990s, again in the name of expanding expression, indicates that the shift reflected in the 1960s and early 1970s has had considerable staying power. Justices appointed by President Ronald Reagan went along with the rulings in the flag burning cases.[30]

The same has been true in cases involving religion. It was Justice Anthony M. Kennedy, a Reagan appointee, who wrote the opinion in a 1992 Rhode Island case (*Lee v. Weisman*) that involved a challenge to the practice of inviting priests, rabbis, or ministers to offer invocation and benediction prayers as part of public school graduation ceremonies.[31] Kennedy found the practice to be in violation of the Establishment Clause despite the fact that clergy who were invited to these events were carefully instructed to prepare nonsectarian invocations and benedictions. If holding religious views or showing respect for the Almighty had been seen as part of "the American way of life," a position that finds support in the writings of George Washington and Abraham Lincoln, the Court in cases like *Lee v. Weisman* was making it difficult for government agencies or officials to promote or protect this "way of life." Put differently, the Court was requiring government to leave more things to chance than had been customary before the 1960s, and even justices appointed by Republican chief executives were abetting this change. Rehnquist, for example, wrote an opinion in a late 1980s Virgin[ia] case that effectively made it very difficult for the states to continue to pr[...]

public figures such as the Rev. Jerry Falwell, a well-known Baptist minister, against the intentional infliction of emotional distress.[32] It also was the Rehnquist Court that defeated repeated congressional efforts to regulate the communication of indecent material to minors over the Internet.[33] Protecting expression from being "chilled" had become more important than protecting the "moral capital" of the society.

It is, in fact, the squeamishness of Justices known for their "conservatism" that reveals just how much water has gone over the constitutional dam since the first decades of the twentieth century. While upholding a Georgia statute regulating X-rated theaters in 1973, Chief Justice Burger felt compelled to add that the Court was doing nothing more than allowing the state to enforce a "morally neutral" statute.[34] Although he had to know that there was no way that the law could be "morally neutral," Burger apparently did not want to be charged with authorizing the government's involvement in legislating morality. Five years later, Justice Lewis Powell, another Nixon appointee, concurred in a decision upholding FCC action against a radio station that had aired a "dirty words" monologue during daytime hours when children might be part of the listening audience. Powell felt compelled to chide Justice John Paul Stevens for authoring an opinion for the Court that seemed to authorize government agencies to render judgments based on the content of expression.[35] Powell wanted to side with the government without opening himself to the charge that he believed that some expression might be more valuable than other expression. The squeamishness of moderate to conservative Justices like Burger and Powell left the government with virtually hollow, because non-principled, victories in those cases where First Amendment claims were subordinated to more traditional appeals to governmental or societal interests. The losses on the rights-based side often turn out to be superficial, while the victories for the government or traditional values end up having a Pyrrhic quality to them. Witness in this connection the reasoning used by Burger to save the display of a Christmas nativity scene in a prominent location in Pawtucket, Rhode Island.[36] All the components of the display were owned by the city of Pawtucket. The nativity scene could stay, according to the Court, because it had become just another ornamental fixture of the holiday season. In short, Burger saved the religious symbol by taking religion out of the symbol—not much of a victory for religion or for the position that religion is good for society. While seemingly giving the city a victory, the Court signaled that it could not find in the Constitution a principled defense of the action taken by government officials to protect an important dimension of the "American way of life." Gone is the day when the Court would uphold government assistance for religion with the declaration that "we are a religious people"—a remark made in an early 1950s case by none other than Justice William Douglas.[37]

"PROGRESSIVE" JURISPRUDENCE: A "BOTTOM LINE" ANALYSIS

The habits of the people and the ability of government to control the governed have been impacted by the jurisprudence that emerged from the theories and policies of the Progressive and New Deal periods. The Court has systematically reduced the scope of the action that government officials might take in the name of self-defense or self-preservation at the same time that it has dangled temptations in front of the people that seemingly are at odds with responsible democratic citizenship. For much of our constitutional history, the Court guarded the capacity of the government to "control" the people, to paraphrase *Federalist* #51, and defended institutions and practices that pointed the people in the direction of socially and politically constructive forms of conduct. There was good political reasoning behind Madison's declaration that the first task of the delegates at the constitutional convention was to devise an arrangement that would "enable the government to control the governed."[38] He understood that civil order requires the control of the factious impulses that are "sown in the nature" of human beings. The leading framers understood that liberty without effective government would produce anarchy and invite tyranny, and the decisions of the Court through the mid-twentieth century generally reflected this thinking. If there have been occasional victories for federalism or the political questions doctrine or state use of the police powers, those victories are the exception and not the rule in modern constitutional jurisprudence. More to the point, if there are occasional victories for federalism or the political questions doctrine or laws based on traditional views of morality, these victories have been exceptions to the general pattern of depreciating appeals to traditional moral values and governmental interests.

There can be little doubt that the recent judicialization of American life has weakened the legislative and executive institutions that the founders believed should be the principal mediating bodies in a modern representative republic. Such end-runs around legislative and executive institutions come with sizable costs. Why even worry about building coalitions to influence electoral outcomes or legislative policy making if the courts are available to provide immediate protection for preferred interests and/or relief against unwanted governmental actions? Success at coalitional politics, the centerpiece of Madison's defense of the large republic, requires considerable effort. Significantly, the return on that effort takes the form of the cultivation of useful habits such as industriousness and moderation. In addition, governance itself is likely to be less factional and more moderate when it is shaped by Madisonian-style coalitional politics. The loss of these things represents a major "cost" associated with the judicialization of American society.

With its amplification of individual rights, its depreciation of the constitutional weight of governmental interests, and its insistence on exposing public action to full view, much of modern jurisprudence leaves political institutions vulnerable to the degenerative forces of radical individualism. At the least, this jurisprudence shrinks what society might do in the name of self-preservation while exposing people who may not be capable of dependable self-control, as well as persons of good repute, to a multitude of dangerous temptations that may make them harder to govern. The flip side of the damage done to political institutions is the harm inflicted on responsible democratic citizenship.

The judicialization of life invites people to become subjects rather than true citizens who possess real control over their way of life. The knowledge that some parties will have difficulty gaining redress through regular governmental processes or that persons can suffer as a result of abuses of political authority makes the liberalization of judicial recourse seem both rational and compassionate. Indeed, it is hard to quarrel with the Court's handling of school desegregation in *Brown v. Board of Education*. Cases such as *Brown*, however, obscure what is required of citizens to preserve a healthy democratic nation. The extension of *Brown* to the judicialization of bullying by school children and of moments of silence in public school classrooms can turn democratic citizens into mere subjects who are invited to place their petitions before judicial officials—with no accompanying lobbying or coalitional politics. The judicialization of such activities leaves Americans with less, not more, control over their own affairs. In the case of the federalization of schoolyard harassment, for example, the Court's decision creates the possibility of transferring control over school affairs from local officials to federal judges—a recipe for building subjects, not citizens.

It is not far-fetched to argue that the practice of seeking either victories without the cost of engaging in long, drawn-out electoral battles or immediate remedies in the form of, say, injunctive relief can corrode habits of good citizenship. Responsible citizenship in a democracy requires a willingness to work at holding officials accountable through political processes, and this is best cultivated by active involvement in the life of the communities in which we live. As the nineteenth-century French political thinker Alexis de Tocqueville knew, people are most likely to become engaged if they are permitted to exercise meaningful control over their own affairs and if they are exposed to the full effects of their decisions. Engaged citizenship was his response to the problem of "soft despotism" in democratic times—a condition marked by enervated and docile citizens who welcome a government that offers to spare them all the cares of living.[39] Judicial decisions that seek to immunize people from the real pains of political life (e.g., the effects of patronage practices, the sometimes tragic consequences of aggressive enforcement of criminal laws, or the mistakes of well-intentioned social workers) along with the propensity to craft national solutions to local problems, undermine the conditions that Tocqueville believed were required for responsible citizenship and for a civilized democracy to exist.

There is abundant evidence that the contemporary judiciary holds a grander view of the role of the courts than did Madison and Marshall. Justice Brennan, to take one example, believed that judges such as himself possessed a heightened understanding of the elements of the fully consummated democratic state and of the kind of cost-benefit calculations that are required to reach this end. Once language, history, and majoritarian preferences are rendered suspect as guides for decision-making, virtually all that remains is the judgment of the members of the judiciary regarding proper action. The judgment of the judges trumps the reasoning of all other persons since the courts are assumed to be entrusted with the final determination of what is acceptable in all significant matters that affect the way of life of the people. For many judges, those judgments are to rest on the "reason and passions" of the times more than on the original thinking that informed the Constitution. In the end, the judiciary is presented as the institution that can best be trusted to mediate disputes in a rights-oriented society where willfulness is an extension of authentic personhood and where moral truths are relegated to the status of personal claims. The result of this reasoning is to depreciate the status of the Constitution as the defining document of the political community. Liberty is left as a principle into which meaning can be "poured" by different persons and groups. But since common opinion, history, language, and nature are rendered problematic as guides for assessing claims, it is hard to see how the burden of sifting through competing views of what is desirable or just can be discharged without engaging in subjective decision-making or inviting factious conflicts.

Judicial officials would do well to remember Madison's teachings on limited government and separation of powers. They also would do well to acquaint themselves with Tocqueville's reflections on responsible democratic citizenship. The Supreme Court would not only strike a blow for democracy by restraining its urge to judicialize American culture and society, but it might discover that a policy of restraint would heighten public respect for the judiciary and for the entire constitutional system.

NOTES

1. *Federalist* #78.

2. *Bush v. Gore*, 531 U.S. 98 (2000).

3. *Planned Parenthood of Southeastern Pennsylvania v. Casey*, 505 U.S. 833, 996 (1992).

4. Ibid. at 996.

5. Benjamin Cardozo, *The Nature of the Judicial Process* (New York: Yale University Press, 1921), 17.

6. Ibid., 43.

7. Ibid., 66.

8. 298 U.S. 238 (1936).

9. 369 U.S. 186 (1962).

10. *Colegrove v. Green*, 328 U.S. 549 (1946). This case involved a federal court challenge to a congressional districting scheme in Illinois.

11. 1 Cranch 137 (1803).

12. 369 U.S. at 211.

13. Ibid., 217.

14. 395 U.S. 486 (1969).

15. 369 U.S. at 269-70.

16. 403 U.S. 388 (1971).

17. *New York Times Co. v. United States*, 403 U.S. 713 (1971).

18. *Clinton v. Jones*, 520 U.S. 681 (1997).

19. It might be argued that the same toleration for the legalization and judicialization of American life is visible in the Rehnquist Court's decision to uphold the special prosecutor law in 1988, *Morrison v. Olson*, 487 U.S. 654. Justice Antonin Scalia submitted a harsh di

that relied on strict separation of powers reasoning to challenge the constitutionality of the independent counsel provisions of the Ethics in Government Act of 1978.

20. *Davis v. Monroe County Board of Education*, 526 U.S. 629 (1999). In 2000, Rehnquist himself refused to uphold a congressional exception to the judicially created Miranda warning.

21. *Griswold v. Connecticut*, 381 U.S. 479 (1965).

22. 1 394 U.S. 557 (1969).

23. See, for example, Justice Harry Blackmun's characterization of the right to privacy as the right to choose a lifestyle in *Roe v. Wade*, 410 U.S. 113 (1973). Blackmun allows the right to an abortion to be limited by appeals to the mother's health or the rights of a viable fetus, but not by traditional appeals to morality. The view that the right to privacy covers the right to choose a lifestyle and to embrace one's own "conception" of one's "place in society" was repeated by the Rehnquist Court in the most important abortion case of the 1990s, *Planned Parenthood of Southeastern Pennsylvania v. Casey*, 505 U.S. 833 (1992). In *Lawrence v. Texas*, 539 U.S. ___ (2003), eleven years after Casey, the Rehnquist Court overturned Texas' sodomy law.

24. 395 U.S. 444 (1969). The Court issued a per curiam opinion in *Brandenburg*. Justice Douglas wrote a separate concurring opinion in which he questioned the appropriateness of the "clear and present danger" test in "the regime of the First Amendment." This represented a movement away from his position in *Dennis v. United States*, 341 U.S. 494 (1951), a First Amendment case involving the prosecution of Communists under the Smith Act for engaging in seditious activities, where Douglas vainly sought to save the defendants from conviction by using a tightened version of Justice Oliver Wendell Holmes's famous test.

25. 274 U.S. 357.

26. *Cohen v. California*, 403 U.S. 15 (1971); *New York Times v. United States*, 403 U.S. 713 (1971).

27. Ibid. at 726-727.

28. 403 U.S. 388 (1971).

29. Ibid. at 430.

30. *Texas v. Johnson*, 491 U.S. 397 (1989). Justice Kennedy, appointed by President Reagan in 1988 and recognizing that his vote would not sit well with conservative Republicans, announced in his concurrence that "sometimes we must make decisions we do not like."

31. *Lee v. Weisman*, 505 U.S. 577 (1992).

32. *Hustler Magazine v. Falwell*, 485 U.S. 46 (1988).

33. See, for example, *Reno v. ACLU*, 521 U.S. 844 (1997); also *Ashcroft v. Free Speech Coalition*, 535 U.S. 234 (2002).

34. *Paris Adult Theatre I v. Slaton*, 413 U.S. 49 (1973).

35. *FCC v. Pacifica Foundation*, 438 U.S. 726 (1978).

36. *Lynch v. Donnelly*, 465 U.S. 668 (1984). In 1995, the Rehnquist Court ruled against the refusal of the University of Virginia, a state institution, to allow student activities fees to support a student-edited Christian magazine on First Amendment freee speech grounds. The University's case was based on the Establishment Clause. See *Rosenberger v. Rector and Visitors of the University of Virginia*, 515 U.S. 819 (1995).

37. *Zorach v. Clauson*, 343 U.S. 306 (1952). Douglas's declaration was repeated by Justice Stewart when dissenting in an early 1960s school prayer case. *Engel v. Vitale*, 370 U.S. 421 (1962). George Washington reminded Americans of the role religion plays in a decent society in his "Farewell Address" of September 19, 1796:

> Of all the dispositions and habits which lead to political prosperity, Religion and morality are indispensable supports. In vain would that man claim the tribute of Patriotism, who should labour to subvert these great Pillars of human happiness, these firmest props of the duties of Men and citizens. The mere Politician, equally with the pious man ought to respect and to cherish them. A volume could not trace all their connections with private and

public felicity. Let it simply be asked where is the security of property, for reputation, for life, if the sense of religious obligation *desert* the oaths, which are the instruments of investigation in Courts of Justice? And let us with caution indulge the supposition, that morality can be maintained without religion. Whatever may be conceded to the influence of refined education on minds of peculiar structure, reason and experience both forbid us to expect that National morality can prevail in exclusion of religious principle.

The Writings of George Washington, ed. John C. Fitzpatrick, (Washington: United States Printing Office, 1940). Vol. 35: 229.

38. *Federalist* # 51.

39. Tocqueville, *Democracy in America*, 246-261.

CHAPTER 8

DECONSTITUTIONALIZATION AND AMERICAN FOREIGN POLICY

The characteristic feature and problem of foreign policy is uncertainty. This simple fact makes it particularly difficult to think about the problem of deconstitutionalization of American foreign policy. Constitutions are, first and foremost, ordering devices within communities, but they also separate one community from another. Constitutions relate to foreign affairs or foreign policy in a different way than they do to domestic politics. The first act of constitution making is to create a distinction between citizens (or nationals) and all other peoples. But once the citizens of the world have differentiated themselves into separate countries, a harmony of interest can neither be presumed nor is it often seen. The second task of constitution making is to empower the new political order with the means to protect itself. It is obvious that a decent life within a political community is preconditioned by that community's relations with its neighbors.

Another way of understanding the distinction is to say that international relations is dominated by necessity—the fear of coercion, fraud, and violence—whereas justice and morality have more likelihood of emerging and succeeding in domestic politics. Yet, maintaining proper domestic politics requires vigilance in the face of international necessity. As Niccolò Machiavelli understood survival is the first task of a political community, for there can be no constitution without security from conquest. The constitutional or moral structure that girds a political community will not survive if gross errors are made in the conduct of foreign policy. But it is also unclear whether a government can ignore justice in the international arena. One reading of the twentieth century suggests that monarchy, communism, fascism, and various other types of tyranny and oligarchy prevalent in the developing world were not as powerful as liberal democracies because they were not as just.

After the United States and its allies won the Cold War it became possible to think more about justice than about necessity. Even after the September 11, 2001, attacks on the World Trade Center and the Pentagon, the United States does not seem to be faced with stark necessity in foreign affairs. Although terrorists may attack the United States, it is not clear that they can destroy it or its political institutions. We seem therefore to be confronted with choices or options that grow out of preferred values, not dire necessity. While it hardly need be said that good and bad choices still determine whether we reduce national pain or stimulate national pleasure, survival no longer seems at stake. Global material progress, American military might, and the political stability of modern liberal democracy may have moderated the tragic consequences of foreign policy errors.

How this new condition might be connected, in a meaningful sense, to the problem of deconstitutionalization is neither clear nor straightforward. But at least this much is clear: the Constitution laid out an extremely flexible process by which foreign policy was to be formulated and implemented. The Constitutional powers of the executive and the legislature are so mixed when it comes to foreign policy that virtually nothing done by either branch could, as such, undermine the Constitution. But a third actor, the Court, has gradually entered the foreign policy arena (sometimes through a very back, back door) in a manner that does threaten to undermine constitutional arrangements. Of course, if survival is no longer at stake, the costs of the Court's activity will be minimal or at least manageable. But, if necessity has not genuinely been subdued, a president could be forced to violate the Constitution—as interpreted by the Court—in order to do his constitutionally assigned job.

THE CONSTITUTIONAL STRUCTURE OF FOREIGN POLICY MAKING

The Constitution seems meticulously clear in ascribing powers over foreign policy. Article I grants to Congress (with the presidential signature or over the presidential veto) powers to regulate foreign policy-related matters in a host of areas, among which are foreign commerce, naturalization of citizens, currency transfer, piracy, other felonies committed on the high seas, international law, declaration of war, the existence of rules of engagement, and maintenance of the armed forces, the authority to suppress insurrections and invasions, and to suspend the "Privilege of the Writ of Habeas Corpus . . . when in Cases of Rebellion or Invasion the public Safety may require it." In the same article the states are effectively prohibited from engaging in their own foreign policy.[1]

Along with other state and federal officials, presidents are required to take an oath supporting the Constitution. More specifically, however, presidential foreign policy powers, as outlined in Article II, begin with the statement that the "executive Power shall be vested in a President of the United States." The President not only is expected to serve as commander in chief of the armed forces, but he is responsible for making treaties and receives opinions from executive officers. The President commissions officers, appoints ambassadors, and receives those from other nations. Finally, the President is required to "take Care that the Laws be faithfully executed."

This division of power does not look particularly ambiguous on its face, yet anyone familiar with the history of American foreign policy knows that the performance of functions has not been nearly as clear as the Constitution makes seem. Articles I and II state that Congress is responsible for establishin parameters and resources available to the President for the purposes of developing a foreign policy, and the President is responsible for implementing that policy. Yet, active and even inactive presidents have often been forced to push the constitutional envelope on the key issues or features of the constitutional distribution of functions. Thus, presidents use force without congressional authorization—as was the case of the Barbary Coast pirates during Thomas Jefferson's presidency, the arming of merchant ships in the Atlantic under Franklin Roosevelt, and the attempted rescue of the crew of the Mayaguez in the presidency of Gerald Ford. Presidents sometimes use executive agreements as substitutes for treaties, as did Dwight Eisenhower in basing U.S. troops in Spain. George Washington did not anticipate how difficult treaty negotiations would be if he actively sought the advice of the Senate, but he quickly learned that the Senate had more diffuse advice than he could use. Since that time, presidents have negotiated treaties with minimal senatorial advice. The daily process of running the executive branch puts the President in intimate and continuous charge of policy. In most instances, foreign policy involves presidential action followed by various types of congressional acquiescence. In foreign affairs, the constitution proposes but practice disposes.

THE CONSTITUTIONAL CONCEPT OF FOREIGN POLICY

Perhaps a better way to grasp the exercise of the foreign policy power under the Constitution is not to begin with the Constitution itself, but with the most influential theorist and teacher of the separation of powers, John Locke. From Locke's perspective, the Constitution would, on the surface, look deficient. The Constitution mixes the foreign policy powers between the President and the Congress. Locke recommended that foreign policy be exclusively an executive power. At a minimum, the founders hid Locke's advice in complexity—if they did not ignore it altogether. To see how the founders misused Locke, it is necessary to look more closely at Locke's argument.

Government comes into being, according to Locke, in order to exercise three powers better and more safely than they can be exercised in a state of nature: legislation, adjudication, and execution. This the Constitution mirrors generally, though the judicial power fares better in the Constitution than it does in Locke's reflections. While Locke's theory concentrated mostly on the relations between the legislative and the executive powers, he also identified a fourth power that is contemporaneous with the creation of civil society; he called it the federative power. This power accompanies the executive power and is vital to the community, but is not executive as such. The federative power holds the community together and protects it from external attack. Locke argued that the federative power is "less capable to be directed by antecedent, standing positive laws than the executive and so must necessarily be left to the prudence and wisdom of those whose hands it is in to be managed for the public good."[2] The federative power normally accompanies the executive because its activities or objects are not subject to legal direction and cannot be anticipated by legislation.

What a nation must do to protect itself and further its interests depends more on how foreign governments behave than on constitutional guarantees. Since the executive is always in being and exercises the force of the community as part of its domestic duties, it is better positioned than the legislature to exercise the federative power. Thus, according to Locke, but apparently not according to the American Constitution makers, the federative or foreign policy power ought to be held almost exclusively by the executive branch.

There is a subsidiary executive power that also has some bearing on Locke's discussion of the executive power. The executive occasionally must exercise the prerogative, which is the "power to act according to discretion for the public good, without the prescription of the law and sometimes even against it."[3] The prerogative permits the executive to take action when unexpected emergencies—most perhaps, arising from outside the constitutional community—occur. The only check on prerogative power is the people's belief of whether its use was successful. Locke explains that the prerogative power is "nothing but the people's permitting their rulers to do several things of their own free choice where the law was silent, and sometimes, too, against the direct letter of the law, for the public good and their acquiescing in it when so done."[4]

The most striking examples of the uses of prerogative in U.S. history were Lincoln's seemingly unconstitutional actions during the Civil War. Lincoln defended his exercise of power by explaining that, "Often a limb must be amputated to save a life; but a life is never wisely given to save a limb. I felt that measures, otherwise unconstitutional, might become lawful by becoming indispensable to the preservation of the Constitution, through the preservation of the nation."[5] With modest reflection it is clear that the core of Lincoln and Locke's argument is that the uncertain environment in the realm of necessity requires more flexibility than formal allocation of constitutional authority permits.

As we have seen, the founders decided to ignore Locke and divide the foreign affairs powers between Congress and the President. It is likely that the Constitution would have been rejected by a majority of Americans in 1787 if the American president exercised the federative power in the same manner as the British king. Whatever the sentiment at the founding, the happy result for Americans has been that the division of the federative power between the legislative and executive branches has offered a flexible means of exercising power in an accountable manner—in some ways superior in Locke's scheme. On the whole, Congress has given presidents support, constructive criticism, and a great deal of discretion to make policy. Moreover, because Congress has most often been a co-sponsor of American foreign policy, the use of the prerogative power as Locke or Lincoln understood it has seldom attracted attention. There have been, after all, very few times when presidents have had to admit that they might have broken the law.

It should not be surprising that the presidential power often predominates over the principle of checks and balances. After all, the relative power of each branch depends on its ability to assert itself, and the executive is in an aus cious position to assert itself. The policy-making process is structured suc important tasks and responsibilities facing the nation at any given time and situation will be performed, and usually performed successfully. There is no guarantee, of course, that wisdom will prevail. At least it can be said that a variety of policy options will be heard—even if the best one is not pursued. The separation of powers structures the foreign policy-making process so that alternatives can be heard and presidents held accountable without provoking a constitutional crisis.

If one were to consider the historical record, it might even be fair to say that, between the President and the Congress, particularly the Senate, almost no exercise of power is unconstitutional as such. Actions are only more or less prudent, more or less politically acceptable. As is implied by Andrew Johnson's impeachment—which on the surface concerned foreign policy (Johnson's confidence in his advice from the Secretary of War)—institutional ambiguity is deeply embedded in the issue of constitutional legitimacy. Nevertheless, it is clear that in most cases both the Constitution and political practice favor presidential supremacy in conducting American foreign policy.

In short, presidents have exercised the federative power and occasionally employed the prerogative power since the origin of the republic. Presidents have bought territory, suppressed pirates, fought secret naval wars, and sent troops to most places around the world with hardly a peep from Congress. When Congress has not empowered presidents to use their discretion in conducting foreign policy, many presidents have used it anyway. When the branches disagree, Article I of the Constitution puts Congress in a position to call presidents to task, as for example it did to President Ronald Reagan during the Iran-Contra affair. Although it has been argued that the separation of powers creates "an invitation to struggle," the Iran-Contra affair is one of the few occasions that the presidential use of foreign-policy making powers or the exercise of the prerogative power encountered genuine congressional opposition.[6]

WILSON AND FOREIGN POLICY

In most instances the interaction between Congress and presidents has been strictly contained within the formal constitutional policy process itself. Nothing illustrates presidential leadership in foreign affairs and how presidents are answerable to Congress for their choices more clearly than the fate of Woodrow Wilson's foreign policy. As president, Wilson successfully maneuvered the country through military adventures in Mexico, presided over three years of American involvement in the European Armageddon, and led the nation into the grande finale of the Great War. As soon as the greatest danger to America since the War of 1812 was over, however, Congress clipped the President's wings.

Wilson acted as if he could conduct American diplomacy in the same manner as could the British Cabinet. Wilson believed that the American Constitution had truncated and prematurely halted the evolution of the nation's political development. Not only did the written constitution of enumerated powers limit those actions of government, but the separation of powers kept both the President and Congress from functioning effectively. Wilson was not averse to the President and Congress having distinct functions, but he maintained that the Constitution did not apportion those functions between the institutions correctly. What Parliament was good at, according to Wilson, was providing criticism and final approval or disapproval of executive action. The debates in Parliament, the votes of confidence, and the questions posed to the government were the proper functions of the Parliament. He believed that Parliament could deliberate on the wisdom of policy, but it was not capable of *making* policy. America's Constitution, on the other hand, empowered Congress to formulate, shape, and even micromanage policy, all to the detriment of the nation. Approving a law or a policy initiative submitted by a responsible government is a far cry from hammering out the policy in committees or continuously second-guessing a presidential initiative.

Wilson made every effort to force relations between the President and the Congress to mirror Parliamentary relations. This effort was evident in the way he structured American foreign policy making during the war but even more so in the debate over the peace. He never received advice from the Senate. He negotiated the peace almost single-handedly, and he expected Congress to accept his lead implicitly. Wilson could not have consulted Congress more minimally—he presented the legislators with an "up or down" vote. It fell to Congress, once the pressure of necessity had lifted, to redress the political balance, which it did immediately in rejecting the Peace of Paris and the League. One can wonder if the British system might not have been preferable in this case, but it does show the constitutional arrangement working in its most typical manner.

More than any other president, Wilson set out to overturn the separation of powers. He pursued this goal with a rhetoric designed to transform the relationship between executive and legislature into a quasi-parliamentary model. Wilson created "the rhetorical presidency" and hoped to use it to overcome the defects of the separation of powers in domestic affairs, and the lack of executive discretion to exercise the federative power in foreign affairs.[7] Wilson failed, partly because as president he did not assert the prerogative power in support of his federative responsibilities, and the power to conduct foreign policy remains, as it did before Wilson, within the legal bounds of the Constitution's creative uncertainty. Of course, some presidents have tried to push the envelope of their power—few with the urgency of Franklin Roosevelt in the Atlantic or Ronald Reagan on behalf of the Contras—and occasionally they have encountered congressional resistance. Presidents, however, have not been unduly hampered in their actions, because in times of crisis Congress has no interest in being responsible for imperiling national security and understands that the legislature cannot lead the nation out of danger. It turns out, then, that in foreign affairs there is little peril from a president overstepping some hypothetical constitutional line. There is no constitutional limit in foreign policy making to deconstitutionalize, there is only congressional opinion of the appropriateness of presidential action.

CLOUDS ON THE HORIZON

But, lest complacency set in, it is important to note that there is a dark cloud on
the constitutional horizon, and it comes from a rather surprising source: the
Court. Locke had envisioned an executive who could act for the good of the
nation subject to the approval of the nation. In America, the impeachment power
is the conduit of public opinion (approval and disapproval). Locke even left
room, in a pinch, for an appeal to heaven (arms). America's single appeal to
heaven was not over the exercise of presidential prerogative, of course, and foreign policy was not really the primary consideration of the Johnson impeachment. Thus it can safely be said that the founders' program has worked re-
markably well.

But, what if the Court interjects itself into that relationship? It is unclear
whether the Constitution envisioned the Court as the primary arbiter of disputes
arising from the separation of powers. Judicial review was anticipated by Hamilton but opposed by Jefferson. Of course in *Marbury v. Madison* the Court empowered itself to nullify part of the Judiciary Act of 1789 in which, it held, Congress had overstepped its constitutional authority to assign original jurisdiction
to the Supreme Court. Since *Marbury* was closely related to the powers of the
Court itself, the Court had a clear interest in the outcome in the case.

Even in cases not dealing directly with foreign affairs, the Court may inad-
vertently destroy the flexibility and accountability that the Constitution has
brought into foreign policy matters. To understand this point more clearly, one
need only consider the holding in *Youngstown Sheet and Tube v. Sawyer*, where
the Court decided that President Harry Truman's authority as commander in
chief did not extend to control of domestic industries even if they were essential
for producing military equipment.[8] But what if the production of war materials
were vital for avoiding military defeat? What if the fate of the nation depended
on the President guaranteeing that key supplies were produced? The ruling in
Youngstown establishes legal prohibitions against the President acting to ensure
domestic production. If such production were necessary for the survival of the
country, the president would be faced with the decision to violate the law or
save the nation. The Constitution, which wisely seems to exclude the Court from
supervising foreign policy, permits Congress to take such prudent calculations
into account.

The same kind of problem arises as the result of *United States v. Nixon*,
where the Court held that it should determine the scope of executive privilege
because it had the authority to define the extent of powers in the other branches.
But what if there were a dispute over whether some information held by the executive needed to be kept secret in order to protect national security? Would it
be prudent for a President to hand over that information under subpoena from
the Court if the nation's security is at stake?

Congress, not the Court, is the branch best able to chasten and rein in the
President, if need be. The reason is simple but compelling. The Court must always declare illegal what violates existing law, and its rulings are precedents for

future cases. If the President acts without legal sanction or in opposition to the law, the Court has no choice but to legalize what in normal times would be a breach of the law or decide against the President in an emergency and jeopardize national security. This stark alternative faced the Court in *Korematsu v. United States*. Justice Robert Jackson's dissenting opinion reflects on the most arbitrary executive power, the use of force. While he admits that force must be used to protect the nation, he insists that the Court cannot legally sanction the violation of constitutional limits in order to justify necessary military actions. "Of course," he writes,

> The existence of a military power resting on force, so vagrant, so centralized, so necessarily heedless of the individual, is an inherent threat to liberty. But I would not lead people to rely on this Court for a review that seems to me wholly delusive. The military reasonable of . . . orders can only be determined by military superiors. If the people ever let command of the war fall into irresponsible and unscrupulous hands, the Court wields no power equal to its restraint. . . . A military commander may overstep the bounds of constitutionality and it is an incident. But if [the Court] review[s] and approve[s], that passing incident become the doctrine of the Constitution.[9]

Since foreign policy is the realm of harsh necessity it sometimes requires that rulers use discretion to meet the threats posed by hostile nations. But a Court is bound by legal prescriptions, and it cannot sanction actions which reach beyond what the Constitution prescribes. Congress, on the other hand, may function without reference to absolute legal criteria, for it operates according to political criteria. The prudential concerns of foreign policy strongly suggest that only Congress should legitimately check the President's exercise of the federative and prerogative powers. For example, it might be wise for Congress to repeal some provisions of the Patriot Act in order to protect civil liberties, and it could do so if the terrorist menace subsides. If the Court were to strike down the law, its decision would become a legal doctrine and would apply even if there were a resurgence of terrorism, leaving the government incapable of protecting the country during some future crisis.

There is one important caveat. It may become more likely and legitimate for the Court to adjudicate foreign policy cases. This is true because the conduct of foreign affairs progressively has come to resemble domestic politics, where order is established and legal rules apply. The absolute predominance of America since the end of the Cold War, coupled with its ability to protect its citizens and punish its opponents across the globe, makes it appear that America is not vulnerable to the harsh necessity commonly associated with the international arena. After all, it is difficult to imagine that the United States could be defeated in war. It is almost inconceivable that any nation or group of nations could overpower the united force of the liberal democracies, which have never had a war among themselves and are all, to a greater or lesser degree, allies of the United States. Moreover, international organizations, most especially the European union, have made the world less dangerous, and globalization of the world's omy has made people interdependent. Just as Wilson had hoped as early as World War I, the realm of necessity seems to be giving way to the realm of freedom in which stability, peace, and order obtain.[10] Of course, once order has been established, the Court could play an important role in applying the law.

Imbued with Wilsonian expectations and the contemporary realities of America's global military, political, and economic reach, citizens, courts, and congressmen may easily lose sight of the special problems of power and justice that have traditionally applied to international relations. Thus if we are to speak of a deconstitutionalized foreign policy-making process today, it is for the following reasons. First, most foreign policy issues look more like domestic issues than they ever have in the past. Second, the United States has joined international organizations that mask the realm of necessity—the harsh reality of international relations—behind political institutions. Third, American power has made it difficult to see foreign policy necessity even if it does exist. Finally, the Court has restructured constitutional expectations in such a way as to obstruct both flexibility of the process and accountability to the people.

As the conditions that affect foreign policy come to mirror those which determine domestic policy, the two spheres become increasingly difficult to separate. As necessity recedes, legal justice necessarily advances. A judicialized foreign policy will be no great predicament if in fact we are at a kind of end of history—a situation in which all people in the world are satisfied with their economic, political, and spiritual conditions. Whether the end of history is possible, given the restlessness of the human soul, is still an open question. The fate of the nation can still be put in jeopardy, in which case it would be highly imprudent to extend the reach of the judiciary any further into the interpretation of presidential powers. In fact, one might fairly argue that presidential indifference to the Court's judgments in a wide variety of cases dealing with the executive may be the only way to reconstitutionalize foreign policy making. If the Court can define the President's domestic power, it can do so with respect to the federative and prerogative powers. National survival may someday depend on denying to the Court that power.

NOTES

1. Article I, Section 9, United States Constitution.
2. John Locke, *The Second Treatise of Government* (Indianapolis: Bobbs Merrill Company, Inc. 1952), 83.
3. Ibid., 92.
4. Ibid., 94.
5. Robert Hirschfield, ed. *The Power of the Presidency*, 2nd ed. (Chicago: Aldine, 1973), 80. Quoted in James Ceaser, Glen Thurow, Jeffrey Tulis, and Joseph Bessette, *American Government: Origins, Institutions and Public Policy*, 4th ed. (Dubuque, IA: Kendall-Hunt Publishing, 1995), 377.
6. Cecil V. Crabb Jr., and Pat M. Holt, *Invitation to Struggle: Congress, the President, and Foreign Policy* (Washington, DC: Congressional Quarterly Press, 1980).

7. James Ceaser, Glen Thurow, Jeffrey Tulis, and Joseph Bessette, "The Rise of the Rhe-torical Presidency," *Presidential Studies Quarterly* 11 (Spring 1981): 223-251.

8. 343 U.S. 579 (1952).

9. 323 U.S. 214 (1944).

10. Roosevelt envisioned the presidency as a bully pulpit and certainly envisioned an active president, but he did not posit the separation of powers as an obsolete stage of British political development. While Wilson could envision the agreements as the necessary and sufficient conditions of the realm of freedom, Roosevelt envisioned preparation to meet the realm of necessity as the first and necessary condition of a new world. Agreements could only register realities of like-mindedness of the great and the prepared. In short, necessity can never be left for a nation.

CHAPTER 9

NATIONAL PERFORMANCE REVIEW AND MADISONIAN CONSTITUTIONALISM: THE PERSISTENCE OF WILSONIAN ADMINISTRATIVE THOUGHT

It is a mistake to conclude from the paucity of information in the Constitution regarding a federal system of administration that leading founders such as James Madison, George Washington, and Alexander Hamilton did not anticipate the significance that administrative activities would acquire in the political order they had fashioned. There was good reason for Hamilton's inclusion of Alexander Pope's couplet on administration in *Federalist* #68: "For forms of government let fools contest—That which is best administered is best." In the same sentence in which he characterized the couplet as "political heresy" for deprecating the importance of constitutional forms, Hamilton observed that "the true test of a good government is its aptitude and tendency to produce a good administration."[1] He understood that good administration would draw the allegiance of the people to the national government while giving federal officials adequate means for "controlling the governed"—something that Madison believed would be critical to a successful experiment in democratic republicanism.[2] Like Hamilton, Madison made specific reference in several *Federalist Papers* to the benefits that would follow from the creation of an effective national system of administration.[3]

The conventional opinion that the founders overlooked administrative issues is clearly a distortion of the historical record. It is the case, however, that they did not elevate administration to the center of political life as did the Progressives and New Dealers of the twentieth century. Hamilton, the founder most closely associated with the defense of a vigorous national system of administration, should not be confused with Woodrow Wilson, who believed that the best democracy would be one that effectively replaced politics with administration. Interestingly, one of the remarkable features of American politics in the twentieth century is the fact that the political face of administrative reform changed little from Wilson to Clinton. Populism and scientific management dominated administrative theory and practice, and the odd synthesis of these concepts represents an important break with the constitutional thought of founders such as Washington, Madison, and Hamilton. The Clinton administration's plan for "reinventing government" essentially repeated Wilson's plea for the country to move beyond the founders' goal of constitutional republicanism to the creation of a perfectly efficient democracy. Indeed, if the administrative thought reflected in the National Performance Review was separated only by degrees from Wilsonianism, it represented a qualitative shift from the vision of a limited, representative government of checks and balances held by most of the leading founders. By the end of the twentieth century, the asserted advantage of a marriage between scientific management principles (efficiency calculations) and populism (relatively unmediated democracy) was an article of faith for many Americans.

ADMINISTRATIVE SCIENCE AND DEMOCRATIC POLITICS

There is little doubt that the dominant reform theorist and practitioner of the first decades of the past century was Woodrow Wilson. Democratic government represented for him the culmination of all political development. By the end of the nineteenth century, democracy was thought to be free of the baggage that caused leading founders such as Madison to give it only a qualified endorsement. Political parties and city governments increasingly came under attack for being insufficiently democratic. For Wilson, the important political undertaking that remained for the United States was to create a perfectly efficient democracy, one in which "good" government is "amenable from day to day to public opinion." He considered the last significant task of statesmanship to devise a political system capable of efficiently implementing the will of a self-conscious and self-directing people.[4] Wilson's "end of history," or messianic reasoning, anticipated the union of political populism with the principles of scientific management. It was not by chance that Wilson wrote an essay on the science of administration in which his arguments complemented the defense of cabinet-style government in some of his earliest writings. In both cases, his objective was to advance the efficient implementation of the popular will. Interestingly, his essay on the science of administration was published as the country was celebrating the centennial of the Constitution—and the allegiance of the people to established practices and institutions meant that fundamental reform would not come easily. For Wilson, the difficulty of the task only magnified the stature of whoever might accomplish it.

In his 1887 essay on administration, Wilson issued a siren call to Americans to embrace the benefits of the scientific study of administration being developed in Europe. Wilson elevated administrative study to new heights in the United States by arguing that properly trained administrators would know both what governments should do and how best to do it. He argued that students of the science of administration must understand what everyone with a fully developed historical consciousness knows about the aims of decent and just societies must also possess technical knowledge about the proper way to advance ends. Wilson's faith in democracy was intimately tied to his belief that the historical moment was approaching when most people would recognize and demand the things that make for a defensible social order. Drawing their guidance from administrative science, government personnel in Wilson's fully consummated democratic state would carry out the policy preferences of a people whose consciousnesses reflected an understanding of "what government can properly and successfully do."[5] The consequence would be a perfectly efficient democratic state—the last stage of political development, according to Wilson.

Management, or administration, emerges as the decisive enterprise if we assume, like Wilson, that public opinion is the "motive power of government," and that democracy depends on the capacity of the people to be thoughtful and trustworthy sovereigns.[6] The only remaining problematic element becomes the execution or implementation of the "will" of the people, hence Wilson's attention to the benefits of cabinet government and his interest in the science of administration. The obvious expectation is that the efficient implementation of an enlightened popular will would result in perceptible improvement in the social welfare. His labors on behalf of the Federal Reserve Act that set up a new banking system and government-driven economic mobilization during World War I, described as "war socialism," are reflections of his deep commitment not only to preserving democracy, but also to perfecting it.

Improving the welfare of the people, of course, was at the heart of the New Deal agenda advanced by President Franklin Roosevelt with the assistance of his famous "Brain Trust." The conviction that government exists to protect the people from "bitter wrongs" was writ large in New Deal-style liberalism. The enjoyment of happiness—not merely protection for the *pursuit* of happiness—became the measure of the respectability of a society, and of the government as well. The objective of New Deal liberals was to free people of the fear that human existence had a tragic quality. In this connection, Franklin Roosevelt conceptualized his task as mobilizing public opinion and interest groups behind policies designed to eliminate the remaining sources of deprivation and intimidation. He combined an ambitious legislative agenda—fifteen proposals were sent to Congress in the first hundred days—with a conscious effort to develop an intimate relationship with the American people through careful use of the media—press conferences and his famous "fireside chats." If the pursuit of comfortable preservation—or "safety and happiness," to borrow from the Declaration of Independence—was an important part of the American psyche going back to colonial times, a commitment from the government to secure safety and happiness was especially attractive to post-Depression Americans.

The 1937 report of the President's Committee on Administrative Management, or Brownlow Report—arguably the most significant administrative document of Roosevelt's presidency—reveals the transformation in thinking that had occurred between the framing of the Constitution in 1787 and the depression of 1937. The president emerges in the report as a political leader (the "leader of [the] people") whose aim ought to be to raise the "level of the happiness and dignity of human life."[7] This language conveys the New Deal vision of the means and ends of democratic government. In a striking passage, the report declares that "there is much bitter wrong to set right in neglected ways of human life."[8] There is here, as in the writings of Wilson, the presumption that proper exertions can correct such "bitter wrong[s]." Political leaders should identify these ills and then mobilize both the public will and the administrative machinery needed to correct them. Of course, the "wrongs" considered bothersome by a citizenry that will not tolerate anything that interferes with personal happiness cannot be ignored. Addressing every complaint invites a type of "dumbing down" of government, subjecting minor inconveniences to political regulation and creating excuses for government officials to occupy themselves with day-to-day annoyances rather than trying to solve more substantive problems. If this vision of an activist and beneficent democratic state inflates the role of government in general, it especially inflates the role of the executive branch.

The concern of founders like Madison that excessively inflating the authority of one department might lead to unchecked or unreflective government was replaced in the 1937 report by the assertion that society benefits from a visible magnification of the authority of the president. If "industrialism" and other social and economic activities were to "serve humanity," to quote New Deal Brain Truster Harold Ickes's *The New Democracy*, then industry must be scientifically supervised by the executive department.[9] Significantly, the Brownlow Report tended to treat governmental activities in managerial terms, for example, fiscal and personnel management. Roosevelt's broad reading of the Constitution's general welfare clause added to the tasks undertaken by government and strengthened the executive branch over the legislative.

If Wilson drew attention to the benefits of administrative science, New Dealers like James Landis placed administration or management close to the center of government. In keeping with the principles of scientific management, Landis called for the effective use of "disinterested expertise" to promote "social regulation."[10] If nothing else, the Depression had revealed that comfortable preservation could not be taken for granted even in the most advanced democratic society of the day. If economic sufficiency could be guaranteed for everyone at the same time that pluralist politics protected political liberty, and principles of efficiency were employed for purposes of wealth maximization and for improving responsiveness to public preferences, then Wilson's project could be completed. Landis and other associates of Roosevelt such as Felix Frankfurter believed that a combination of properly arranged administrative procedures, effective public accountability, and presidential oversight of governmental affairs would allow the country to merge the benefits of modern science and technology with the principles of democratic government. If Roosevelt and his aides sometimes displayed impatience with the bureaucracy, their unhappiness arose from the conviction that that part of the government was not adequately serving public needs as articulated by elected officials and their political assistants. Once there is agreement that the government has a moral as well as constitutional obligation *to do* whatever it *can do* to advance the general welfare, allow parchment formalities or merely institutional intransigence to interfere w fective action becomes intolerable. Importantly, any impatience citizens exhibited with the bureaucracy was not evidence of a principled objection to bureaucratic expansionism. New Dealers clearly invited the people to expect more of government than did founders such as Madison and Washington. New Deal thinking played on the desire of the people for solutions to social and economic problems that had been considered insurmountable barriers to comfortable preservation for the many. In fact, post-Depression America was ripe for the reformist rhetoric and the promised action of the New Dealers. If the Wilsonian liberals were apostles of change, the later New Deal liberals had become defenders of an accepted faith in the beneficent powers of government. This faith insinuated itself so completely into the American political culture that even President Reagan, the most formidable Republican critic of New Dealerism in the last half of the century, finally had to make his peace with President Carter's Department of Education.

THE CLINTON ADMINISTRATION'S PLANS TO "REINVENT" GOVERNMENT

In an incident as remarkable for the attention it did not get as for the message it conveyed, President Clinton announced only minutes after assuming the presidency from George Bush that each generation of Americans gets to define what it means to be an American. That such a reference in an inaugural address to the malleability of the American republic would elicit little commentary or criticism is evidence of the enormous influence that Progressive and New Deal thinking continues to exercise in American politics. Clinton wedded his view of a pliable American republic to a conviction that late-twentieth-century Americans were comfortable with an activist national government eager to protect all rights and redress all injuries. It was in this connection that he announced after the tragic high school shooting in Littleton, Colorado, that the federal government was prepared to send a legion of federally financed counselors to help the local community recover from the shock of the tragedy. Clinton's eagerness to speak out on issues such as Internet viruses and his decision to abruptly leave an international conference halfway around the world to be back in the United States when a major hurricane struck several southeastern states in 1999 are additional evidence of his commitment to ubiquitous government. He took for granted that it was no longer problematic to employ the largesse of the national government to use the advances of modern science to solve the daily problems of the American people. His assumptions reveal that government, somewhat ironically, has been simultaneously miniaturized (attending to smaller and smaller concerns) and magnified (requiring attention to more and more matters).

Entities such as the Federal Emergency Management Agency (FEMA) and the Food and Drug Administration (FDA) are responsible for the implementation of policies and directives that follow from the philosophy of palliative government. The assumption that most Americans want protection for all rights and redress of all grievances—that they yearn for non-tragic existence—makes the concerns of government coterminous with life itself. By the end of the twentieth century, the benefits of a union of the principles of organizational science and populism were an article of faith. In Wilsonian fashion, the major task was to determine how best to implement an agenda based on the pursuit of a tragedy-free existence.

It is precisely the implementation or execution of policy that Vice President Al Gore made the centerpiece of the "national performance review" that he undertook on behalf of the Clinton administration and that was unveiled with great fanfare in 1993. The title selected for the project reflects the attention being given to the efficient delivery of governmental services by the end of the century: "Creating a Government that Works Better and Costs Less."[11] The resemblance to the second part of Wilson's description of the objectives of administrative study in his influential essay of 1887 is uncanny: "It is the object of administrative study to discover, first, what government can properly and successfully do, and, secondly, how it can do these proper things with the utmost possible efficiency and at the least possible cost either of money or of energy."[12] The "Introduction" to the 1993 *Report of the National Performance Review* (NPR) includes a reference to Wilson at the same time that it treats the "modern bureaucratic state" in completely trouble-free terms.[13] The report looks to the perfection of the modern bureaucratic state, which is equated with the efficient satisfaction of citizen/consumer preferences. The modern pursuit of equality and justice as conceptualized by the NPR invites, even necessitates, an expansion of government regulations.

There is a significant parallel between the emphasis given to the satisfaction of popular preferences in the National Performance Review and the use of polls and focus groups for campaign purposes. The NPR assumes the legitimacy and desirability, if not necessarily the sufficiency, of "focus group" governance. The "Introduction" to the 1993 NPR speaks of "deliver[ing] what the people want" and "treat[ing] taxpayers like customers."[14] Running through the report is the assumption that popular preferences are unquestionable. The critical problems have to do not with the legitimacy of the desires of the people, but with the government's capacity to satisfy those desires efficiently. Hence the assertion that "the central issue we face is not *what* government does, but *how* it works." The report links the "crisis" in government with the fact that the "people simply feel that government doesn't work."[15] Since popular desires or feelings are radically changeable, the authors of the NPR call for a government "culture that promotes reinvention."[16] Administrative processes must be as malleable as public desires, government employees as adaptable as shifting popular preferences. In line with the argument that the protection of impulsive expression is necessary to true democracy, the authors of the NPR make a virtue of governmental responsiveness to popular impulsiveness—democratic government arguably is reinvented as fundamentally impulsive government.[17] It is not surprising that managing the executive department's reactions to current events had become a round-the-clock occupation for the Clinton White House, with several media briefing scheduled each day.

The impression that unmediated public opinion should drive government follows from language in the 1993 NPR that conveys the distinct impression that the Clinton administration was joining forces with the people in a classic battle against unresponsive government. Significantly, the report has an "outsider" flavor to it. Its authors present themselves as part of a larger "we" bent on reforming governmental processes. The people are encouraged, seemingly even instructed, to join in this endeavor. Witness the following language from the third report of the NPR (1995):

> Americans are frustrated, irritated, confused, even angry about our government—about the cost, and the hassle, and the inflexible rules, and the uncooperative attitude. But we're even angrier that our great dream seems to be slipping away—the dream of a government that is "of the people, by the people, and for the people," a government that isn't "them" but "us." [18]

The image of a united "we" who must hold the government accountable to our collective interests reappears at the very end of the 1995 report: "When it comes to government's management of our money, we need to be able to 'take it to the bank.' We need to be sure that our government is managing professionally the work we expect it to do and, when it needs to spend our money, spending it wisely."[19] There is something ironic about language that legitimates popular displeasure with the government being used by people who are part of the governing body. Very little separates this approach to governing from campaign politics. Going beyond the practice of candidates who seek to ingratiate themselves with voters by echoing their complaints, however, the "insider" authors of the NPR consciously play the role of serious cheerleaders of discontent. Rather than merely acknowledging existing sources of unhappiness, the rhetoric of the report seems designed to incite popular discontent. The language of the report is reminiscent not only of late-nineteenth-century populism, but of the righteous indignation associated with anti-establishment movements of the 1960s that faulted the national government for engaging in immoral, and not just unwise, actions.

Enmeshed with this populist attack on government inefficiency in general are criticisms of Congress for not cooperating with attempts by the Clinton administration to "reinvent" government. The attacks focus as much on substantive policy issues as on structural or institutional reforms. The most biting criticisms are ideological in nature. With reference to a disfavored piece of pork legislation, the authors wax eloquent on the perversity of legislative choices: "If Congress is proposing to cut back benefits to the needy, or trim badly needed investments in education, training, and infrastructure, how can we continue to support a tea-taster?"[20] Again, the "we versus they" strategy assumes that increased assistance for the needy or added investments in education are desirable, just as improvements in efficiency are presumed to be without any problems. It is clear upon examination that the NPR is not principally about efficiency, but about advancing a particular social agenda, that is, an agenda consistent with a modern, and moral, view of what government "should" be doing, to paraphrase Wilson. The NPR's authors find its social agenda incontestable, hence the severity of the attack on anything—including both sources of "inefficiency" and partisan policy conflicts—that threatens to delay or derail the full achievement of desired goals. The declaration that this effort has the full support of the American people constitutes a ploy in the partisan battle over the proper boundaries of governmental activity.

As noted above, the language of these reports should not be mistaken for anti-government thinking. The documents constitute a clarion call for a government that is perfectly efficient in what it does—and the expectation is that it should be doing plenty. The 1995 report confirms that the NPR is not a blueprint for smaller government. While acknowledging that a "great debate continues over what government should do," the authors of the report assert for the people that "*we* know what basics *we* expect to get: protection from enemies here and abroad, clean air and water, food that's safe to eat and toys that are safe for our kids to play with, help in emergencies, safe workplaces, *and so on*. We don't want to get rid of government; we want it to work better and cost less."[21] The laundry list of things for government to do could hardly be more extensive.

Evidence that the Clinton administration had no quarrel with the modern bureaucratic state is abundant. The Circuit Court of Appeals for the District of Columbia touched a sensitive nerve with administration officials when it ruled in 1999 that the EPA's interpretation of the Clean Air Act amounted to an unconstitutional delegation of legislative power.[22] The courts of appeals decision carried important implications for the exercise of discretionary rule-making powers by all federal agencies. This was not lost on Clinton administration officials, who saw the decision as one of "extraordinary governmental concern."[23] They feared the loss of broad rule-making powers by executive agencies that could be employed as supplementary devices for the advancement of the administration's political agenda. The appellate court's decision in *Browner v. American Trucking Association* was especially distressing to persons who welcome a paternalistic government in the form of a benevolent and powerful administrative state, in other words, to the partisans of "big government" who were the principal cheerleaders for President Clinton's goodies-laden State of the Union Address that marked the official beginning of his last year in office.[24] These efforts to extend the regulatory reach of the national government continued to the last days of the Clinton Administration with OSHA's announcement of new rules aimed at reducing repetitive motion injuries in the workplace and a request by the Agriculture Department that Congress empower it to regulate the sale of all food items, including items sold as part of fund-raising projects, in the vicinity of school cafeterias. By one estimate, the Clinton administration added 25,000-plus pages of new regulations during the three months preceding the inauguration of George W. Bush, a Republican president.

The Clinton's administration's appeal for the reinvention of government ha an almost irresistible quality. Whether they label themselves liberals or cons vatives, Democrats or Republicans, most political officials view Progre and the New Deal as beneficial, or at least tolerable, "additives" that made the American political system both more democratic and more just. Representatives of the major political parties freely endorse the use of governmental power to address perceived wrongs. Palliative government, and also transformational government based on emotional appeals to compassion, is in vogue.[25] Nor did "big government" disappear under Clinton's successor—witness not only the creation of the Department of Homeland Security under George W. Bush, but his support for a prescription drug benefit under Medicare as well as the ambitious "No Child Left Behind" program.[26] The marriage of populism and scientific management principles has had a mesmerizing effect. Most public figures with reservations about the results of this marriage are at a loss about how to object, as is evident in the public relations disaster suffered by Newt Gingrich and his Republican congressional allies when Clinton blamed them for the infamous budget impasse that shut down the government in the mid-1990s.

It would be wrong, however, to suggest that the NPR escaped unscathed. Typical objections focused on what might be termed technical and strategic problems—for example, criticism that the failure to include Congress as a partner in the crafting of the NPR increased the difficulties associated with implementing proposed reforms. Another early criticism arose out of the belief that the toll on middle management positions resulting from full implementation of the workforce reduction proposals would seriously interfere with the goal of optimizing efficiency.[27] More serious than these technical or strategic problems, however, are the constitutional implications of the system-wide reforms envisioned by the Clinton administration.

Several constitutional problems are evident in the role the NPR assigns the bureaucracy in the governmental system. The authors of the NPR envision a streamlined system of administration that bestows considerable power on agencies to manage their own affairs. An entire section of the 1993 report is devoted to "decentralizing decision-making power."[28] This is not a formula, however, for creating the statesman-like bureaucracy that scholars such as John Rohr and Herbert Storing thought might fill the role of the original Senate, that is, an institution that could appeal to its collective knowledge as well as the experience and constitutional oath of its members to legitimize the exercise of large discretionary authority to advance significant national interests.[29] On the surface it might appear that the Clinton administration had just such a role in mind for the bureaucracy when it permitted the Food and Drug Administration to assume authority to impose wide-ranging regulations on the cigarette industry without explicit congressional approval, and even arguably in the face of legislative disapproval.[30] The plan to reinvent government, however, calls upon government agencies to act in a fashion that resembles what the founders expected of the House of Representatives rather than the original Senate. A better image would be of an activist House that responds to popular demands for government benefits.[31] The insistence that agencies treat citizens as customers whose preferences should drive administrative action, at the same time that White House officials encourage people to demand more of government, undermines the possibility for statesman-like decision-making by the bureaucracy. Significantly, Woodrow Wilson also had undermined the possibility of a principled defense of statesman-like governance with his insistence that true democratic government treats citizen preferences as the proper starting and ending points for legitimate policy formulation.[32] The NPR's customer-friendly approach to government fits well with the increasing reliance on devices such as the initiative, recall, and referendum touted by Progressives as important instruments of self-government or democracy.[33] It might be added that California's recall election of 2003 drew sustenance from the same political "spring" that nourished the NPR.

NPR AND MADISONIAN CONSTITUTIONALISM

If founders like Madison understood that democratic impulses could easily undermine the requisites of competent and decent republicanism, Progressives and New Dealers did not see an alternative to popular preferences as a source of legitimacy for public policies. True, they sought to create a new social consciousness that would embrace an activist state committed to the advancement of the general well-being of the people. But in practice what they ended up cultivating was the conviction that public preferences, whether arising out of a properly developed social consciousness or not, should drive government action. It is this conception of the relationship of the people to government that is reflected in the "customer service" orientation of the National Performance Review. By the 1990s, the citizen/customers who would be driving administrative action had bought into the position that government properly could be asked to assure them a tragicless existence. Another version of this position is reflected in "dignity theories" that see the affirmation of individual dignity—represented in the theory that people should be assisted in their pursuit of preferred ways of life or lifestyles—as the fundamental litmus test of proper government action.[34] If nothing else, the rhetoric of the NPR unleashes the forces of direct popular government or government based on unmediated public preferences that Madison and the other leading founders believed had to be contained. The institutions associated with constitutionalism were critical to the success of this enterprise. Madison understood full well what he was saying when he declared in *Federalist* #51 that the first task of the delegates at the Constitutional Convention was to create a government capable of "controlling the governed."[35] His version of such a government combines representative institutions with devices for checking and channeling human impulses in order to advance the common good. He also wanted officials to draw authority from institutions such as the presidency itself rather than to rely on the transient will of the people.[36]

A system of administration grounded in principles of efficiency and driven by transient popular preferences stands at odds with both the structure and ends of the constitutional order envisioned by the founders. There is nothing in the model set out in the NPR to protect the original system of separated and divided powers. Insofar as Perot-like complaints about "gridlock" resonated with electorate, the Clinton administration's seemingly cavalier treatment of t tem of separated powers was unlikely to provoke great resistance. If it is dangerous for the people to be blind to the utility of the institutional division of powers, it is no less dangerous to create a bureaucratic culture that is not grounded in a due sensitivity to the special role of each branch in supporting decent and competent democratic government. An activist bureaucracy whose popular legitimacy is tied to the advancement of a social agenda catering to the desire of the people for a tragic free existence may end up looking "democratic," but in fact it may constitute a genuine threat to a quality democracy that treats people as citizens and not as subjects. The maniacal pursuit of efficiency or of "libertarian dignity" as well as the practice of treating popular preferences (which are practically unlimited) as sacred carries the potential for overwhelming limited government and endangering true human liberty.

Madison and other early leaders such as Washington and Marshall believed that the success of the American experiment in democratic government depended on a citizenry capable of self-discipline and possessed of at least a rudimentary understanding of principles of self-government and due process of law. Jefferson's case for independence of the American colonies rested on the argument that the American people were ready for self-government, which requires an understanding of one's rights and a capacity to judge whether a government is providing reasonable protection for those rights. Self-government is not possible without the ability to understand the threat of dangers such as seeking immediate gratification of preferences at the expense of the long-term interests of society. Beyond sound reasoning, a democratic citizenry must be capable of acting in accord with the dictates of reason by, for example, refraining from discounting the future too heavily in the interest of satisfying current desires. If this knowledge must be present in the citizen body for the American constitutional system to achieve the great aims associated with that system, it is even more imperative that persons in governing positions, including positions in the bureaucracy, possess such knowledge and that they be prepared to act on it as well. Madison and other leading founders understood that it is a mistake to conceive of civil society simply in institutional or procedural terms, as the mere aggregation of free associations and independent governing institutions operating under principles of due process and guarantees for free speech or privacy rights. They recognized that a nation will not be able to sustain a decent and competent democratic government, and create free citizens rather than subjects, if its institutions are not supported by a society whose members are distinguished by habits of industry, thoughtful self-control, and obedience to the law—in other words, a social culture whose moral core matches the considerable demands placed on the members of a modern democratic society. Madison and other early statesmen, and Lincoln after them, understood that successful democratic republics are fragile and must be carefully nurtured and preserved. Their preservation over time is not something to be taken for granted. Tocqueville had the same message for his readers at the very end of *Democracy in America*: "Providence did not make mankind entirely free or completely enslaved. Providence has, in truth, drawn a predestined circle around each man beyond which he cannot pass; but within those vast limits man is strong and free, and so are peoples. . . . [I]t depends upon [the nations of our day] whether equality is to lead to servitude or freedom, knowledge or barbarism, prosperity or wretchedness."[37]

NOTES

1. *Federalist* #68.

2. *Federalist* #51.

3. Ibid.

4. See David E. Marion, "Alexander Hamilton and Woodrow Wilson on the Spirit and Form of Responsible Republican Government," *Review of Politics* 42 (July 1980): 319-328.

5. Woodrow Wilson, "The Study of Administration," *Political Science Quarterly* 2 (1887): 197.

6. Ibid., 216. Also see Wilson, *The New Freedom*, 231. Wilson's futile efforts to secure American participation in the League of Nations were particularly troubling in light of his declaration that public opinion was becoming increasingly enlightened.

7. United States, Executive Department, *Report of the President's Committee on Administrative Management* (Washington, DC: Government Printing Office, 1938), 1, 2.

8. Ibid., 2

9. Harold Ickes, *The New Democracy* (New York: Norton, 1934), 77, 121.

10. James O. Freedman, *Crisis and Legitimacy* (Cambridge: Cambridge University Press, 1978), 45. The appeal to "disinterested expertise" was commonplace within the scientific management movement. See generally, Frederick Winslow Taylor, *The Principles of Scientific Management* (New York: Norton, 1947), esp. 5-8, 140-144.

11. "Creating a Government that Works Better and Costs Less," *Report of the National Performance Review* (Washington, DC: Government Printing Office, 1993) [hereafter referred to as NPR].

12. Woodrow Wilson, "The Study of Administration," 197.

13. The argument that the United States may appropriately be described as a modern administrative state was given expression by Justice Byron White in *Immigration and Naturalization Service v. Chadha*, a major mid-1980s separation of powers case. 462 U.S. 919 (1983).

14. NPR, 8, 2. The elevation of citizen preferences to center stage is reminiscent of the call for "maximum feasible participation" by the poor in antipoverty programs in the late 1960s. This period also witnessed increased lobbying for radical decentralization of public schools in places like New York City, and the inclusion of ombudsmen or grievance offices within government agencies. An excellent examination of these developments can be found in Herbert Kaufman, "Administrative Decentralization and Political Power," in *Classics of Public Administration*, eds. Jay Shafritz and Albert Hyde (Fort Worth, TX: Harcourt, Brace & Co., 1997), esp. 291-293.

15. Ibid., 2.

16. Ibid., 123. The commitment to transformative administration did not disappear with the election of George W. Bush in 2000. The Senior Executive Service's website in 2003 proclaims that the "men and women" in the SES are "charged with leading the continuing transformation of the federal government." www.opm.gov/ses/.

17. For the argument that the First Amendment protects the expression of emotions as well as ideas, see Justice Harlan's opinion for the United States Supreme Court in *Cohen v. California*, 403 U.S. 15 (1971).

18. "Common Sense Government: Works Better & Costs Less," 2-3. *Third Report of the National Performance Review* (Washington, DC: Government Printing Office, 1995).

19. Ibid., 85.

20. Ibid., 77.

21. Ibid., 4-5, emphasis added.

22. *Browner v. American Trucking Association.* "Issue Arcane; Implications Sweeping," *Richmond Times-Dispatch*, May 15, 2000, A2. The case made it to the United States Supreme Court as *Whitman, Administrator of EPA v. American Trucking Association.* In his opinion for the Court, Justice Scalia ruled that the Environmental Protection Agency could not construe the relevant statute in a way that "completely nullifies textually applicable provisions meant to limit its discretion," 531 U.S. 457 (2001).

23. Ibid.

24. Among other things, Clinton lobbied Congress during his last year for additional federal funds for teacher training programs and the rebuilding or refurbishing of schools—historically matters left to the states and localities.

25. For a popularized defense of transformative leadership see James MacGregor Burns, *Leadership* (New York: Harper & Row, 1978).

26. Federal spending increases were considerably higher than inflation under George W. Bush. David Westphal, "Spending Rises Feed Deficit," *Richmond Times-Dispatch*, September 4, 2003, A2.

27. Donald Kettl, *Reinventing Government? Appraising the National Performance Review* (Washington, DC: The Brookings Institution, 1994).

28. NPR, ch. 3.

29. See John Rohr, *To Run a Constitution* (Lawrence: University of Kansas Press, 1986); Herbert Storing, "Political Parties and the Bureaucracy," in *Political Parties, U.S.A.* (Chicago: Rand McNally, 1964), 19.

30. *F.D.A. v. Brown & Williamson*, 529 U.S. 120 (2000).

31. See James Q. Wilson, "The Rise of the Bureaucratic State," in *Current Issues in Public Administration*, ed. Frederick S. Lane, (New York: St. Martin's, 1982).

32. See David E. Marion, "Wilson's 1887 Essay: Telling 'Noble Lies'?" in *The Wilson Influence on Public Administration: From Theory to Practice*, ed. Paul P. Van Riper, (Washington, D.C.: The American Society for Public Administration 1990), 48-49.

33. David Broder, *Democracy Derailed* (New York: Harcourt, 2000). Broder provides a critical review of the growing use of the initiative as an alternative to representative government.

34. See Jerry Mashaw, "Administrative Due Process: The Quest for a Dignity Theory," *Boston University Law Review* 61 (1981): 885, and David E. Marion, *Justice William J Brennan: The Law and Politics of 'Libertarian Dignity'* (Lanham, MD: Rowman & Littlefield, 1997).

35. *Federalist #51*.

36. For a thoughtful examination of the comparative benefits of reliance on institutions versus reliance on appeals to the people, see Ceaser, Thurow, Tulis, Bessette, "The Rise of the Rhetorical Presidency."

37. Tocqueville, *Democracy in America*, 705.

CONCLUSION

THE ELECTION OF 2000
A CASE STUDY IN DECONSTITUTIONALIZATION

This book was conceived in the midst of the impeachment crisis of 1999 and was completed in the immediate aftermath of the second Iraq War and its danger-laden reconstruction. In between occurred the disputed election of 2000, and it may be appropriate to take a brief look at that remarkable event. Many books will no doubt be written about the aftermath of November 7, 2000, and most of them will show that both political camps, the courts, the media, the people, and the press each made decisions based on perceptions of political or corporate self-interests. However, we would note that while each actor, each institution, and each group made decisions based on individual calculations of relatively short-term consequences, the progress of deconstitutionalization was both wonderfully illustrated and immeasurably advanced by these decisions. If the process that we have discussed in this book proves to be a continuing trend—and includes some of the adverse consequences that we have identified—we may one day look back on these days as a crucial moment in the deconstitutionalization of the United States when even political people who claimed to be most opposed to these tendencies contributed to their development.

As we have argued, one of the chief characteristics of "deconstitutionalized" government is the need to ground political legitimacy in immediate, identifiable, and measurable popular support rather than in institutional standing or constitutional powers. Normally, the outcomes of presidential elections in the United States are determined by the constitutional majority dictated by the Electoral College. In almost all cases, this constitutional majority is clear and unambiguous, but in 2000, the day after the election found neither candidate in possession of a clear constitutional majority. This unique situation left the American people looking for some alternative method of persuading themselves that the presidency would devolve upon the appropriate candidate, and each candidate's camp in turn found an opportunity to define the legitimacy of its title to be called "President-elect" on some other standard, if only the supporters could persuade the American people that the source of their candidate's legitimacy was appropriately democratic one.

Vice President Al Gore's camp immediately began to stress the importance of the fact that Gore had won the popular vote on November 7. Al Gore himself, as well as various different groups in the Democratic party, argued on and off over the next thirty-six days that only Gore could claim presidential legitimacy and that the source of his legitimacy lay in a popular mandate expressed through the votes of the people counted as a single national electorate. The single most astonishing discovery of the 2000 interregnum was the fact that this claim to legitimacy proved almost entirely unsuccessful. One poll revealed that nearly fifteen days after the election during which every Democratic spokesman stressed Gore's still-growing lead in the ongoing popular vote counts, some 40 percent of the American people *did not know* Gore had won the popular vote and *even fewer* considered that the fact that he had the most popular votes made him the presumptive President-elect.

Many commentators had long argued that the Electoral College could survive only so long as the EC winner was also the popular vote winner and that if the two ever disagreed, the resulting outcry would spell the end of the Electoral College. In 2000, this assumption proved to be utterly false when even during a month in which there was essentially *no* Electoral College winner, the popular vote winner was incapable of making a credible claim to the presidency. This remarkable fact might be looked upon as evidence of the enduring power of *constitutionalism*; we might conclude that the American people accept the constitutional rules for selecting a president and accept constraint by those rules as legitimate. However, we think that it would be a mistake to accept this reading of Vice President Gore's failure to persuade the American people that his popular vote lead constituted title to the Presidency. If anything, Gore's claim to the Presidency based on his popular vote plurality may have proved ineffective not because it was a deconstitutionalizing contention but because it was too constitutional and placed too much emphasis on the importance of a "formal" election process and too little on establishing a connection with the most recent strains of "popular opinion."

Furthermore we must note that Gore's strategy to gain legitimacy on the basis of the popular vote was only one of many that he adopted during the election dispute. Some of the arguments were not necessarily tied to, or even consistent with, the principle that clear election by the popular vote was grounds for presidential legitimacy.

The most deconstitutionalizing statements by the Democrats came in early December when Gore's representatives argued that requests for possession of ballots were possible under the Freedom of Information Act, that the counting of votes would continue even if George W. Bush became president, and that they expected that these private counts would eventually revealed that Gore had won Florida and the election. Democrats expected that a groundswell of public indignation would cripple Bush's power as president and might even lead to an alteration of the outcome, removing Bush and installing Gore. While there was, of course, *no* constitutional method by which Al Gore, who would be by that time a private citizen and completely removed from the long statutory line of presidential succession, could be made president after the fact to correct some injustice, Democrats did not hesitate to suggest that a way might be found to overcome any institutional impediments to placing "the right man" in the White House. Even when conceding that this outcome was impossible, Gore's surrogates did not hesitate to threaten to use the "proof" of Gore's victory as justification for thwarting any and all presidential actions by a would-be President Bush who, they warned, could be effectively transformed into a lame duck within the first 100 days of his election. As recent history has shown, presidents of many contemporary non-constitutional democracies have been forced to step down when popular pressures against their claim to the office became too powerful. In some of these cases, the leader of the opposition party has been successfully installed as at least interim president when the office became vacant. Indonesia in 1998, Peru in 2000, and the Philippines in 2001 are only a few of many examples that might be cited. Gore supporters—most notably the Reverend Jesse Jackson— insisted that such a deconstitutionalized transfer of power was possible, or at least ought to be possible, in the United States as well.

Gore's several strategies were part of a long series of moves and counter-moves in which Gore and his followers were not the only ones maneuvering for a claim to legitimacy or making judgments about such claims. Governor George W. Bush also put a number of teams on the ground in Florida to press his entitlement to the presidency. He also used a combination of public relations and legal maneuvers to try to "sell" the idea that he was the rightful President-elect. In one sense, Bush's position was "constitutionalist" in that he argued that he had, in fact, won the constitutional majority defined by the Electoral College, but in many important regards, Bush's moves, just like Gore's, revealed an unabashed acceptance of the idea that contemporaneous popular support as expressed in daily polls was the true source of political legitimacy.

It is perhaps particularly worthy of note to point out that the parade of supporters of both candidates revealed an astonishing coordination between the various branches and divisions of government in the United States. Governors and members of the House and the Senate figured prominently among the spokespersons for the two campaigns both on the ground in Florida and on television and radio programs covering the event.

During the 2000 dispute, the national news media covered the activities of the two camps in what not so long ago would have been considered a most astonishing fashion. The new organizations accepted as fact, and as appropriate, that each and every statement emanating from the two camps was only "spin." In doing so, they made it clear that they considered the election a contest in which the real goal was control of popular opinion: not to *be* the winner of the November 7 election, but to be thought of as "the winner" on whatever day really mattered whether December 12, December 18, January 6, January 20, or only "to day." CNN assigned John King to report "the spin" from the Gore camp Candy Crowley to report "the spin" from the Bush camp. These reporte asked on occasion to report what they thought "the spin" on unfolding events *would be* even before they spoke to anyone from the camps to actually hear "the spin" from the source. The initial success of a nightly "news" program called "The Spin Room" seems to have derived from the pleasure that the general public took from calling in to rate which "spins" they thought were most clever, or to take their own turn "spinning" for the candidate of their choice. The never-quite-stated assumption of all this coverage was that there was, and is, no such thing as an unequivocal, legitimate, constitutional claim to office, and that all claims to power are contingent, temporary, and grounded on momentary popular support.

CRISIS, DEMOCRACY, AND DECONSTITUTIONALIZATION

We argue that there is an ongoing process that we have identified as "deconstitutionalization." Like most political transformations that happen as laws and institutions pass through the shifting political circumstances and evolving political ideas that constitute political history, deconstitutionalization often appears to be the inevitable consequence of some pre-ordained evolutionary process. However, changes in our political institutions are, in fact, the result of conscious decisions made by individual human beings. To say that these decisions were "conscious" is not to say that their consequences were deliberately chosen, because generally both the few and the many failed to see the long-term outcomes of their political actions. It is to say, however, that political actors and thinkers, making choices that seem to make sense in the situations in which they found themselves and that were generally oriented toward what they took to be their own self-interest at the moment, were together responsible for changing institutions. Institutional change does not "just happen."

We have presented the ideas of Lincoln, Wilson, and Roosevelt in order to highlight three important shifts in American political history brought about because of slavery and civil war, industrialization, and depression—the greatest challenges to face the nation. In each case there were compelling reasons to go beyond the constitutional order laid out in the principles of Madison. It should not be surprising that Lincoln, the leader closest in time to Madison, was also the most familiar with the costs of restructuring the Constitution. Wilson was more sanguine about recasting the Constitution because he put his faith in the progressive movement of history. Roosevelt, ever the politician, more or less ignored the theoretical problems associated with democracy and constitutional government and sought to legitimate a pragmatic approach to lawmaking based on the right of the people to define their own needs and wants.

We have also pointed out that governmental power increases during a crisis, most often as a consequence of war, and retracts when the crisis passes. We predict that the extraordinary authority given to President Bush to fight terrorism under the Patriot Act will be rescinded if and when threats diminish. Deconstitutionalization does not occur, as Arthur M. Schlesinger Jr. maintains in *The Imperial Presidency*, because presidents accrue power during crises and fail to return it in tranquil times, but rather because the very success of America's constitutionally constructed democracy has all but blinded people to the need for constitutional limits on democratic rule.[1] In every instance of crisis that we present in this book, the response to an emergency was to diminish the forms of the Constitution and increase the authority of the people. The cure for the ills of democracy has been more democracy.

It might be argued that we have overstated our case and that the Constitution is as alive today in spirit—if not in form—as it was during most of America's history. Polls indicate that Americans respect and perhaps even cherish their political institutions. Yet polls also show that the populace is upset and disappointed that the government does not do more for them. A substantial majority of people believes that government is not responsive enough to their needs because politicians are corrupt and because elected officials have failed "to listen to the people." Americans want quick solutions to their problems, ones free of the need for tedious and time-consuming consensus building laid out in Madison's constitutional blueprint. The courts have added to this expectation of swiftness by politicizing nearly almost all issues in contemporary life and then ruling on them, not so much to protect the forms of the Constitution, but to promote the interests of the people.

We conclude, therefore, with the contention that the real cause of the deconstitutionalization of America is the ferocious engine of democracy, a phenomenon that seeks inexorably to sweep aside all restraints on the power of the many. Democracy is now taken to be *the* regime, and its sad history of failures and shortcomings, so visible to America's founders, has been all but forgotten.[2]

This book was written in hope that it might remind people of the need for constitutional government. The honorable purpose associated with constitutional government can be stated as a question: Can the mass of human beings control their own lives and destinies? Until the founding of the American nation, the clear answer to that question would have been no, because people in the past needed monarchs or strongmen to guide their political future. The American Constitution held out the hope that ordinary people were capable of deciding their own fates, and in doing so it immeasurably elevated the dignity of common people. The complex interplay of enumerated powers, which limited the power of the state; separate branches of government, which draw their powers from the people in different ways; and federalism, which left much of the day-to-day administrative decisions at the local level, was intended to provide the people with the opportunity to govern themselves and also teach them the limits beyond which democratic self-government would become self-destructive. If we forget those limits, we might lose not only our Constitution, but also our dignity and honor.

NOTES

1. Arthur M. Schlesinger Jr., *The Imperial Presidency* (New York: Popular Library, 1974).

2. Michael P. Riccards, *The Ferocious Engine of Democracy: A History of the American Presidency* (Lanham, MD: Rowman & Littlefield, 1995).

SELECTED BIBLIOGRAPHY

Abbot, Philip. *The Exemplary Presidency*. Amherst: University of Massachusetts Press, 1990.

Andrews, Wayne, ed. *The Autobiography of Theodore Roosevelt*. New York: Scribner's, 1958.

Bagehot, Walter. *The English Constitution*. Ithaca, NY: Cornell University Press, 1963.

Barrus, Roger, and John Eastby, eds. *America Through the Looking Glass: A Constitutionalist Critique of the 1992 Election*. Lanham, MD: Rowman & Littlefield, 1994.

Broder, David. *Democracy Derailed*. New York: Harcourt, 2000.

Burns, James MacGregor. *Leadership*. New York: Harper & Row, 1978.

____. *Roosevelt: The Lion and the Fox*. New York: Harcourt, Brace, Jovanovich, 1956.

Cardozo, Benjamin. *The Nature of the Judicial Process*. New Haven, CT: Yale University Press, 1921.

Ceaser, James, Glen Thurow, Jeffrey Tulis, and Joseph Bessette. *American Government: Origins, Institutions and Public Policy*. Dubuque, IA: Kendall-Hunt, 1995.

____. "The Rise of the Rhetorical Presidency," *Presidential Studies Quarterly* 11 (Spring 1981): 223-251.

Ceaser, James. *Presidential Selection: Theory and Development*. Princeton, NJ: Princeton University Press, 1979.

Commanger, Henry Steele, ed. *Documents of American History*. New York: Appleton, Century, Crofts, 1963.

Crabb, Cecil V., Jr., and Pat M. Holt. *Invitation to Struggle: Congress, the President, and Foreign Policy*. Washington, DC: Congressional Quarterly Press, 1980.

Croly, Herbert. *Progressive Democracy*. New York: The MacMillan Company, 1914.

Davidson, Roger. *The Postreform Congress*. New York: St. Martin's Press, 1991.

Diamond, Martin. "The American Idea of Man: The View from the Founding." In *The Americans: 1976*. Edited by Irving Kristol and Paul H. Weaver. Lexington, MA: Lexington Books, 1976.

Fitzpatrick John C., ed. *The Writings of George Washington*. Washington, DC: Government Printing Office, 1940.

Freedman, James O. *Crisis and Legitimacy*. Cambridge: Cambridge University Press, 1978.

Fukuyama, Francis. "The End of History." *The National Interest* 16 (Summer 1989): 3-18.

Fusfeld, Daniel. *The Economic Thought of Franklin D. Roosevelt and the Origins of the New Deal*. New York: Columbia University Press, 1956.

Galbraith, John Kenneth. *American Capitalism*. Boston: Houghton Mifflin, 1952.

Greer, Thomas H. *What Roosevelt Thought: The Social and Political Ideas of Franklin Roosevelt.* East Lansing: Michigan State University Press, 1958.

Hamilton, Alexander, James Madison, and John Jay. *The Federalist Papers.* http://liberty online.hypeermall.com/Federalist/.

Harris, John F. "Clinton Never Liked the Media: But Don't Ask Him Why." *The Washington Post* (31 December 2000): B1, B2.

———. "Policy and Politics by the Numbers." *The Washington Post* (31 December 2000): A1, A10.

Hirschfield, Robert, ed. *The Power of the Presidency.* Chicago: Aldine, 1973.

Hobbes, Thomas. *Leviathan, or The Matter, Forme, and Power of a Commonwealth, Ecclesiastical and Civill.* Edited by C. B. Macpherson. New York: Penguin Books, 1981.

Hofstadter, Richard, ed. *The Progressive Movement: 1900-1915.* Englewood Cliffs, NJ: Prentice-Hall, 1963.

Hoover, Herbert. *The Memoirs of Herbert Hoover.* New York: Macmillan, 1952.

Hunt, Gaillard, ed. *The Writings of James Madison.* New York: G. Putnam's Sons, 1901.

Ickes, Harold. *The New Democracy.* New York: Norton, 1934.

Jaffa, Harry V. *A New Birth of Freedom: Abraham Lincoln and the Coming of the Civil War.* Lanham, MD: Rowman & Littlefield, 2000.

Kaufman, Herbert. "Administrative Decentralization and Political Power." In *Classics of Public Administration.* Edited by Jay Shafritz and Albert Hyde. Fort Worth, TX: Harcourt, Brace, & Co., 1997.

Kettl, Donald. "Reinventing Government? Appraising the National Performance Review." Washington, DC: The Brookings Institution, 1994.

King, Anthony. "Running Scared." *Atlantic Monthly* (January 1997): 41-61.

Koch, Adrienne, and William Peden, eds. *The Life and Selected Writings of Thomas Jefferson.* New York: Modern Library, 1944.

Lerner, Max, ed. *The Prince and the Discourses.* New York: Modern Library, 1940.

Lincoln, Abraham. *Abraham Lincoln: Speeches and Writings.* New York: The Library of America, 1989.

Link Arthur S. *Woodrow Wilson and the Progressive Era: 1910-1917.* New York: Harper & Row, 1954.

Locke, John. *The Second Treatise of Government.* Indianapolis, IN: Bobbs Merrill, 1952.

Machiavelli, Niccolò. *The Prince and the Discourses.* Edited by Max Lerner. New York: Modern Library, 1940.

Madison, James. *Notes of the Debates of the Federal Convention.* Edited by Andrienne Koch. New York: Norton Library, 1968.

———. "Vices of the Political System of the United States." In *The Writings of James Madison.* Edited by Jack N. Rabocov. New York: The Library of America, 1999.

Marion, David. "Alexander Hamilton and Woodrow Wilson on the Spirit and Form of a Responsible Republican Government." *Review of Politics* 42 (July 1980): 309-328.

———. *Justice William J. Brennan: The Law and Politics of 'Libertarian Dignity.'* Lanham, MD: Rowman & Littlefield, 1997.

———. "Wilson's 1887 Essay: Telling 'Noble Lies'?" In *The Wilson Influence on Public Administration: From Theory to Practice.* Edited by Paul P. Van Riper. Washington, DC: The American Society for Public Administration, 1990.

Mashaw, Jerry. "Administrative Due Process: The Quest for a Dignity Theory." *Boston University Law Review* 61 (1981).

McClellan, James, and M. E. Bradford, eds. *Elliot's Debates.* Richmond, VA: James River Press, 1989.

Meyers, Marvin, ed. *The Mind of the Founder: Sources of the Political Thought of James Madison*. Hanover, NH: University Press of New England, 1981.

Milkis, Sidney M., and Michael Nelson. *The American Presidency: Origins and Development, 1776-1990*. Washington, DC: Congressional Quarterly Press, 1990.

Moley, Raymond. *After Seven Years*. New York: Harper & Brothers, 1939.

Montesquieu, Comte de. *The Spirit of the Laws*. Translated by Anne M. Cohler, Basia Carolyn Miller, and Harold Samuel Stone. Cambridge: Cambridge University Press, 1989.

Morgan, Ted. *FDR: A Biography*. New York: Simon and Schuster, 1985.

Nichols, David K. *The Myth of the Modern Presidency*. University Park: Pennsylvania University Press, 1994.

Noonan, Peggy. "Why Bush Failed." *New York Times* (5 November 1992): A35.

Peterson, Merrill D., ed. *The Portable Thomas Jefferson*. New York: Penguin Books, 1975.

Rauch, Jonathan. "Father Superior: Our Greatest Modern President." *The New Republic* 22 (2000): 22-25.

Riccards, Michael P. *The Ferocious Engine of Democracy: A History of the American Presidency*. Lanham, MD: Rowman & Littlefield, 1995.

Rohr, John. *To Run a Constitution*. Lawrence: University of Kansas Press, 1986.

Roosevelt, Franklin D. *The Public Papers and Addresses of Franklin D. Roosevelt*. New York: Random House, 1938.

Rossum, Ralph. *Federalism, The Supreme Court, and the Seventeenth Amendment: The Irony of Constitutional Democracy*. Lanham, MD: Lexington Books, 2001.

Schlesinger, Arthur M., Jr. *The Coming of the New Deal*. Boston: Houghton Mifflin, 1958.

——. *The Crisis of the Old Order*. Boston: Houghton Mifflin, 1957.

——. *The Imperial Presidency*. New York: Popular Library, 1974.

——. *The Politics of Upheaval*. Boston: Houghton Mifflin, 1960.

Sinclair, Barbara. *Unorthodox Lawmaking: New Legislative Processes in the U.S. Congress*. Washington, DC: Congressional Quarterly Press, 1997.

Smith, Adam. *The Wealth of Nations*. New York: Modern Library, 1937.

Swift, Elaine K. *The Making of an American Senate: Reconstitutive Change in Congress, 1787-1841*. Ann Arbor: Michigan University Press, 1996.

Stark, Steven. "Too Representative Government." *Atlantic Monthly* (May 1995).

Storing, Herbert. "Political Parties and the Bureaucracy." In *Political Parties, U.S.A.* Edited by Robert Goldwin. Chicago: Rand McNally, 1964.

Syrett, Harold, ed. *The Papers of Alexander Hamilton*, 26 vols. New York: Columbia University Press, 1961-1979.

Taylor, Frederick Winslow. *The Principles of Scientific Management*. New York: Norton, 1947.

Thucydides. *History of the Peloponnesian War*. Translated by Charles Foster Smith. Cambridge, MA: Harvard University Press, 1969.

Tocqueville, Alexis de. *Democracy in America*. Translated by George Lawrence. Garden City, New York: Doubleday, 1969.

Toynbee, Arnold J. *Survey of International Affairs: 1931*. London: Oxford University Press, 1932.

Westphal, David. "Spending Rises Feed Deficit." *Richmond Times-Dispatch* (4 September 2003): A2.

Wilson, James Q. "The Rise of the Bureaucratic State." In *Current Issues in Publ¹ ministration*. Edited by Frederick S. Lane. New York: St. Martin's, 1982.

Wilson, Woodrow. "Cabinet Government in the United States." In *Selected Literary and Political Papers and Addresses of Woodrow Wilson* (New York: Grosset and Dunlap, 1925), vol. 1: 1-30.

———. *Congressional Government: A Study in American Politics*, intro. Walter Lippmann (Gloucester, MA: Peter Smith 1885, 1956, 1973).

———. *Constitutional Government in the United States*. New York: Columbia University Press, 1908.

———. "Division and Reunion: 1829-1889." In *Epochs of American History*. New York: Longmans, Green and Co., 1893, 1898, 1902.

———. *Leaders of Men*. Edited by T. H. V. Motter. Princeton, NJ: Princeton University Press, 1952.

———. "Mere Literature and other Essays." In *Selected Literary and Political Papers*. Vol. 3. New York: Grosset & Dunlap, 1926-27.

———. *The New Freedom*. Introduction by W. E. Leuchtenberg. Englewood Cliffs, NJ: Prentice-Hall, 1964.

———. *The State: Elements of Historical and Practical Politics*. New York: DC Heath, Inc., 1908.

———. "The Study of Administration." *Political Science Quarterly* 2 (1887).

Young, James Sterling. *The Washington Community*. New York: Columbia University Press, 1966.

Zinn, Howard, ed. *New Deal Thought*. Indianapolis: Bobbs-Merrill, 1966.

INDEX

Abolitionists, 22, 28, 29, 30, 31, 32, 33, 40
Adams, John, 104
Antifederalist, 82
Articles of Confederation, 12, 21, 80, 82, 98, 99

Bagehot, Walter, 56, 57, 59, 62, 63
Brennan, William, 114, 115
Bush, George H.W., 7, 107
Bush, George W., 7, 95, 109, 150, 151, 152, 153

Calhoun, John C., 44, 88
Ceaser, James, 50
Civil War, 25-6, 28, 90
Clinton, William Jefferson, vii, ix, 7, 117, 145, 148n24
Congress, 72, 79-97; bicameralism, 81, 84, Bush, G.W. and, 95; Clinton and, 104, 108, 142, 143, 144, 148n24; committees in, 51, 53, 58; the Court and, ix, 90, 91, 92, 97n28, 97n32, 116, 117, 119, 120, 124n20; Croly [Herbert] on, 89; debate in, 88, 89; democratization and, 85; effectiveness of, 94, 95; election to, 86; election of 1854 to, 34; expectations of, 94, 95; *Federalist Papers* on, 81, 82, 89; foreign policy and 127-34; founders and, 79-83; Hamilton on, 90; impeachment and, vii, viii; Lincoln and, 26, 33, 42, 43, 44, 48n3, 104; Mexican War and, 104; New Deal and, 106, 38; Nixon and, 104; Pierce [Franklin] and, 34; Perot and, 6, 11n9; powers of, 81, 84, 89, 90, 92, 97; President and, vii, viii, 67, 98; Progressives and, 81; Republicans in, ix, 76, 95, 108, 144; Roosevelt, F. D. and, 67, 72; slavery and, 36, 37, 38, 39, 40; tyranny and, 80; Wilson and, 53, 57, 58, 63, 79, 87, 89, 90, 91, 92, 95, constitution[alism] as ordering device, 126; citizenship and, 126; collective action and, 51; democracy

and, 108; economics and, 97; English government and, 25, 56, 61, 66n15; foreign policy and, 126; limited government and, 82; literary, 50, 54, 60, 79; organic, 50, 55, 62, 64, 79
Constitution [of the United States], 9, 10, 22, 64, 81, 110, 123; administration and, 136; Anglo-Saxon [British] heritage of, 55, 58, 92; authority in, 51; *Baker v. Carr* and, 116; Berger Court and, 117; capitalism and, 68; Cardoza and, 113; changes and, 85; "comprehensive" character of, 113, 114, 115, 117; Congress [legislature] and, 79, 82, 83, 90, 1; convention, 20, 21, 79, 88, 90; depreciation of, 127; democratic character of, 11; *Dred Scott* and, 37; federalist character of, 13; foreign policy and, 105, 127, 128, 130, judicial review and, 132, 133; Lecompton Constitution and, 39; liberals and, 114; limited character of, 82; Lincoln and, 43, 45; as living, ix, 153; Locke and, 129; losing, 154; Madison and, 25; nationalist character of, 12; novelty of, 55; power in, 97; practice and, 60, 61; presidential authority and, 27, 67, 98, 103, 104; rational deliberation and, 18, 22; republican or democratic, 50; Roosevelt, F. D. and, 67, 68; Roosevelt, T. and, 105; single-member districts and, 86; slavery and, 32, 34, 37, 39, 40; social equilibrium and, 18; virtue and, 19; way of life and, 120; Whig character, 63; Wilson and, 50, 54, 130, 131, 137; written character of, 56, 58, 60, 63

Declaration of Independence, 80, 138; African-Americans and, 35, 36; Constitution and, 83; Jefferson and, 10, 25, 27, 80; Lincoln and, 37, 3⁹ 45; meaning of, 9, 10, 25, 27, 46; self-interest and, 46

ABOUT THE AUTHORS

ROGER M. BARRUS is Professor and Chair of the Department of Political Science at Hampden-Sydney College. He has published articles in the areas of American government, politics, and foreign policy, and political philosophy. He was co-editor of *America Through the Looking Glass; A Constitutionalist Critique of the 1992 Election* (Rowman & Littlefield, 1994).

JOHN H. EASTBY is Director of the Western Culture Program and Professor of Political Science at Hampden-Sydney College. He is author of *Functionalism and Interdependence* (University Press of America, 1985) and co-editor of *America Through the Looking Glass; A Constitutionalist Critique of the 1992 Election* (Rowman & Littlefield, 1994).

JOSEPH H. LANE JR. is Assistant Professor of Political Science at Emory & Henry College. His work has been published in the *American Political Science Review* and *Review of Politics*. He is currently completing a monograph entitled *Green Paradoxes: Rousseau and the Roots of Environmentalist Thought.*

DAVID E. MARION is Director of the Wilson Center for Leadership in the Public Interest at Hampden-Sydney College and Senior Scholar at the Bill of Rights Institute located in Arlington, Virginia. He is the author of *The Jurisprudence of Justice William J. Brennan Jr.: The Law and Politics of "Libertarian Dignity"* (Rowman & Littlefield, 1997), winner of the Choice Best Academic Book Award.

JAMES F. PONTUSO is Professor of Political Science at Hampden-Sydney College. He is author of *Václav Havel: Civic Responsibility in the Postmodern Age* (Rowman & Littlefield, 2004), and *Assault on Ideology: Solzhenitsyn's Political Thought,* (Lexington Books, 2004). He is editor of *Political Philosophy Comes to Rick's: Casablanca and American Civic Culture* (Lexington Books, 2005).